Male Homosexuality
in Modern Japan

Male Homosexuality in Modern Japan
Cultural Myths and Social Realities

Mark J. McLelland

CURZON

First Published in 2000
by Curzon Press
Richmond, Surrey
http://www.curzonpress.co.uk

© 2000 Mark J. McLelland

Typeset in Sabon by LaserScript Ltd, Mitcham, Surrey
Printed and bound in Great Britain by
Biddles Ltd, Guildford and King's Lynn

British Library Cataloguing in Publication Data
A catalogue record of this book is available from the British Library

Library of Congress Cataloguing in Publication Data
A catalogue record for this book has been requested

ISBN 0–7007–1300–X (hbk)
ISBN 0–7007–1425–1 (pbk)

Contents

Acknowledgements

This book has its origin in a doctoral thesis written in the Japanese Studies Department of the University of Hong Kong and I would like to thank my then supervisors, Kirsten Refsing and Okano Masazumi, who stopped me from straying too far down strange paths. Thanks is due also to Wim Lunsing who provided a great deal of help at all stages of the project and to James Robeson who read an early draft and pointed out factual inaccuracies and structural problems; to Sabine Frühstuck, Sharon Kinsella and Megumi Maderdonner who corrected my understanding of Japanese women's comics; to Murakami Fuminobu who pointed out some of the many errors in my Japanese transliteration and translation; and to James Valentine and Roger Goodman for their comments and criticisms. I would also like to thank Karen Kelsky for sharing her insight into the 'rhetorical functions' of Japanese women's media discourse.

Thanks is also due to the many gay men in Japan without whose help chapters 7 and 8 could not have been written. I am also grateful to Susan and Mitsuru Sakuraba without whose couch my interviews could not have been conducted so comfortably. Thanks must go to Nakata Kazuo whose bedroom houses a veritable archive of material relating to homosexuality in Japan and to Ōhama George who kindly made available the tapescripts of his own interviews with Japanese gay men. Alasdair, Alysha and Andrew should be thanked, too, for providing a comfortable home environment while I was absorbed in the writing of this book. Many other people have helped me in different ways, but I would finally like to thank Chantal Stoughton for her editorial input and enthusiastic encouragement.

Some of the material in the book has already been published in the context of a number of academic journals and I would like to thank the editors for the opportunity to present my work to a wider audience. An early draft of chapter 3 appeared in *The New Zealand Journal of Asian Studies,* and early drafts of chapters 4 and 5 appeared in *The Journal of Gender Studies* and *The US-Japan*

Women's Journal English Supplement respectively. Other material presented in the book received an airing in *Intersections* and *The Journal of Communication Inquiry*.

I would like to thank Biburosu, Hakusensha and Shōgakkan for permission to reproduce illustrations. I have made every effort to contact other copyright holders. If the copyright holders of other illustrations reproduced in the book would kindly contact the publishers, I will make sure to include them in subsequent editions.

Please note, all Japanese personal names occur in Japanese order: surname first.

Mark McLelland,
Brisbane

While we can make our identities, we cannot do so exactly as we please ... as many of us find ourselves racialized, biologized, minoritized, somehow reduced rather than enabled by our bodies and our histories, our special diacritics which become our prisons.

Arjun Appadurai

Illustrations

A plate section is found between pages 148 and 149

1 'New Half from Shinjuku:' this magazine advert for a Tokyo theme park features a transvestite man. The caption at the bottom reads 'I came from Shinjuku' (the site of Tokyo's pre-eminent gay town).

2 This car sticker reads *okama ni chūi* which can be read as 'watch your behind' or 'watch out for *okama*'.

3 The original *okama*: a pot for cooking rice.

4 School boys in love, from the women's manga *B-Boy*. The caption reads 'The last day we will walk in the same uniform.' (Courtesy of Biburosu publications.)

5 School girls in love, from the women's manga *EG*.

6 The character 'Mel', from the women's manga *New York New York*. (Courtesy of Hakusensha publications.)

7 In this scene from the women's manga *A Cruel God Reigns*, Jeremy is being tied up and raped by his step-father. (Courtesy of Shōgakkan.)

8 School boys make love in the women's manga *XY*. The top caption reads 'Does it feel good ...?'.

9 In this comic from the gay magazine *Barazoku*, the 'beautiful boy' image of women's manga is rejected. The 'ugly boy' (on the left) is preferred by his team mates because of his superb skill at fellatio.

10 This feature article from the gay magazine *G-Men* describes how enjoying gay sex in a university sports club depends upon seniority. The chart places 'god' at the apex followed by the third years, second years and freshmen. The title of 'CASE 1' literally reads 'seniors eat juniors.'

11 These symbols from the personal ads in *G-Men* help the reader to identify his 'type'. Included are symbols for age, facial hair, SM, and fetishes.

12 In this feature from the gay magazine *Samson*, which caters to men who like older men, the father figure says, 'Put yourself in my care (*amaete goran*) without hesitation.' Note the use of *amae*, a frequent term in transgenerational relationships.

13 In this scene from *Iron Man*, the hero meets his new boss for the first time. The boss is marked as homosexual both by his name, Kamasu, which incorporates the *kama* of *okama*, and by the rear view of his buttocks. He is ostensibly practising golf.

14 This advertisement for a host agency called 'Shibuya Dicks' describes the agency as a specialist in 'huge cocks'. The prices for its 'delivery' service are clearly marked ¥20,000 for two hours and ¥30,000 for the night. It also advertises part-time positions for men aged between 18 and 30 who possess 'big roots'.

15 Some ads which use English are obviously inviting a foreign clientele but others use English (often incorrectly) because it is considered sexy as in Boys Culb (sic) which describes itself in Japanized English as a 'sexy boys' oasis'. The bottom ad offers part-time positions to 'short-haired university students who are active in sports clubs' as both hosts and video models.

16 'Boys love' is not limited to women's manga. This ad from a gay magazine is for a phone line specialising in sexy stories about school boys. The young boy says 'I'm ... coooommmming.'

17 IZAM, the beautiful cross-dressed lead singer of the boy-band *SHAZNA*, is also popular elsewhere in Asia. This article was featured in a Hong Kong magazine.

Chapter 1

Introduction

Whose homosexuality?

The subject of this book is elusive as it is by no means clear who, exactly, is to be included in the concept of 'male homosexual' even in English; in Japanese, as will be described below, problems with terminology are even more serious. In the west, recent developments in lesbian and gay studies (*see* for example, Dorenkamp and Henke 1995) as well as in the study of sexuality generally have led towards the increasing problematisation of all terms used in a nominalising manner which try to name a person in terms of the gender of his or her preferred sexual partner. This shift has largely been due to the influence of postmodern ideas which have entered academia via feminism and gender studies, and yet it is not new. Even in the late 1940s, Alfred Kinsey, in the first large-scale empirical survey of the sex life of American men ever conducted, was warning against the use of terms like 'homosexual' and 'heterosexual' as nouns describing distinct types of people. He writes:

> Males do not represent two discrete populations, heterosexual and homosexual. The world is not divided into sheep and goats ... It is a fundamental of taxonomy that nature rarely deals with discrete categories. Only the human mind invents categories and tries to force facts into separate pigeon-holes. The living world is a continuum in each and every one of its aspects. The sooner we learn this concerning human behavior the sooner we shall reach a sounder understanding of the realities of sex (1948: 639).

Although I endorse Kinsey's warning against the desire to organise human sexuality into tidy categories, I am sceptical that the 'realities of sex' can ever be fully understood, not because of deficiencies in our methods of approach which are, after all, humanly produced and therefore culturally encoded, but because 'sex' is an ideological and not an empirical concept. In coming to this understanding, I have been much influenced by the historical work of Michel Foucault who has argued that in the nineteenth century in western cultures, 'sex' came to be constructed as a distinct category of acts which held the secret to understanding human behaviour. He says:

> All along the great lines which the development of the deployment of sexuality has followed since the nineteenth century, one sees the elaboration of this idea that there exists something other than bodies, organs, somatic localizations, functions, anatamo-physiological systems, sensations, and pleasures; something else and something more, with intrinsic properties and laws of its own: 'sex' (1990: 152–3).

Arising from this increased attention paid to sex was the new division of people into two opposite and mutually exclusive sexual types, the homo- and heterosexual. As Foucault argues, sodomy, which had previously been understood as simply a category of forbidden acts, at the end of the nineteenth century became transposed onto a certain kind of person or body: *the homosexual*. He comments that 'the sodomite had been a temporary aberration; the homosexual was now a species' (1990: 42). This has resulted in a situation, common throughout Anglo-American culture where 'of the very many dimensions along which the genital activity of one person can be differentiated from that of another ... precisely one, the gender of object choice ... has remained as *the* dimension denoted by the now ubiquitous category of "sexual orientation"' (Sedgwick 1990: 8). However, I shall be arguing that although this binary division of people into two sexual types according to the gender of their sexual partners has, for many people, established itself as the primary paradigm for understanding human sexuality in most western societies, its applicability is questionable in Japan which has not, until very recently, entertained the notion that 'sexuality' connotes an 'identity.'

Foucault's insight is fundamental to the approach I take to (homo)sexuality throughout this book. I do not try to explain, in terms of a grand meta-narrative, the 'meaning' of the various representations of homosexuality in modern-day Japan; nor do I contrast representations of homosexual men created by the media with actual homosexual men whose self-understanding is somehow more 'real.' Instead, I try to show how the many different understandings of the implications of same-sex love between men are caught up in a number of 'discourses' which variously position them as more or less personally and socially desirable. For instance, I found that the popular media represent 'homosexual' men as simultaneously funny and sympathetic and dangerous and despicable; they are sometimes represented as a threat to the family and society and then, in other discourses, reinscribed as women's best friends and ideal partners. In certain contexts, homosexual sex is spoken of as 'disgusting' (*kimochi warui*) and yet graphic representations of love between beautiful boys (*bishōnen*) are often represented as more romantic and pure than relationships between men and women. Similarly, men who experience same-sex attraction themselves also give contradictory accounts of its significance. Some feel themselves to be part of an oppressed minority, others feel that their sex lives have no impact on the roles they play in everyday life. It is clear that the myriad representations of homosexuality in Japanese culture cannot be judged in terms of a pre-existent, unitary, empirical sexual experience shared by all homosexual men equally. In the realm of human sexual relations, there are no ideal types, either homo- or heterosexual.

Throughout the book I have had to resist the temptation to oppose the relatively fluid understandings of sexuality held by many of my Japanese interviewees with a monolithic 'gay identity' supposedly held by western homosexual men and women. Although intellectually I know that none of the terms 'gay identity,' 'homosexual identity' or 'lesbian identity' can be found in writing prior to the mid-1970s (Epstein 1998: 134) and are therefore very culturally and historically specific, the amount of media discussion given to 'gay pride' and its inverse, the 'gay threat' in many western societies does encourage a rather essentialist reading of sexual identity (*see* Signorili 1994). As Knopp (1990) points out 'most of North America's large cities (and many smaller ones) now contain at least one predominantly gay neighbourhood.' This visibility of lesbian and gay people living in close association in large urban areas does suggest parallels with ethnic communities who also choose to live with other members of their 'minority group.' The idea of a lesbian and gay minority identity is also encouraged by 'an anti-gay counter movement' (Knopp 1990) which encourages an us-against-them mentality on both sides of the homo/hetero divide.

Yet, although it was clear by the mid-1980s that, as Gayle Rubin famously pointed out 'in modern, western, industrial societies, homosexuality has acquired much of the institutional structure of the ethnic group' (1998: 112), empirical studies of so-called 'gay communities' have failed to give coherent content to the notion of a 'gay' or 'homosexual' identity. In fact, studies of homosexuality and AIDS transmission such as those carried out by Dowsett (1996) in Australia and Coxon (1996) in Britain question the usefulness of identity labels such as 'gay' altogether and instead speak of 'men who have sex with men.' In their extensive interviews with partners in 'non-heterosexual relationships' Heaphy et al. (1998) also found that the terms 'lesbian,' 'gay,' and 'bisexual' were often resisted by their interviewees and that the understandings of these terms sometimes differed between interviewee and interviewer. They also discovered that the different partners in a relationship also sometimes differed in their acceptance of labels. That these differences in interpretation can arise in a context in which both the interviewee and researcher share, to a large extent, a common culture, should draw attention to the problems which arise when 'sexuality' is analysed across cultures.

Although the 'ethnic' self-characterization of lesbians and gays in the US may have made sense given that society's long history of civil-rights struggles and widespread legal restrictions on the expression of same-sex sexuality, there is no reason to assume that this particular formulation will endure. As Altman states, 'the idea of "gay/lesbian" as a sociological category is only about one hundred years old, and its survival even in Western developed countries cannot be taken for granted' (1996: 79) (see also Altman et al. 1988). As Neil Miller (1993) comments in his journalistic account of 'gay life' around the world 'the terms "gay" and "straight" revealed themselves to be Western cultural concepts that confused more than they elucidated' (1993: 68–9). It is therefore ironic that some Japanese gay-rights activists look to western models, the efficacy of which are already widely disputed in some western societies. The role of these imported models in Japan is unclear: 'America' serves as a sign of liberation for many Japanese homosexual men whilst simultaneously being rejected by others. It is misleading, then, to set up 'gay identity' as something that the west has developed which Japan somehow lacks, despite the fact that some Japanese homosexual men, gay rights activists in particular, do present this argument.

The lexicon of same-sex love

At this point it is important to explain the terms I will be using to discuss homosexuality in Japan. By 'homosexuality' I mean, simply, same-sex sexual desire. When I speak of homosexual men, I am therefore referring to men who experience sexual desire primarily directed at other men. However, I do not accept the binary homo/ hetero division which suggests that 'homosexual' men do not or cannot express themselves sexually with women. It became clear during my fieldwork in Japan that many of my interviewees had experienced sexual relations with women and several of them anticipated resuming sexual relations with women at some point in the future. I avoid the use of the term 'bisexual' as a default category to tidily file away all those men whose sexual activity cannot be neatly described as hetero- or homosexual as the notion of bisexuality, attending as it does only to the sex of the genitals involved, is insensitive to motivation. For instance, some of my interviewees initiated sexual interactions with women whereas others simply responded to the sexual initiative of their female partners. Some enjoyed the experience and sought out opportunities to repeat it, others didn't. What was enjoyable about the experience was also different for many. For several men it was not orgasm which was most pleasurable, but the sense of emotional empathy and sharing which they established with their female partners, an empathy which they stressed was generally lacking with male partners, although the sex with men was often more intense. It may be possible to describe men like this as *homo*sexual but hetero-emotional. I also came across stories about homosexual men visiting female prostitutes and enjoying, not the sex *per se*, but the experience of being able to order (or being ordered) to perform certain acts (such as licking feet). Also, some men manage to perform sexually with women, but only by fantasizing that their partner is a man: is this interaction therefore really homosexual?

Hence, I am reticent throughout about the use of all sexual nomenclature which attempts to establish fixed categories. I will, however, say that all the men I interviewed were, for the purposes of orgasmic satisfaction, more inclined to seek out male partners and none of them was, at the time of interview, sexually involved with a woman. To this extent, then, I speak of them as 'homosexual.' In so doing, I am aware that I am crowding together a host of different experiences and developmental life-cycles under a single term. As recent research has shown 'developmental sequences vary tremen- dously' (Epstein 1998: 146) with regard to when, how and if a man who engages in same-sex sexual acts comes to identify as 'homo- sexual.' Goode also points out that 'regarding oneself as gay – in the vocabulary of some, recognising that one *is* a homosexual – is not something that happens automatically,' adding that 'there is a considerable independence between engaging in homosexual behavior – and even recognizing that what one is doing, is, in fact, "homosexual behavior" – and adopting a homosexual identity' (1997: 262). The biographies of the men I interviewed problematise the use of fixed categories for describing an individual in terms of his sexual behaviour.

For the sake of variety, I also use the terms 'gay men' and 'same-sex desiring men' although by these terms I mean nothing other than men who predominantly experience sexual desire towards other men. When the gay men I cite refer to themselves, I generally include in parentheses their preferred Japanese term for describing themselves so that the nuance attached can be assessed by the reader. For non-Japanese speaking readers, I discuss in the next section of this chapter the various lexical items used at present in Japan to describe same-sex desiring men and outline the problems that an English speaker faces when trying to render these terms, which have been produced in a sexual culture quite different from that of Anglo-American societies, into English.

Closely connected with the idea that each individual possesses a sexual identity is the notion that he or she also has a gender identity. The common-sense understanding of this term involves the correlation between certain biological features (the possession of male or female sexual organs) with a diverse complex of dress codes, speech patterns and mannerisms, as well as ways of thinking, feeling and acting which are understood to be either 'masculine' (i.e. characteristic of male bodies) or 'feminine' (i.e. characteristic of female bodies). I follow postmodern feminist writers such as Judith Butler (1990), Eve Kosofsky Sedgwick (1990) and Monique Wittig (1992) as well as Queer theorists such as Jonathan Dollimore (1991) in arguing that 'gender,' like 'sex' is a social fiction. These theorists argue that the notion 'woman' is the binary opposite of 'man' and fixes the place of both in the field of gender relations which are based on ideology not biology. Dollimore, in particular, has argued that this binary opposition is ultimately unstable and as such is the site of considerable anxiety and paranoia, particularly on the part of men who have the most to lose if gender can be shown to be negotiable as opposed to natural. I use these ideas when I show that it is the sexuality of Japanese *women* which has traditionally been a site of anxiety for men, as illustrated in the negative attention female sexuality is given in the popular press, television and manga. Male sexuality is very much tied in with male gender role and is represented as dominating and controlling female responses in much the same way that men dominate and control women in the public sphere. It is therefore problematic in a male-dominated society like Japan to represent men as sexual in relation to other men without radically re-examining what it means to be gendered male. Popular culture deals with this problem by representing homosexual men as essentially women *manqué*; since they fail convincingly to 'pass' as women, they are not represented as sexually active as no 'real' man would find them desirable. I wish to show that the pervasive representation of homosexual men as 'feminine' is ideologically motivated as it is not possible to show two gender-normative men in a sexual interaction without bringing into doubt the 'natural' ground of male gender which is maintained through the sexual domination of women.

It is perhaps not surprising then, that it is in women's comics that men are most often represented as sexually involved with other men, but, as I argue in chapter 4, this is made possible only to the extent that these characters are not really 'men' but *bishōnen* (beautiful youths) who are in fact regendered, uniting the best of 'masculine' and 'feminine' in a kind of androgynous ideal. These youths are biologically male but the gender they 'perform' is not characteristically masculine. I argue that the figure of the homosexual *bishōnen*, the creation of women manga artists, is one example of gender 'performativity' as outlined by Judith Butler (1990), a key concept to which I will return in later chapters.

Japanese terms describing same-sex attraction

There has been a marked change over time in the nature of the vocabulary used to describe male same-sex attraction. During the Tokugawa period (1600–1867), the *nanshoku* (sometimes transcribed as *danshoku* and meaning 'male eroticism') code contained a wide variety of terms for describing the partners involved in homosexual acts depending upon such factors as age (their junior or senior role), status, and the context in which the acts took place. These terms were gradually replaced by translations of sexological terminology derived from European languages which focused on homosexual identity such as 'Urning' and *dōseiaisha* (same-sex-love person) or homosexual acts such as *dōsei kōsatsu* (same-sex intercourse). The novelist Mishima Yukio ([1951–3] 1973, vol. 5), writing just after the war, was still using the traditional term *danshoku* which he neologises as *danshokuka* (or *danshoku*-ist) to denote male homosexuals, although he does refer to the American usage of the word 'gay.' Older informants among my interviewees such as Sato and Hara informed me that as late as the early-1970s, vocabulary derived from the *nanshoku* code was still in use to describe same-sex acts among men but that by the end of the decade this kind of terminology had completely disappeared, being replaced by English loan words.

The prominence of cross-dressed individuals featured in the media means that cross-dressing is the main paradigm Japanese people have for understanding non-normative sexualities. Thus, homosexual men are understood to be *okama* (literally a 'pot' but meaning something similar to the English word 'queen') and are usually represented as cross-dressed and effeminate. The use of the term *okama* derives from the slang usage of the term to refer to the buttocks and thereby to anal sex (Long 1996: 216) which is considered to be the definitive sexual act engaged in by homosexual men, although the status of the active partner in this act is uncertain. However, use of this term is extremely loose and it can be used to describe a man who displays any transgender attribute. For instance, an article in the current-affairs magazine *AERA* (1 March 1999) on men who adopt female names and personae in order to participate in women-only Internet chat lines, describes such men as *netto okama* (Net *okama*), although here there is no relation between the adoption of a female name and same-sex attraction.

Japanese homosexual women are sometimes described using another 'pot' metaphor, *onabe* (meaning 'pan') a parallel term to *okama* which only has meaning in relation to it (Long 1996: 215). However, this term is less well known than the English loan word *rezu* (from lesbian). *Onabe* are represented as the opposite of *okama*, being masculine in both dress and demeanour. Yet this term, too, is difficult to pin down. For instance, an article in the magazine *Da Vinchi* (March 1999), describes the relationship between a *nyūhāfu* (new half: male-to-female transsexual) and an *onabe*. But it is not possible to translate *onabe* as 'lesbian' in this context, for, as the person identified as an *onabe* explains, s/he clearly understands him/herself to be a man, albeit without a penis. One further term connected with the 'pot' metaphor is the word *okoge* which is literally the burnt rice which sticks to the bottom of the pot and is a term for 'fag hag' (straight women who like to hang around gay men) but this is not generally understood, despite the popular 1992 movie of that name (discussed in chapter 5).

The idea that same-sex attraction necessarily involves some kind of transgenderism or desire to be like or even become the opposite of one's biological sex is constantly reinforced by Japanese media which discuss homosexuality and transgenderism in the same context. For example, in the same edition of the popular magazine *Da Vinchi* (March 1999) discussed above, there is an article on cross-dressing boy bands entitled 'Do you like men who are too beautiful?' The lead article includes interviews with some of the cross-dressed performers and goes into the history of cross-dressing in the Japanese music and theatre industry. Given the number of *katakana* (an indigenous alphabet for transcribing foreign words) terms introduced in these articles, the writers provide a glossary entitled 'Words to help you understand individuals who have gone beyond their sex (*sei wo koeta*).' The first word defined is *gei* (gay) which is glossed as 'male homosexual' (*dansei dōseiaisha*); other words describing male homosexuals such as *homo* and *okama* are described as 'offensive.' Also defined are *rezubian* ('female homosexual'), *nonke* (gay slang for 'heterosexual'), *toransusekusharu* ('transsexual,' persons who want to change their biological sex through an operation), *toransujendā* ('transgender,' persons who expresses themselves through the gender opposite to their biological sex but do not want an operation), *toransubuesutaito* ('transvestite,' a person who wants to dress as the opposite sex because of a 'fetish'), and *nyūhāfu* (male-to-female transsexuals or male-to-female transgendered individuals who have 'come out' [*kamu auto*] and work in the sex industry [*fūzoku*]). In this list it is not at all clear how gay men and lesbians want to 'go beyond' their sex or what, if anything, they have to do with transgendered individuals. The boys who cross-dress professionally as part of their stage act (described as *imēji kei*, or 'image group') state that their cross-dressing has nothing to do with same-sex desire and the couple described as an *onabe* and a *nyūhāfu* are not 'homosexual' but transsexual. It is therefore not clear why the subject of homosexuality should come up at all in this context.

So pervasive is the understanding of gay men as necessarily cross-dressed or transgendered that it has even found its way into some sex-education literature. For example, one book entitled *Kore kara no seikyōiku: shō chū kōkōsei no nayami ni kotaeru* (Sex education from now on: [you] can reply to junior-, middle- and high- school students' troubles; Matsuoka Hiroshi 1981) has thirteen lines under the heading of 'homosexuality' (*dōseiai*) but the examples cited are entirely about cross-dressing. The author refers to a worried high-school boy who says 'I feel interested in dressing as a woman (*josō*) and I wear women's underclothes every day' (1981: 65); although the boy does not refer to any same-sex attraction, it is assumed that the desire to cross-dress is in itself symptomatic of homosexuality. The author states that men who cross-dress cannot forget the way they were dressed up as girls and spoiled (*kawaigatte moratta*) by their elder sisters. Although it is acknowledged that not *all* men who like to wear women's clothes are homosexual since some men simply like to dress in girls' clothes but 'don't especially want to become girls,' the implication is that real homosexuals not only like to dress as girls but actually want to become them (1981: 65). It is difficult to find representations of gay men other than those in specifically gay media which challenge this taken-for-granted assumption.

Thus, Japanese gay men who want to come out about their sexual preference are faced with a problem when it comes to choosing a term to describe themselves as most of the terms currently available tend to conflate homosexual attraction with cross-dressing and transgenderism. This problem is clearly expressed in the following extract from a campus broadsheet produced and distributed by a gay male student in 1994:

> Before I wrote my first article, the first thing I had to think about was 'what on earth should I call myself?' ... The people who read my first message probably realise that I am 'gay' – that's English, isn't it? But there isn't a word in Japanese. For example, *dōseiaisha* is a medical word and it has a discriminatory nuance, isn't it rather like a sick person? Then there's the word *homo* but that's English too and it's used on the television to make fun of people. I really wanted to use the word '*gei*' in *katakana*. But, are you listening? Regarding '*gei*,' you think of gay boys and gay bars, don't you get the image of a man who cross-dresses (*josō no hito*). (Reproduced in Ōhama 1994; my translation).

It is clear, then, that Japanese has a wide variety of terms relating to what Valentine refers to as 'queer sexualities,' some indigenous and others borrowed from English. However, as Valentine comments 'The multitude of designations in Japan for queer sexualities may sound as if there are subtle discriminations being made between different types of sexual orientation. Yet the assorted categories tend to be interchangeable' (1997a: 108). Significantly, there seem to be fewer terms applying to sexually nonconformist women. This was also noted by Valentine who argues that 'lesbian relationships are still accorded less acknowledgement and visibility and face a more restricted battery of concepts' (1997a: 98). This comes as no surprise, and as I argue in chapter 4, Japanese media tend to only pay attention to women's sexuality when it relates to men. The difficulty of giving content to the terms discussed above is apparent in some definitions given in a guide book to Tokyo's sex scene (Altbooks 1998: 167). In a discussion of cross-dressing 'image clubs' where straight men can go to be made up as women, the writer is keen to distinguish these straight men from *okama* and *nyūhāfu* with whom they might be conflated. The definition of *okama* is given as 'a male homosexual who likes to cross-dress' (*josō wo konomu dansei dōseiaisha*) whereas a *nyūhāfu* is defined as 'a male homosexual who has had a sex change operation.' These definitions suggest that male homosexuals who do not like to cross-dress exist, but also that a *nyūhāfu*, even after the operation, is still regarded as a 'male homosexual.' However, this apparently clear distinction between *okama* and *nyūhāfu* is confused by a report about a Thai '*okama* kickboxer' in the Internet sports magazine *XUSXUS* (8 July 1999). This individual who, on account of the female hormones s/he is taking, 'has breasts which have expanded like a dream' is reported as undergoing a sex-change operation, after which s/he hopes to become an 'actress' (*joyū*). However, s/he is referred to in the headline as an *okama*, not a *nyūhāfu*. Significantly, after transitioning, s/he says that his/her aims are to 'try to make people laugh or even sing,' thus reinforcing the notion that the best place for an individual who crosses gender lines is the entertainment world.

Furthermore, same-sex desiring men themselves differ as to the nuance attached to words describing homosexuality. The gay activist Fushimi Noriaki (1991: 10) offers the following suggestions: *homo* has the 'dark image of a pervert;' *okama* has the 'nuance of a transsexual (*toransusekushuaru*) and transvestite (*josō*).' *Dōseiaisha* 'seems to suggest a sick person.' Personally, he prefers 'gay' (*gei*) and 'homosexual' (*homosekushuaru*), particularly the former because of its connection with the 'American liberation movement' (*Amerika no riberēshon undō*). Fushimi is one of a number of gay rights activists who is attempting to reappropriate the word *gei* and rid it of its transgender connotations, instead stressing its traditional use as a self-applied label in the American movement for gay rights. However, as Valentine argues, many same-sex desiring men are cautious about accepting 'gay' as a label because:

In terms of identification, *gei* carries implications of a political stance or movement, of sexuality defining self, and hence of coming out. Thus, in Japan identification as 'gay' is unlikely for those who are not part of the gay commercial scene or who do not conceptualize themselves primarily in terms of sexuality (1997a: 101).

Valentine's view is very much supported by data relating to self-perception collected from my interviewees, discussed in chapter 7.

Research approach

My first impressions of the nature and role of homosexuality in Japan came through living and working there, first as an exchange student and later as an editor in a publishing company. At this time I was active in Tokyo's large 'gay scene' which is primarily located in the Ni-chome (second ward) district of Shinjuku. I had a large number of gay (male) friends and picked up a considerable amount of biographical information over the years. I also watched Japanese television, read comic books and magazines, and went to the cinema where I was surprised to find, given the general silence about the topic of homosexuality noticeable among my straight friends and colleagues, that there was a considerable amount of media discourse about it. I thus knew that there were a large number of Japanese gay men (enough to keep over 200 gay bars in Shinjuku alone in business) and that images of homosexuality were visible in Japanese popular culture. So, when I was told that there were few homosexuals in Japan, or even that there were none, as not infrequently happened, I simply assumed that my friends were being disingenuous and attempting to hide from the inquisitive foreigner aspects of Japanese culture which they saw as undesirable. Homosexuality thus became the 'h-word' which along with the 'b-word' (*burakumin*: a hereditary sub-caste facing discrimination due to their ancestors' connection with work considered polluting) I, and my foreign friends, knew from experience never to bring up in conversation. However, as I began to research the topic of homosexuality in a more disciplined fashion, I became aware that through suspecting my Japanese friends of being less than honest, I was actually imposing my own ethnocentric understanding of homosexuality onto Japan. When I and my Japanese friends spoke about 'homosexuality' we were talking about rather different things. I came to see that 'being gay' as a self-proclaimed identity was indeed rare in Japan, not necessarily because Japanese people were less open or more repressed than some supposed Euro-American ideal, but because sexuality, unlike gender, is not commonly understood to be the basis of 'identity' in Japan.

This was brought home to me not so much by reading the work of theorists like James Valentine (1997a; 1997b) who also argues this point, but in reading a book of interviews collected by a criminal-science lecturer and researcher at Chūō University, Yajima Masami (1997) which contains the life stories of twenty homosexual men of widely differing ages, educational backgrounds and occupations. It would be difficult, using this material, to construct any kind of common understanding of homosexuality shared by these men whose only shared attribute is a desire for genital interactions with members of their own sex. Intrigued by the very different under-standings of homosexuality and the role and significance of same-sex desire in the lives of these men, I myself conducted sixteen interviews with homosexual men, the results of which are discussed in chapters 7 and 8.

In shaping my ideas, I have also been influenced by a great deal of printed material in the Japanese language which deals with homo-sexuality. Much of the material written before the nineties has a highly ideological slant and tries to account for, justify or explain away the practice of homosexual desire in earlier periods of Japanese history (for example, Minakata [1940] 1991; Inagaki [1963] 1993). More recent work dating from Japan's 'gay boom' in the early-1990s differs from that mentioned above in that much is written by men and women who identify as gay or lesbian. This material too has a distinct ideological slant, many writers using American models of gay rights and gay liberation which set up a persecuted 'minority' against a persecuting 'majority' (such as Itō Satoru 1996; Fushimi 1991). I use material from my interviews with homosexual men to problematise this picture which is not apparent in the experience of all the men I spoke to. There are also many other books written about gay men, either as expressions of sympathy and support (Kurigi 1996) or for their shock value (Kiyohara 1994). Considerable academic attention has also been paid to homosexuality in recent years with issues of high-brow journals such as *Gendai no esupuri* (August 1990), *Eureka* (May 1993), *imago* (November 1995; May 1996), and *Gendai shisō* (May 1997) being dedicated to homosexual topics. The work of lesbian and gay activists and researchers is also being published, as in the two collections *Kuia sutadiizu 96/97* (Queer studies 96/97). I draw on this material extensively commenting on its value as I do so throughout the following chapters.

I have also used a great deal of material taken from popular culture such as magazines, newspapers, comic books, television shows and movies as well as material produced by the gay community itself, specifically gay magazines, videos, and gay sites on the Internet. As I argued above in relation to the stories told by homosexual men about their same-sex desire and its significance in their lives, material taken from popular culture too, does not contain a single unitary discourse as to the nature and meaning of homosexual desire. However, these discourses of homosexuality are not completely random although they often do conflict with each other. Incidental references to, or representations of, homosexuality are so common in Japanese media that it is impossible for me to discuss every context in which they occur. So, in the following chapters I shall be attempting to isolate certain common themes or ways of conceptualizing homosexuality apparent in Japanese popular culture and show how these representations are variously resisted, negotiated or rejected by same-sex desiring men themselves.

As mentioned above, my preliminary understanding of homosexuality in Japan was gained through a period of residence in Tokyo, totalling about five years, between 1988 and 1994. However, much of the information in this book was collected during three trips to Japan undertaken between 1997 and 1999. Much of the literature search was done while taking a language course at Senshu University, Kawasaki-shi, from December 1997 to March 1998. Most of the interviews were completed during a month's stay in Tokyo in July/ August 1998. Follow-up work with some of my interviewees was also conducted in another month's trip to Japan in December/January 1998/9. In addition to this total of five months fieldwork in Japan, I have been in regular e-mail and postal contact with many Japanese gay friends who have very kindly provided me with photocopies of relevant newspaper and magazine articles as well as videos of television programmes and an update on new books published about homosexuality. I am particularly indebted to one friend in particular whose room is a veritable library and resource centre for the study of homosexuality in Japan, crammed full as it is with books, magazines, comics, videos and photocopies of material relating to a wide variety of homosexual topics spanning a period of over ten years. I spent several days looking through this material and refer to just a tiny fraction of it in the following chapters.

Chapter 7 of this book would not have been possible without the cooperation of the sixteen men who agreed to be interviewed by me. Some of these men were friends of mine from before I started this project, however, most of my interviewees were contacted via the Internet: they either replied to advertisements I had placed on gay websites, or I replied to their advertisements. Sometimes people I had contacted through the Internet would refer me to their friends who were interested in participating in the project. Some of the men were happy to be interviewed via e-mail but either did not want to meet face to face, or it was impossible to find a mutually agreeable time and location to meet. Some of the men I met consented only to chat informally about their experience and did not want to be taped, others agreed to meet for a more lengthy discussion and were happy for the interview to be recorded. I always allowed my interviewees to choose the language of the interview. About half chose English. This is because most of the men who bothered to reply to my advertisement were '*gaisen*' (primarily interested in foreign men) for whom English was the preferred medium of conversation. However, at crucial points in the interview, I often asked them to rephrase a certain phrase or idea in Japanese or give me the Japanese term for the English word they were using.

My method of contacting Japanese homosexual men has necessarily resulted in *gaisen* being over represented, so I cannot claim that my research sample is representative of Japanese gay men in general. But, as Flowers et al. (2000: 71) point out 'representative samples of men who have sex with men are almost impossible to attain,' and other means of meeting up with Japanese men would have produced their own biases. However, to give a better idea of the wide range of experience characteristic of Japanese homosexual men, I have regularly referred to interviews taken from the collection by Yajima (1997) throughout the book. I have come across little in Yajima's collection to suggest that the information given by my interviewees is in any sense unrepresentative; Yajima's informants share similar common points and differences to my own. I have also referred, when relevant, to the tapescript of six interviews with gay men kindly supplied to me by Ōhama George (1994) and the recent collection of interviews by Summerhawk et al. (1998), as well as to biographical information appearing on gay men's homepages and other sites on the Internet.

At this point, it is important to say something about research ethics. I put out a number of advertisements in both English and

Japanese on the Internet, some mentioning that I was a researcher involved in a project about homosexuality in Japan, and others simply containing some biographical information and stating that I wanted to make Japanese gay friends. I did this because I wanted to meet as many different kinds of people as possible. Some of the men who responded to my 'research' messages actually wanted me to tell them about gay life in Japan whereas respondents to my 'friends' advertisement soon changed their minds about meeting me when I told them I was a researcher. Several men I corresponded with felt uncomfortable about meeting me in my guise of researcher. For example, I received the following reply from a man who had initially responded to my 'friends' advertisement:

> Please note that I am in the closet, with few gay experiences. I don't really know whether I am gay or not. I have not read many books and novels about gays. I have never been to gay bars. I don't have much knowledge about gay life in Japan. So, I have nothing to tell you about your research ... thank you for your frank approach but I hesitate to see you if you only expressed interest in me in view of your study.

This man was precisely the kind of person I wanted to meet, for it was very easy for me to go to gay bars and strike up conversations with gay men on the scene, and I could read Japanese gay books myself. However, contacting ordinary gay men who lived ordinary lives without much interaction with the gay community was actually quite difficult. Because I found that most of the men who replied to my friends advertisement, if I told them beforehand that I was a researcher, declined to meet me, I stopped divulging this information in advance. However, I found that once I had met a person and established communication, if I then mentioned my project, most men were happy to tell me about their personal experiences, although I did have several refusals. Consequently, all the men whose biographies are included in chapter 7 knew beforehand that details about their lives would possibly be used in my book.

Chapter outline

I have organized the material in the book into ten chapters. In order to contextualise the discussion of the forms that homosexual representation take in contemporary Japan, I have written, in chapter 2, a general outline of the shifts in perception which have characterised Japanese understandings of homosexuality since the Tokugawa period. However, this historical work really requires a book in itself, and as there are considerable gaps in the literature, especially covering the change from Tokugawa to Meiji and again covering the period immediately following the Second World War, I have been unable to deal with this topic in the depth that it deserves. I have, however, tried to avoid speculation, and have simply discussed the literature such as it exists.

Chapters 3, 4 and 5 look at the different manifestations of what is perhaps the most pervasive trope for conceptualising homosexual desire at present in Japan, that of the homosexual man as gender-deviant (i.e. somehow 'feminine'). In chapter 3, I look at the common image of the *okama* as he appears on television, in comics and in the popular press. I draw attention to how the figure of the *okama* is understood as humorous and even harmless, yet when the possibility that homosexual desire might actually be acted upon is entertained, the homosexual is transposed into a figure of fear. A rather different representation of homosexual men is analysed in chapter 4 which looks at the extraordinarily large genre of boy-love (*shōnen'ai*) manga which is written by and read primarily by women. I try to account for why at times very graphic representations of male homosexual sex should be so attractive to young women. In doing so I look at the treatment of female sexuality in the Japanese media generally and then relate this treatment to images of heterosexual sex in comics and pornographic videos marketed at men. I argue that heterosexual sex in Japan is heavily 'scripted' in terms *other* than romance and that love between members of the same sex, although difficult and ultimately tragic, is seen as somehow more pure than sex between men and women which is related either to prostitution or the reproductive demands of the family system. I argue that the emphasis upon fantasy and escape in this genre means that these representations mean little to actual homosexual men.

In chapter 5, I draw upon the material discussed in the preceding two chapters to argue that many women in Japan have constructed a fantasy image of the gay man as a kind of transgender ideal, uniting the best aspects of both men and women in one body. This has led to a number of women, alienated from traditional models of masculinity, seeking marriage partnerships with gay men who believe that such a marriage will offer them a better deal. I also look at how homosexual men themselves view marriage and argue that same-sex attraction is by no means understood to mean that marriage to a woman is either impossible or undesirable. I raise the question as to whether the apparent re-evaluation of the marriage relationship currently being considered by some women and gay men signifies a general shift in the understanding of marriage and the central role of the family in Japanese society, concluding probably not: the same-sex couple, married with children is still perceived as something which could only exist in 'other' societies.

Chapter 6 focuses on representations of homosexuality in specifically gay media, focusing especially on gay magazines, pornographic videos and the Internet. I avoid setting these images up as the 'genuine' representation of same-sex desire in terms of which all other images need to be judged. I try to show that gay media 'script' homosexual acts and produce a vision of the homosexual body in a manner similar to mainstream media, although the representations obviously differ. In gay media the homosexual body is constructed, not as an androgynous intermediary between the sexes, but as a hyper-masculine figure whose interests are very much oriented around sex, not romance.

Chapter 7 contains the lifestories of sixteen Japanese homosexual men with whom I conducted interviews. I decided to go into this material at length because although there is now a large amount of material published in Japanese by gay men who are 'out' about their sexual orientation, these men live in rather different worlds from the men I interviewed. Indeed, through 'coming out,' gay men such as Itō Satoru, Fushimi Noriaki and Nishino Kōji have become media personalities (*tarento*) whose particular 'talent,' it could be argued, is publicising their difference in a society where homogeneity is, perhaps, overvalued. Few of my interviewees see taking such a step as either necessary or beneficial. So, I wanted to give a voice to the large number of ordinary homosexual men whose stories tend not to be picked up by the media and reported upon and whose lives would not make it into a book because they resemble so closely the lives of other people.

In chapter 8, I discuss a number of the issues which were brought up by my informants and attempt to relate them to the opinions and concerns of other gay men who have published books, written in gay magazines and on the Internet. I show how difficult it is to support any of the stereotypes about homosexual men in Japan as their life experiences and attitudes in general are so varied and complex.

Based on the interview data and discussion in chapters 7 and 8, chapter 9 addresses the notion of 'gay identity' in Japan. I argue that although images of homosexuality in the mass media present the homosexual man in terms of a certain identity (one that is understood as differently gendered rather than differently sexed), homosexual men themselves are more likely to represent their same-sex desire in terms of sexual acts which have little impact or significance for their self-image or identity. Hence, although there are now well-publicised Japanese gay activists who have adopted a western agenda of gay identity and gay rights, many ordinary Japanese gay men remain sceptical about the usefulness of this discourse in a Japanese context. Finally, in the Afterword I suggest that although American-style identity discourse is increasing in volume in Japan, because of cultural differences it remains to be seen just how the idea of a 'gay identity' will be negotiated and accepted by Japanese society, if indeed it will be accepted at all.

Chapter 2

Homosexuality in Japanese History

Introduction

Male homosexuality has a long and well-attested tradition in Japan going back at least a thousand years. However, until recently the notion of *the homosexual* as a distinct type of sexual being has not been apparent in Japanese culture. Although there are clearly documented traditions of homosexual relationships occurring in a variety of contexts such as the Buddhist monastery, the samurai castle and the kabuki theatre, each with its own distinct terms and etiquette, same-sex eroticism was understood as simply one kind of erotic enjoyment which was not considered to exclude opposite-sex attraction. However, despite the fact that same-sex eroticism is celebrated in much of premodern Japanese art, poetry and literature, this has little relevance for the way in which homosexuality is understood today either by the wider society or by homosexual men themselves.

In this chapter, I briefly outline the various ways in which homosexual desire has been understood and represented over time, pointing out both the continuities and discontinuities that exist between characteristically modern and traditional understandings.

Tokugawa homosexualities

Tokugawa-period (1600–1867) Japan has probably the best recorded tradition of male same-sex love in world history. Period novels (Ihara Saikaku [1682] transl. 1964; [1687] transl. 1990; [1688] transl. 1983), poetry (Schalow 1996), and art (Screech 1998) all provide extensive representations of the varieties of homosexual love practised. Incidental information gleaned from biographies (Shively 1970), news scandals and official records (Leupp 1995) as well as testimony from foreign visitors (edited by Cooper 1965) show how widely practised was male-male eroticism throughout all strata of

society. Tokugawa (homo)sexuality has recently been widely discussed in both English (Watanabe & Iwata 1989; Leupp 1992, 1995,
1996; Schalow 1996; Furukawa 1994) and in Japanese (Hanasaki
1980; Shibayama 1993; Hiratsuka 1994). These researchers amply
illustrate the widespread prevalence of homosexual relations among
men of samurai class as well as among urbanites generally.

I shall summarise the forms these same-sex practices took and the
ways in which they were scripted. Leupp (1992: 98) argues that the
overriding paradigm for all male same-sex sexual encounters in
Tokugawa Japan followed what Foucault termed 'the principle of
isomorphism between sexual relations and social relations.' That is,
the behaviour in sexual relations mirrored the status and power
differentials inherent in the greater society. This is also affirmed by
Furukawa who states that 'the samurai model is a homosexual
relationship based on the fixed framework of the older *nenja*, who
loves, and the younger *chigo*, who is loved' (1994: 100).

In accordance with this principle, the younger partner, termed
chigo or *wakashū* was the passive subject of an elder male's (*nenja*)
sexual advances and acts. There were four main contexts in which
same-sex practices seem to have occurred. Firstly, within the
Buddhist priesthood there was a long tradition of boy love which in
popular imagination went back to the eighth-century monk Kūkai
who was supposed to have introduced the practice from China
(Schalow 1992). The pattern here was for a young boy serving as an
acolyte (*chigo*) to be the beloved of a senior monk or abbot. Both
illustrated scrolls and stories dating from the fourteenth century
testify to the homoerotic (if not always sexual) nature of the
relationship between acolytes and their preceptors (Childs 1980;
Guth 1987; Watanabe & Iwata 1989). Ihara Saikaku takes it for
granted in his work dealing with male love, *Nanshoku ōkagami*
(Great mirror of male love, [1687], transl. Schalow 1990) that
priests are interested in pursuing boy actors and prostitutes. A
series of Tokugawa-period jokes and humorous stories collected by
Levy (1973) also suggests that the sexual relationship between
monks and acolytes was a general assumption. One example will
suffice to give a flavour of this collection: a monk falls from a tree
whilst cutting firewood and pierces his rectum on a stump; his
acolyte replies 'isn't that your karma?'(1973: 129).

Furthermore, as pointed out by Leupp (1992: 98), sexual relations
between masters and servants (young apprentices) were common and
widely accepted. That these boys should prostitute themselves for

money or favours is well attested, Hidaka comments that 'servant boys were ... loved by their shop masters and *bantō* [manager] clerks for whom they had to work very obediently in any circumstances' (1982: 96). Young salesmen who were sent out to peddle their master's wares seem to have also offered themselves; Statler (1961) suggests that peddlers of Chinese medicine would sell themselves as well as their merchandise and Leupp (1995) argues that aloeswood salesmen sometimes doubled as prostitutes. The sexual tryst in Fukuroi in Shōzan Koikawa's *Fifty-three Stages of the Tōkaidō* (an irreverent spoof on Hiroshige Andō's famous woodblock prints of the same name) shows a travelling salesman anally penetrating his errand boy whose smaller genitals and scant pubic hair mark him as pubescent. Interestingly, the boy is also represented with an erection and the couple are locked together in a kiss suggesting that the sentiment was mutual (Hidaka 1982: 33). Leupp also refers to the Dutch envoy Engelbert Kaempfer's account of a trip to Edo which took place at the end of the seventeenth century where he notes the existence of a number of boy prostitutes posing as sellers of medicinal plaster. Apparently, the commissioner escorting the mission was so excited by the sight of these boys that he delayed the procession for a half hour while he sampled their wares (Leupp 1995: 68). The system of apprenticeship which meant that boys were contracted to an established craftsman or trader for up to twenty years meant that many boys and young men would be living under the same roof, frequently sharing the same sleeping space. These men were unable to marry until they were set up in their own trade or practice which they were rarely in a position to do until their forties (if ever). Thus, in the absence of a discourse stigmatising same-sex relationships, it was entirely to be expected that older men would establish emotional and sexual bonds with the younger boys who shared their living space.

The third context in which homosexual love was practised was within the samurai strata of Tokugawa society where same-sex romantic relationships were represented in terms of an elite discourse which valorized the love of men over the love of women. Yamamoto Jōchō's *Hagakure* (In the shade of leaves [1717], transl. Wilson 1979) is a key text for understanding the crucial role that same-sex relationships played in the extremely homosocial samurai environment. The book illustrates the high moral seriousness which could attend same-sex bonds. Ikegami Eiko is one of a growing number of commentators who are stressing that the nature of samurai culture cannot be understood without 'taking the prevailing sentiments and erotic aesthetics of male-male love into consideration' (1995: 210). It is finally becoming clear that homosexuality was not a behaviour 'tolerated' by the Tokugawa government but was an elite social practice with a style, etiquette and aesthetic of its own. The final arena in which same-sex sexual acts could be enacted was within the floating world (*ukiyo*) of theatres and brothels. Both actors and prostitutes occupied a similar social position in the eyes of the authorities and the theatre and brothel districts were situated close together on the outskirts of the cities. The history of the kabuki theatre in Japan had, from the beginning, been tied up with prostitution and the original actresses in 'women's kabuki' had been banned from the stage because of the disturbances caused by fights among the audience over their post-performance favours (Shiveley 1968). However, the appearance of beautiful youths in women's roles caused much the same problem, leading to the banning of youths appearing as women. Women's roles therefore came to be performed by specialised adult female-role players (*onnagata*). That the sexual charms of both young male-role actors (*yarō*) and female-impersonators *(onnagata)* caused a commotion is clear from a reading of period actor-almanacs (Dunn and Torigoe 1969), literary and pictorial descriptions of the floating world (Douglas and Slinger 1981; Screech 1998) and government surveillance of the theatres which was designed to monitor the disturbances caused by fights over the favours of these actors and not to criminalize the attraction itself (Shively 1968).

As well as actor/prostitutes, there were brothels dedicated to supplying boys for male patrons. These boys were termed *kagema* and serviced customers in *kagema chaya* (teashops) which were clustered together in designated areas of the city (Hanasaki 1980). Unlike liaisons between samurai which depended upon a difference in age, sexual relations with *kagema*, who were often transgendered, were based on gender differentiation, with the *kagema* playing the role of woman (or passive insertee) (Furukawa 1994: 100). Like their female counterparts, these boys had often been kidnapped or sold by their parents and had little prospect of escape into a better life. They could be required to continue sexually servicing customers till well beyond their teens through the fictive playing of the *role* of boy which was achieved by keeping a boy's unshaven forelocks and distinctive open-sleeved kimono. Such a prostitute is encountered by the fourteen-year-old Yonosuke, hero of Ihara Saikaku's ([1682], transl. Kuwata 1964) *Kōshoku ichidai otoko* (Life of an amorous man), who, despite being younger in age, takes the sexually active role with the much older prostitute.

It is clear from the above that it was not so much 'homosexuality' which was common in Tokugawa-period Japan but a proliferation of 'homosexualities,' that is, a variety of sexual interactions, the only common factor among which was the sex (not necessarily the 'gender') of the participants. These styles were context specific and their performance was governed by a strict etiquette which was embodied in popular culture. The scenarios were already scripted in *shunga* (erotic pictures), *ukiyo-zōshi* (floating-world stories), Buddhist stories and fables, kabuki dramas and samurai 'how to' manuals.

The Meiji discourse of sexual deviance

However, the richly documented tradition of male homosexuality which existed in the Tokugawa period did not survive into Meiji (1868–1911), although pockets of overt homosexual practice do seem to have persisted into the Taisho period (1912–25). As Mizushima (1973: 270) points out 'there is much less written evidence of overt homosexual activities during the Meiji period, raising the question whether actual homosexual behaviour declined or whether it merely disappeared from view.' The Meiji period saw the development of new discourses framing homosexuality deriving from recently evolved sexological discourses imported from the west (Furukawa 1994).

The contest between older understandings of *nanshoku* (male eroticism) as part of the samurai code of honour and new sexological discourses positing homosexuality as a deviant and dangerous passion is illustrated in an autobiographical passage from Mori Ōgai's *Wita sekusuarisu* (Vita sexualis, [1909] 1971). The book was published in 1909 but Ōgai is referring to incidents which took place during his school days some twenty years previously. He writes that it was in the school dormitory that he first learned of *nanshoku* (1971: 116). At this time, he writes that 'looked at from the perspective of sexual attraction (*seiyokuteki ni kansatsu shite miru to*), there were two groups of students' (1971: 119). One group, the 'dandies' (*nampa*) affected elegance in their dress and manners, were avid readers of pornographic books and chased after geisha. This group was despised by the 'hard liners' (*kōha*) who were more masculine in their attire and preferred to read stories glorifying *nanshoku*. Ōgai says that this latter group was in the minority but only because his school was in Tokyo and this group consisted of men from Kyushu, particularly

Kumamoto (1971: 118). The 'hard liners' were interested in younger boys and at one time Ōgai seems to have become the object of their attention, understanding this attention solely in sexual terms, stating that he was looked at as a prospective 'receptive homosexual partner' (*nanshoku no ukemi*). The adult Ōgai conceives of the passive role in homosexual sex as suiting a *specific kind of person*, for he says 'I had no *predisposition* to be an Urning' (*boku ni wa* Urning *taru soshitsu wa nai*) (1971: 117). Ōgai uses the term '*Urning*' in Roman letters, showing that he had been influenced by German sexology which employed this term, deriving from the sexological work of Karl Heinrichs Ulrichs (1825–95) who coined the term '*Urning*' from a reference to Uranus in Plato's *Symposium* (Spencer 1995: 290). Ulrichs considered homosexual orientation to be inborn (and therefore natural) and to be characteristic of a specific type of person: the *Urning*. However, it is very unlikely that the youths pursuing the young Ōgai could have conceived of themselves in this way, their sexuality still being constructed in terms of the previous *nanshoku* code which valorised the love of men over and above that of women as part of a militaristic lifestyle extolling masculine virtue and despising feminine weakness.

At this time militaristic discourse still tolerated if not celebrated intimate friendships among fellow soldiers. Watanabe cites an excerpt from a letter from a German observer of the Manchurian War (1880–83) who writes:

> Many officers have told me of scenes where a soldier in love with another had fought at the risk of his own life, rushing willingly to the death spot. This is not simply due to the warrior spirit and contempt for death characteristic of the Japanese soldier, but also to their passion for another soldier ... (Watanabe and Iwata 1989: 122).

Basil Chamberlain, writing at the beginning of the twentieth century, praises the Japanese army, observing that 'the intercourse between officers and men is frank and intimate' (1905: 44). He also states that 'the newcomer may smile to behold two or three soldiers strolling along hand in hand, as if they were Dresden shepherdesses' (1905: 46) but he is quick to point out 'there is no effeminacy here' (1905: 46). This eroticised camaraderie seems to have more in common with the previous understanding of *nanshoku* as a set of values grounded in a certain homosocial lifestyle, than with the competing discourse which posits homosexuality as simply a deviant sexual act. It is therefore no surprise that the discourse of *nanshoku* should have survived longer in relatively 'traditional' areas such as Kagoshima in Kyushu as well as in the extremely homosocial environment of the military and boys schools and universities.

Sodomy (*keikan*) had, in fact, been made a criminal act in article 266 of the Meiji legal code in 1873 (Furukawa 1994: 108) although it seems hardly ever to have been punished. In the table of crimes from 1876–1881 there are only twenty instances of sodomy listed (0.01 per cent of the total number of offences) (Furukawa 1994: 110). This article was finally removed from the code in 1881, ironically at the instigation of a western legal expert, the French Boissonade[1] (1994: 110). The brief criminalisation of the act of sodomy reinforced the idea that it was a deviant and dangerous act. Turn-of-the-century newspaper reports are full of accounts criticizing the continued practice of *nanshoku* among military-academy students because of its adverse effect upon discipline. The vocabulary used in these articles: 'the "horrible depravity" of *nanshoku* among students, "roundup of immoral student groups, the acts of animals," "the loose morals of idiot students," and "no end to the depravity of students"' (Furukawa 1994: 112) illustrates the new conceptualisation of *nanshoku* as consisting of a deviant sexual act. Furukawa argues that such newspaper reports were part of an 'anti-sodomy campaign' centred in Tokyo which was only partly successful as vestiges of the old *nanshoku* code survived in isolated places such as Kagoshima until well into the Taisho period. He argues that:

> The equation of homosexuality with sodomy and criminality never achieved wide circulation in Japanese society whether through the sodomy ordinance of early Meiji or the anti-sodomy campaign in the latter half of the period. The *keikan* code as a mode of understanding circulated only in a limited sphere, centred on the law, and did not go beyond that to reach society generally (1994: 114).

Significantly, homosexuality at this time was still conceptualised as a masculine and even masculinizing practice. It was associated with the military and with male homosocial environments such as schools and universities. Nor was homosexuality yet understood as a minority activity, rather it was viewed as an activity that young men were prone to engage in. A report in *Eastern World* on 19 February 1898 says, 'Male homosexuality ... is so widespread among the students of Tokyo that adolescent boys cannot go out at night' (cited in Watanabe and Iwata 1989: 122). It was not male homosexuality *per se* which was stigmatised at this time, but the whole issue of 'youthful sexuality' which came to be understood as a problem in need of medical investigation and intervention. That young men would inevitably sexually misbehave whether it be by sodomising younger boys or squandering their tutorial money on geisha seems to have been taken for granted. So, despite Mori Ōgai's (imported) understanding of homosexuality as a criminal *act* (sodomy) specific to certain bodies (*Urnings*), popular culture saw it as a wider problem afflicting youth in general, much as we might view drug abuse today. The problematisation of youthful sexuality came at a time when the category of 'youth' itself was being formulated. The old samurai system where status was inherited had given way to a new system in which status was achieved. What signified in Meiji Japan was not so much an individual's family background as his educational background, particularly enrolment in specific courses of the imperial universities. Thus a great deal depended upon how a young man managed his youth and how he exploited his opportunities for social advancement (*shusse*) (Kinmouth 1981). The issue of sex, both hetero- and homosexual, was seen as a potentially damaging distraction from which a young man needed protection. That commentators were anxious about the kind of precedent that youthful indulgence in inappropriate acts might have on the future leaders of Japan is clear from the report of a journalist who wrote in the *Mancho-ho* of 18 May 1899, that he hoped the government would take measures against 'habitual conduct of such bestiality amongst the future lawyers, officers and teachers of Japan' (cited in Watanabe and Iwata 1989: 122).

Post-war understandings of homosexuality

The defeat of Japan at the end of the Second World War led to the American Occupation during which time a new constitution was drafted along western lines. However, anti-homosexual statutes and regulations, still common in many American states as well as in most European countries at this time, were not introduced into Japan (Pinkerton and Abramson 1997) which meant there was no change in the official policy which largely ignored same-sex sexuality as it existed between men.

Information about male homosexuality during this post-war period is relatively sparse. There are however, scenes in Mishima Yukio's novel *Kinjiki* (Forbidden colours [1951–3]; 1973: vol. 5) which describe a small bar scene for gay men in Tokyo just after the war. Although he maintains the indigenous term *danshokuka* to refer to 'homosexual' men, Mishima is aware of the effect mixing with foreign (particularly American) gay men was having upon Japanese young men. In a chapter entitled *Gay Party* (the title is in Roman alphabet in English) Mishima glosses 'gay' as 'American slang for *danshokuka*', (1973: 200) which suggests that its usage was not widely understood outside 'gay circles' or what Mishima terms *gei no shakai* (1973: 203). This chapter describes a Christmas party attended by many American gay men from the Occupation forces, most of whom had 'kept' Japanese boys as lovers. Yuichi, the 'hero' of the novel is introduced to the gay scene by a lover whom he meets in a cruise spot in Hibiya Park. He continues to meet lovers at a variety of cruise spots, at parties like the one described above and at a bar in the Ginza, called 'Rudon's.' This bar, however, was not exclusively gay but was popular among gay men because of the beautiful boys installed as waiters by the proprietor. Mishima makes no reference to exclusively gay bars and there is no mention of Shinjuku Ni-chome which is now the major site of gay venues in Tokyo. Hiratsuka (1994: 141) confirms that after the war gay bars were uncommon but that there were bars where the 'hostesses' (*okami*) were cross-dressing (*josō*) men. Although these bars were termed 'gay bars' (*gei bā*), the clientele was straight, consisting of hostesses from the *mizu shōbai* (entertainment trade) and their 'boys' (*wakamono*). He states that 'homosexual men (*homo no dansei*) were not made very welcome' (1994: 141).

The 1998 Bessatsu Takarajima edition dedicated to *Ura Tōkyō kankō* (Backstreet Tokyo sightseeing) has a brief potted history of gay bars in Japan from the end of the Second World War to the present written by a gay editor and writer, Ogura Tō. He argues that after the war the gay bar scene in Tokyo was small and closely linked with prostitution. He mentions the first bar to become well known immediately after the war was located in the Ginza area and known as the 'Brunswick.' In the 1950s, the number of bars increased to about twenty but most of them were filled with hustlers (1998: 146). He says that the system at these bars was similar to present-day host bars where the client would enter, have a drink and then select a partner from among the boys working at the club. Then he could either go to some hotel with the boy, or retire for a brief period to a separate room in the club. However, he also comments that these bars functioned as a safe space for gay men to meet with each other and it was not entirely unknown for men to meet with love partners there. He argues that the modern gay bar which serves more as a 'communication space' (*komyunikēshon supēsu*) than a venue to meet sex partners evolved out of these hustler bars, and many such bars began to accumulate in Shinjuku Ni-chome. At present, this area has over 200 gay bars (1998: 147).

It is relevant at this point to discuss further the work of Mishima Yukio (1925–1970), mentioned above, if only because he is often presented in the west as Japan's preeminent 'gay' writer[2]. Although he wrote twenty-three novels and over ninety short stories as well as plays, poetry and travel pieces, the theme of homosexuality is only given extended coverage in two of his novels: *Kamen no kokuhaku* (Confessions of a mask) ([1949] 1973: vol. 3) and *Kinjiki* (Forbidden colours) ([1951–3] 1973: vol. 5), one short story: *Onnagata* ([1952], transl. Donald Keene 1996), and a non-fiction work dealing with a classical Japanese text on *bushidō*, or the Way of the Warrior, *Hagakure nyūmon* (Introduction to *Hagakure*) ([1968], transl. Catherine Sparling 1977). Mishima's novel *Kinjiki* is interesting in its nostalgic references to the previous Japanese tradition of *nanshoku* which he contrasts with the pitiable lives lived by modern homosexuals. However, he does not idealise heterosexual love as he shares the misogyny apparent in some of the discourses surrounding Tokugawa-period *nanshoku* which represent women as unworthy love objects. Mishima's treatment of homosexuality is marked by an undercurrent of anxiety and self-doubt, even self-hatred. He conceives of homosexual men as a distinct subgroup who are forced to associate with each other in order to appease their sexual desire which is characterised as a misfortune. The alienation of homosexual men from mainstream society is emphasized in scenes contrasting the hidden, furtive activities of gay men which take place behind closed doors in bars or in 'closed' public spaces such as park bushes and toilets with the open manner in which heterosexual people, particularly families, go about their business. He speaks of Sunday, commonly known as family day in Japan, as 'miserable for homosexuals (*danshokuka*)' (1973, vol. 5: 236). However, Mishima is equally dismissive of straight society and the meaningless roles which both men and women are required to enact. Mishima makes homosexuality visible but as a separate world; in doing so he only problematises it and offers few positive images. It must, however, be stressed that Mishima is not denigrating modern-day homosexuality at the expense of some supposed ideal of heterosexual masculinity, as

he makes clear in his scathing attack on modern Japanese men in
Hagakure nyūmon. In this text Mishima portrays heterosexual
Japanese men as effeminate and emasculated, suggesting that the
loss of the discourse of *nanshoku* has led to the effeminization of
men in general. Mishima seems to be dissatisfied with modern
masculinity in general and sees the austere tradition of *nanshoku* as
upheld by Yamamoto as an ideal for all men, irrespective of sexual
orientation.

Mishima had read a great deal of western sexology which he
frequently alludes to in his work, as in *Kamen no kokuhaku*
(Confessions of a mask, [1949] 1973: vol. 3), his first novel to deal
extensively with sexual desire, specifically homosexual desire, written
when he was just twenty four. Here he refers to the theories of
Magnus Hirschfeld to explain his sadomasochistic attraction to a
picture of St. Sebastian the sight of which occasions his first
ejaculation, and the start of what he refers to throughout as his
'bad habit' (*akushū*) (1973: 191). Mishima details the young
narrator's (often understood to be Mishima himself) growing
awareness of how his same-sex passions stigmatise him as different
from other men. This is a slow process, for as he points out, he had no
idea that the homosexual desires he felt belonged to him alone:
'although I already had all the usual information about sex, I was not
yet troubled with the feeling of being different' (1973: 220). He writes
that 'I knew nothing about other boys. I did not know that at night all
other boys apart from me had dreams in which women ... were
stripped of their clothing' (1973: 242). As the sex manuals he read all
stated that erections were a spontaneous occurrence prior to coitus, he
assumed that he too would experience an erection when the time
came. He therefore understood sex with women to be quite a separate
issue from the desire that he felt towards other boys (1973: 242). The
same misogyny that is apparent in *Kinjiki* also runs through this
earlier work. Part of the 'mask' that Mishima hides behind is his
ability to court (and break the hearts of) girls. He deliberately seduces
the younger sister of a boy to whom he is sexually attracted and,
having once kissed her, begins to distance himself. There is little to
suggest in either the hero of *Kinjiki* or the narrator of *Kamen no
kokuhaku* that homosexual men might be friends with women, or
empathise with their subordinate position.

Although Mishima is often appropriated as a Japanese gay icon by
western readers and features in translation in compendiums of 'gay
literature' published in the west, he is not commonly understood to

have been homosexual in Japanese society (Starrs 1994: 98) and is not an icon to Japanese gay men. Although a book of memoirs about Mishima by Fukushima Jirō, who claims to have been one of his lovers, was published in 1998, it was soon withdrawn from sale after Mishima's family threatened legal action. The kind of tortured interiority displayed by his characters, both gay and straight, who constantly obsess over their sex lives, often resulting in murder or suicide, have little to recommend them as role models. Many of the Japanese gay men I spoke to about Mishima seemed unaware of the homoerotic content in his novels and regarded them as somewhat old-fashioned[3].

By the late 1960s, the sexual revolution which was taking place across Europe and America does seem to have had some effect in Japan and anxieties about changes in 'sexuality' are regularly reported in the media and new-wave fiction and films became increasingly bold in representing sexual liasons which disrupted hetero-normative mainstream discourses. The 1968 movie *Bara no sōretsu* (Funeral procession of roses) (Matsumoto Toshio) is described by Murray (1994: 406) as 'the first Japanese film to deal with homosexuality' and is valuable for its portrayal of the late-sixties gay scene. However, it is essentially a gay take on the Oedipus myth about a young cross-dressing man (the famous Japanese transvestite star 'Peter') who ends up killing his mother and sleeping with his father, ending with Peter gouging his eyes out upon the discovery of his lover's real identity. Another 1968 film, *Kuroi tokage* (Black lizard) (Fukasaku Kinji) also stars a transvestite actor, Maruyama Akihiro, who in his transgender role has 'homoerotic' interests in girls as well as sexual interest in men. In a bizarre scene, Mishima Yukio, who adapted the original novel for a stage version, appears as a naked human statue in the evil Maruyama's museum filled with beautiful bodies, both male and female. Mishima's well-attested obsession with body-building and his own and others' bodies may be partly responsible for the myth of gay men's 'narcissism' discussed later in chapter 3[4].

During the 1970s, representations of homosexual sex broke into the mainstream in women's manga fiction (*see* chapter 4) and an increasing number of writers began to include homosexual themes in their work. Murakami Ryū has consistently featured homosexual sex in his work, starting with the Akutagawa-prize winning novel *Kagirinaku tōmei ni chikaku buru* (Almost transparent blue 1976) followed by *Koin rokkā beibiizu (*Coin-locker babies 1980). However, the homosexual sex is used in these novels in much the same way as is drug abuse; it is presented as alienated, anti-social and ultimately self-destructive. Murakami focuses on these underground topics in a sustained attack on Japan's conformist culture which stresses homogeneity. However, the sadomasochistic drug-taking subcultures that he describes can hardly be upheld as positive images for those Japanese people who would like to break down the fierce social insistence upon sexual conformity to the family system. It was also during the 1970s that explicitly gay pornography began to be published in magazines aimed at a gay market, starting with the magazine *Barazoku* (Rose clan) first published in 1972 (Lunsing 1995).

Japan's 'gay boom'

I first became aware that Japan was going through a 'gay boom' (*gei būmu*) in the early-1990s when three movies dealing with gay men were released in quick succession from 1992–3. These were *Okoge* (Murata Takehiro 1992), *Kira kira hikaru* (Matsuoka George 1992; released in English as *Twinkle*), and *Hatachi no binetsu* (Hashiguchi Ryōsuke 1993; released in English as *A Touch of Fever*). Although all these movies deal with gay men as their central characters, I remember being surprised at the time that the audiences watching them seemed to be almost entirely made up of young women. After having watched the films and discussed their contents with Japanese gay friends, I began to think that these movies were not, in fact, about gay men at all, but were media fantasies which used the popularity of male homosexuality with young women to increase numbers at the box-office. I discuss *Okoge* and *Kira kira hikaru* and the way in which gay men are constructed in these movies in a manner meant to attract women in chapter 5.

Mass-audience media such as television also fuelled the boom by airing discussions and dramas focused on homosexuality. However, as Buckley (1994: 174) mentions, although male gay couples were included in a popular Japanese television dating game in 1992, 'the day when lesbian couples might also appear in prime-time programming seems far away' (1994: 174). The 'gay boom' was therefore in many respects an increase in the visibility of gay men. Just as the new movies dealt only with love between men, so did *Dōsōkai* (Classmates), Japan's first soap drama to graphically represent a gay love affair between men, which was aired in 1993. Unfortunately, not all these more 'realistic' representations of gay men are necessarily more positive than the pervasive images of gay men as transgendered objects of fun. These images of gay men in the popular media will be discussed in chapter 3.

Media interest in (male) homosexuality was not limited to movies and television alone, as a number of popular magazines also featured articles on gay men and gay lifestyle. There were so many articles and discussions in a wide variety of media that it is impossible for one researcher to give an account of them all. However, I will mention a number that I myself have come across. One of the pioneering articles appeared in the magazine *CREA* (February 1991) entitled *Gei runessansu '91* (Gay renaissance '91). Other articles appeared in such magazines as *Takarajima* (9 December 1993), entitled 'Gay men themselves tell all there is to know about the meaning of love between men' (*Gei jishin ga katari tsukushita otoko to otoko ga ai shi au imi*); *Hot Dog* (10 January 1994), entitled 'Homosexuality: the latest situation' (*Dōseiai: saishin jijō*); and *Marco Polo* (February 1994), entitled 'Gays in ordinary clothes' (*Fudangi no gei*). Articles on homosexuality have continued to be published sporadically, but as gay men are no longer interesting *per se*, they have tended to focus on increasingly bizarre and unusual situations such as the report in *Da Vinchi* (March 1999) on the sexual relationship between an *onabe* and a *nyūhāfu*. More high-brow publications discussing the issues of sexuality and gender from an academic perspective have also appeared in journals. These included an issue of *Gendai no esupuri* (August 1990) entitled 'Images of transgender' (*Toransujendā genshō*) and an issue of *EUREKA* (May 1993) on 'Gay culture' (*Gei karuchā*).

For the first time, knowledge about Japan's 'gay scene' became freely available in mainstream publications and a range of imported vocabulary for discussing sexuality was more widely dispersed. For example, the *Hot Dog* report mentioned above included interviews with three gay men and one lesbian, introduced the gay rights group OCCUR (*akā*), provided a glossary of 'gay vocabulary' including terms such as homophobia (*homofobia*), coming out (*kaminguauto*) and acceptance (*akuseputansu*). In a section entitled 'Communication,' the article also provided descriptions of and maps for a variety of gay venues as well as the titles of a number of gay publications. Yet although these articles sometimes included a token lesbian, they were primarily interested in male homosexuality. Buckley also notices this, commenting that 'special gay-culture issues of major critical theory journals over the last several years have focused on male homosexuality and made minimal if any reference to lesbianism' (1994: 179).

Sexuality in Japan is almost invariably understood from a male standpoint. Hence, the Tokugawa concept of *nanshoku* (literally male-eroticism) was understood as love between men, whereas the contrasting term *joshoku* (literally female-eroticism) referred to love between men and women. Similarly, the modern term *homopurei* (homosexual-play) which refers to sex between men is parallelled by *rezupurei* (lesbian-play) which refers, not to sex between women, but to sex between biological women and straight men dressed as women (Altbooks 1998: 172). Lesbianism has, however, been given a certain space in journals dealing with critiques of sexuality deriving from feminism. Buckley says the fact that 'special-focus issues on gender and sexuality have become common among mainstream journals of culture, literature and philosophy is indicative of the currency of the new discourse of sexuality within the contemporary Japanese intellectual and cultural landscape'(1994: 179). This academic interest in gender and sexuality does not seem to have abated, there having been issues of *imago* (November 1995) on 'Gay liberation' (*Gei riberēshon*) and (May 1996) on 'Sexuality' (*Sekushuariti*) as well as *Gendai shisō* (May 1997) on 'Lesbian and gay studies' (*Rezubian/ gei sutadiizu*). Many of these special editions feature interviews with, as well as articles written by, Japanese (and foreign) lesbians and gays. In 1996, the first edition of *Kuia sutadiizu* (Queer studies) was published, dedicated to new postmodern analyses of gender and sexuality. This was followed by another edition in 1997. The discourse of sexuality in these special editions is full of *katakana* loan words which transliterate the new, trendy vocabulary of postmodern 'Queer Studies.' However, very little mention is made of Japan's own heritage of homosexual culture and practice, and like Queer Studies in the west, the actual impact of these sophisticated intellectual debates is questionable. Despite the availability of information about new theories of sexuality in these popular intellectual journals, this academic discourse does not seem to have impacted at all upon the lives of the men I interviewed and many of the concepts current in this literature do not seem to have filtered through into daily use.

This media interest in homosexuality has created a wider market for homosexual-themed material, including that written and produced by gay men and women themselves. Thus writers such as Fushimi Noriaki were able to describe their own coming out experiences. Fushimi's (1991) *Puraibēto gei raifu* (Private gay life) has a great deal of useful biographical information as well as sections answering commonly asked questions about gay life, an outline of his own coming out process, and a discussion of the meaning of such terms as gender and sexuality in a Japanese context. The novelist Nishino Kōji's *Shinjuku Ni-chome de kimi ni attara* (When I meet you in Shinjuku Ni-chome, 1992) describes the infamous Ni-chome district of Shinjuku, long associated with sexual deviance, from the perspective of its inhabitants. These books were followed by works such as Kiyohara Munetaki's (1994) *Homotaimu* (Homo time), a sensationalist expose of Japan's gay scene written by a gay-porn photographer who had a long time association with the gay commercial world. This book does tend to exaggerate the more newsworthy and therefore bizarre aspects of the commercial gay scene but is also full of interesting anecdotal information about characters and places. The 'gay couple' (*gei kappuru*), Itō Satoru and Yanase Ryūta's (1994) book of advice entitled *Otoko to otoko no ren'ai nōto* (Notes of male-male love) also contains important biographical information about their individual coming out process and the difficulties they faced with both sets of parents as well as society at large (*seken*)[5] when establishing a home together. Other books such as Itō Satoru's (1996) *Dōseiai no kiso chiskiski* (Basic information about homosexuality) and Yamamoto Naohide's (1997) *Sekushuaru raitsu* (Sexual rights) attempt to give realistic information about (primarily male) homosexuality and adopt American models in arguing that diversity in human sexualities must be respected and acknowledged in legal reforms.

There has also been a boom in gay erotic fiction such as Hiruma Hisao's (1990) novel *Yes Yes Yes*; Tate Shirō's (1993) collection of short stories, *Asakusa uramiuta* (The bitter songs of Asakusa); and Sato Hiroaki's (1994) collection of tanka poetry, *Bathhouse*, all of which contain sexually explicit scenes (*see* English excerpts in Stephen Miller 1996). New, small scale art-house movies have also been tackling the theme of homosexuality in a more direct and erotic manner. Such movies include *Rasen no sobyō* (Rough sketch of a spiral) (Kojima Yasufumi 1990), the first documentary film about gay life in Japan. The production of a genre of *bara-eiga* (*bara*, or 'rose' designating homosexuality) which actually began in the mid-1980s has also continued into the 1990s with new directors such as Oki Hiroyuki whose troubled characters roam around Japan looking for love and sex, as in *Yūei kinshi* (Swimming prohibited) (1989), *Kankei* (Infection) (1990), *Matsumae-kun no senritsu* (Melody for Buddy Matsumae) (1992), *Hachigatsu no kuchibiru* (The lips of August)

(1994), and *Anata ga suki desu dai suki desu* (I love you, I love you very much) (1994). Although several of these movies have been given late-night runs at a popular art-house cinema in Shibuya (Rayns 1995), they are essentially underground movies.

There now seems to be an interest in the issue of 'sexuality' generally and many other writers who do not identify themselves as lesbian or gay have also contributed to the debate on homosexuality. These include Kurigi Chieko's (1996) rather idealistic treatment of homosexuality in America, *Amerika no geitachi: ai to kaihō no monogatari* (America's gays: a story of love and liberation); Yajima Masami's (1997) very informative collection of interviews with a wide range of Japanese same-sex desiring men, *Dansei dōseiaisha no raifuhisutorii* (Homosexual men's life stories); and many feminist works including the special edition on 'Sexuality,' volume 6 of *Nihon no feminizumu* (Japan's feminism, 1995) edited by the prominent Japanese feminist Ueno Chizuko who has published widely on the topic of (homo)sexuality. There is also a proliferation in the number of works dealing with masculinity (*otokorashisa*) termed men's studies (*dansei gaku*). Itō Kimio's (1996) book *Otokorashisa no yukue* (The whereabouts of masculinity) first published in 1993 discusses the supposed crisis in masculinity in post-war Japan. There are also a number of booklets published by the Men's Center Japan (*menzu sentā Japan*) based in Osaka which deal with this crisis in male identity and role, including *Otokorashisa kara jibunrashisa e* (From masculinity to individuality) which applies to men a feminist discourse, common in Japanese women's writings, of refusing gender roles in favour of some presumed pre-existent, genuine selfhood. The discourse of 'individuality' (*jibunrashisa*, literally 'like-oneself-ness') was common among both women and gay men I spoke to and seems much more widespread than that of 'identity' which only exists in Japanese as a *katakana* loan word and was seldom used by my informants.

The influence of the gay boom is questionable. Ishino and Wakabayashi comment that although the media treat gay and lesbian lifestyles as 'a fashionable subject ... the approach of the media is still voyeuristic,' citing instances of journalists going 'under cover' to expose the supposedly enticing secrets of Japan's gay world (1996: 100). The gay activist Itō Satoru also complains about the Japanese media's candid-camera techniques, citing a particularly offensive documentary entitled 'Things you should be scared of' (*Kowakute ikenai koto*) which featured a straight journalist hanging around in a gay cruising area waiting to be approached by a gay man (Summerhawk et al. 1998: 90). Itō argues that the reason why gay issues are sensationalised by the Japanese media is because 'to feature homosexuals whose daily lives are really no different from hetero-sexuals does not make interesting programming' (1998: 90). Although many of the representations of gay men in movies, television and print did move beyond the stereotype of gay men as gender inverts, the increased number of *discourses* dealing with homosexuality in Japan has not led to the increased visibility of homosexually-identified men and women on a grass-roots level, and it is still possible to come across young Japanese people who deny that there are, in fact, any gay people in Japan. However, for young men growing up in Japan today with a same-sex preference, the discovery of a community of like-minded people is no longer left to chance, as seems to have been the experience of older homosexual men whose interviews appear in chapter 7. The existence of a 'gay scene' and gay magazines and even gay-rights networks is acknowledged and discussed in popular media. The publishing company Bessatsu Takarajima, for example, publishes an annual guide to *Backstreet Tokyo Sightseeing* which situates gay bars along with other 'back-street' (*ura*) phenomena such as drugs, gambling, and sexual fetishes. Although this publication sustains the idea that homosexuality is a disreputable thing best hidden, it can at least be purchased and kept by gay men without fear of its discovery leading to family suspicion, a reason given by several of my interviewees as to why they did not read books or magazines which specifically addressed homosexuality. More will be said about the gay boom and its influence on the lives of homosexual men when I discuss material from my interviews in chapters 7 and 8.

Homosexuality before the law

Finally, it is important to consider how legal constructions of homosexuality have influenced how mainstream society relates to homosexual men. Unlike in most western nations, consenting same-sex genital interactions between men are unregulated by law in Japan. This may sound surprising in the context of the often fierce debates which have raged around the lowering of the age of consent for *male* homosexual acts in some European countries; however, it must be remembered that most western legal codes have always ignored sexual interaction between women which has seldom been considered a threat. In Japan, although the age of consent for sexual acts for women who have sex with men is thirteen, this does not extend to same-sex acts between men or between women. According to Article 177 of the penal code, thirteen is the youngest age at which a girl is considered capable of consent. It reads:

> Article 177 (rape) A person who, through violence or intimidation, has sexual intercourse with a female person of not less than thirteen years of age commits the crime of rape ... The same applies to a person who has sexual intercourse with a female person under thirteen years of age (Blakemore 1954: 113).

However, as Ikegami Chizuko points out, with regard to the above law 'men are not included.' She says that 'in a word this means that anything can be done to young boys (*shōnen*). For example, even if a thirty-year-old man has sex with a twelve-year-old boy, because there is no regulation against it, this man does not commit a crime (*tsumi ni narimasen*)' (1996: 164).

A Japanese lawyer friend of mine also confirmed that 'all Japanese laws relating to sex are constructed on the assumption that it is something that happens between men and women' (personal communication). However, he did point out that there was an article prohibiting 'indecent behaviour' perpetrated by violence or threat on either a man or a woman, irrespective of age (Article 176 of the Criminal Code). This reads:

> Article 176 (indecency through compulsion) A person who, through violence or intimidation, commits an indecent act with a male or female person of not less than thirteen years of age shall be punished with imprisonment at forced labor of not less than six months ... The same applies to a person who commits an indecent act with a male or female person under thirteen years of age (Blakemore 1954: 112).

Yet, this prohibition would seem to be aimed more at the 'violence and threat' involved than the 'indecent behaviour.' My informant suggested that in a case where a boy brought a charge against a man accusing him of unwelcome sexual advances, the man could be charged with inflicting bodily injury (*shōgai-zai*), assault (*bōkō-zai*) or forced obscenity (*kyōsei-waisetsu-zai*) but not rape. He added that consenting sexual relations between a man and boy could not be prosecuted through national law, but that as each prefecture had its own statutes relating to 'established usage' (*jōrei*) which cover such things as prostitution, it was conceivable that in certain prefectures in Japan there were regulations concerning same-sex sexual interactions. However, I have not been able to establish this[6]. Furthermore, Article 180 of the Criminal Code makes clear that even when the above crimes take place, the police will only take action upon receiving a complaint: 'Article 180 (complaint) The crimes provided in the preceding four Articles shall be prosecuted only on complaint' (Blakemore 1954: 115) which suggests that the Japanese legal system has a largely hands-off approach when it comes to investigating and prosecuting sexual crimes.

Pinkerton and Abramson in their contribution to West and Green's (1997) *Sociolegal Control of Homosexuality: A Multi-National Comparison* also state that 'there are ... no legal proscriptions of homosexuality in Japan, nor any laws concerning the practice of sodomy' (1997: 67). They argue that homosexual behaviour is controlled by 'societal rather than statutory regulations' (1997: 67). They refer to the history of what might be termed 'Tokugawa bisexuality' discussed above to show that Japanese society traditionally permitted a wide range of non-reproductive sexual styles, both homo- and heterosexual, so long as they did not interfere with the primacy of the family unit and the imperative to produce descendants (1997: 70). They argue that 'only recently has the notion of homosexuality as an orientation, rather than simply a behavioural option, emerged as a theoretical construct' (1997: 70). It is possible that the invisibility of homosexuality before the law reflects the general lack of discussion of homosexuality as a lifestyle choice in Japanese society. Just as in western societies, lesbianism was seldom legislated against because it was either considered not to occur or was not perceived as a threat, so too in Japan, male homosexuality is considered to be either extremely rare, or when it does occur, of little social significance.

Male prostitution is common in Japan and, as pointed out in chapter 6, host bars openly advertise sexual services provided for their clients on an 'eat in' or take home basis. As Hatano and Shimazaki argue (1997: 821), the laws against female prostitution are somewhat 'nebulous,' permitting a wide array of sexual services to be provided in a variety of clubs, cabarets, coffee shops and bars. With regard to male prostitution, the law is even less likely to interfere unless the boys involved are under age eighteen, or the club has broken some law, such as employing illegal foreign workers (1997: 821). Kiyohara (1994) argues that even boys who identify as straight sometimes get involved in casual male prostitution in order to pay their way through college. Such a situation is portrayed in the 'gay boom' movie *A Touch of Fever* (Hashiguchi Ryōsuke 1993).

The law in Japan is seldom used to protect against discrimination based on sexual orientation. However, a key anti-discrimination case was launched against the Tokyo Board of Education by the gay rights' group OCCUR (*akā*) when the group was denied access to a recreation and conference centre in Tokyo. The account of this incident given in Pinkerton and Abramson (1997: 81–2) makes it seem like a simple act of discrimination; they state that 'a small group of self-identified gay and lesbian youth known as OCCUR was forbidden access by the municipal government to a publicly funded facility, the Fuchū Youth House, after openly proclaiming their sexual orientation.' Yet the account of this incident given to me by Japanese gay friends who followed the news stories as well as that given by Itō Satoru (1996: 91–2) suggest that it was more complex. It was actually the group's request to use the facility for a second time that was turned down. During the group's first stay at the facility, a number of individuals had 'come out' to members of other groups who were also staying at the centre which resulted in some of OCCUR's members being verbally harassed (Itō 1996: 91–2). Although they complained to the manager, nothing was done about the harassment and when the group attempted to book the centre for a second meeting, they were turned down. When they asked the management for a reason, they were told that 'In order that the Fuchū Youth House should be used in a wholesome manner, there is a strict rule separating men's and women's rooms. Since there is the chance that homosexuals sharing the same room may have sex, it is not possible to allow homosexuals to use the boarding facilities' (Itō 1996: 91–2). This prompted OCCUR to file a law suit, the first ever in Japan to be based on a case of discrimination against sexual orientation. In 1994, the ruling came down on the side of the gay-rights group and awarded them damages. In ruling in support of OCCUR, the judge rejected the local government's arguments that 'allowing homosexuals to use youth facilities will have a bad effect on young people' (Itō 1996: 96). Although this court case was successful, OCCUR's actions were by no means unanimously supported by the gay men I spoke to who argued that the incident was needlessly provoked by some of the group's members unnecessary self-disclosure. I will say more about OCCUR and other gay rights groups and many gay men's ambivalent feelings about them in chapters 8 and 9.

It is clear that just because there is no legal provision against homosexual acts in Japan this does not mean that discrimination is unheard of. However, unlike gay rights groups in Europe and America which have organised around the need to fight for changes to discriminatory regulations encoded in the law, Japanese homosexual people face no *legal* discrimination. This means they are less likely to identify as a minority group stigmatised by legal regulations which distinguish them from a majority as happens in countries like the UK which maintains a higher age of consent for (male) homosexual sex and places restrictions on the situations in which such acts can take place and the number of men who can be involved.

Conclusion

It is apparent that there has been a continuous, well-attested history of genital same-sex interactions taking place between Japanese men from the Tokugawa period until today. However, the frames in which these interactions have been placed and understood differ markedly, making it difficult to speak of a unitary history of 'homosexuality.' During the Tokugawa period, although *nanshoku* (eroticism between men) was often contrasted with *joshoku* (eroticism between men and women), and the relative merits of each debated, there was no clear understanding that these two 'ways' (*michi*) represented opposite or mutually contradictory 'orientations.' Period literature and art has many representations of men enjoying both ways of love consecutively as well as simultaneously, and there are no contemporary terms which can be said to translate the modern understanding of the 'homosexual,' defined as a man congenitally incapable of making love to women.

However, in the Meiji period, intellectuals such as Mori Ōgai who were influenced by recently developed western understandings of a problematic realm of human experience termed 'sexuality' began to conceive of homosexual desire as specific to a certain kind of person: in Mori Ōgai's (borrowed) terminology, the 'Urning.' However, that this notion of homosexuality as a specific form of sexual desire which excluded heterosexual interests was not widely understood even by the Taisho period is clear from newspaper reports complaining about the predatory activities of university students who were out to seduce, not young girls, but young boys. Their predatory desires are not pathologised because of the inappropriateness of the love object (seduction of young girls would not have been considered preferable) but because they are symptomatic of ill-discipline. During this period the category of 'youth' became problematic, and young men were increasingly monitored to ensure they performed appropriate gender roles associated with adult men.

Although the amount of literary and academic attention paid to homosexuality may seem sparse during the post-war period, the attention is not comparatively less than that accorded to what was still considered a criminal act in most western countries. Also, despite the lack of official recognition of gay men in popular culture, there does seem to have been a thriving service industry catering to their needs, an industry which provides over 200 gay bars in a single area of Tokyo alone. However, it was not until the 'gay boom' of the early-1990s that the existence of a 'minority' of lesbians and gay men was recognised in Japanese popular culture. Yet, it is not at all clear that the gay boom is about giving voice to a previously silenced or occluded group of people. Several gay boom movies, for example, co-opt gay men as women's best friends, projecting all the qualities women supposedly find attractive onto gay men and 'othering' all the negative aspects onto straight men. Articles in the popular press actually serve to manufacture the idea of a 'gay identity' by only giving voice to that small minority of Japanese same-sex desiring individuals whose personal circumstances make it possible to be 'out' about their preference. Also, academic and intellectual discourse in highbrow journals discusses 'sexuality' in terms imported from North America and Europe which implicitly assume that such a thing as 'sexuality' exists, that it is differently expressed by different people and that these differences are so fundamental to human nature that one's individuality or identity must be founded upon them. Same-sex desiring individuals are thus minoritised while a supposed heterosexual majority, for whom same-sex desire is a constitutional impossibility, is encouraged to be more understanding. The gay boom simply displays an 'interesting' or newsworthy minority to the majority gaze. How some homosexual men understand themselves in relation to this proliferation of discourses will be discussed in chapters 7 and 8.

Chapter 3

Just Like a Girl: Images of Homosexual Men as Feminine

Introduction

To a certain extent Japanese popular culture tends to conflate same-sex desire with transgenderism and transsexualism. This is because, as James Valentine has pointed out, in Japan 'sexuality (unlike gender) is not a major source of identity, and those whose sexual orientation is toward the same sex are identified as differently gendered' (1997a: 97). Hence, the most prevalent images of gender nonconformists, particularly on television, are cross-dressed men. During my fieldwork in Japan I saw numerous television programmes, printed articles and advertisements which focused on transvestism/transsexualism, usually with humorous intent. In fact, these representations are so frequent that the Japanese media (and by extension, Japanese people) can be said to be fascinated by them. The gay activist and writer, Itō Satoru (1996: 45) refers to a research project conducted by the gay rights organisation OCCUR, which in one week of evening-time viewing found fourteen separate incidents of homosexuality or transsexualism treated as an object of humour or contempt[7]. I will first describe a few television programmes I myself observed which illustrate this and then discuss some examples from popular print media which also conflate homosexuality and transgenderism with humorous intent. Finally, I will look at how homosexuals who 'pass' are treated in the Japanese media, suggesting that when these figures are represented as passing from the outside to the inside of social life, they cease to be funny and are instead regarded as a threat.

Homosexuality and cross-dressing in the Japanese entertainment world

As pointed out in the introduction, the prominence of cross-dressed and transgendered 'talents' (*tarento*) in the entertainment media has resulted in the image of the *okama* becoming the most recognisable representation of non-normative sexuality in Japan. However, due to the historical association between cross-dressing and the entertainment world, not all cross-dressed or cross-gendered individuals in that world are understood to be homosexual. In fact the Japanese people I spoke to keenly resist that interpretation. The situation then, is rather complex. Japanese people seem to identify homosexuality with cross-dressing and transgenderism but when the cross-dressing takes place in specific social spaces such as the television, the entertainment world, and entertainment areas (such as Tokyo's Shinjuku district) they are reluctant to read this as an expression of sexual identity, preferring to see it as an individual's act or performance. An illustration of this is the annual *Kōhaku uta gassen* (Red and white song contest) which takes place on NHK's Channel 1 on New Year's Eve. The contest features a men's and women's team made up of that year's most successful media personalities who take turns to sing. Their performances are evaluated by a team of judges who then decide which team has won. On 31 December 1997, I was watching the programme with two English friends new to Japan. When the women's team compere, Wada Akiko, came on my friends both insisted that she was a man. Although a woman, Wada does have a very masculine appearance. She is tall, with broad shoulders, short hair and a deep, booming voice which is excellent for belting out the tear-jerking popular songs in Japan known as *enka*. Her gender performance is somewhat masculine, she does not use the hyper-feminine speech used by other female personalities and is somewhat forward and aggressive in her interaction with men.

Another gender-nonconformist star and a prominent personality in the men's team was Mikawa Ken'ichi who, when he appeared in a woman's kimono and make up, was taken to be a woman by my friends. They were quite perplexed as to why key representatives of the men's and women's teams should be transgendered and asked a Japanese friend of mine about it the next day. He was defensive, at first denying that there was anything masculine about Wada and then explaining Mikawa's cross-dressing as a publicity stunt aimed at bolstering his failing popularity. (Although why cross-dressing should make a star more popular was left unexplained.) My friends insisted that Mikawa was 'obviously' gay, whereas my Japanese friend insisted that he was not. This exchange was interesting for two reasons. Firstly it shows how indelibly etched is the association in the English mind between effeminacy and homosexuality: a man who dresses and behaves as a woman is 'obviously' gay. And secondly, it shows the reluctance of Japanese people to make inferences about a person's inner experience based on outward performance *in certain contexts*. Japanese people understand the entertainment world to be quite separate from reality and a transgendered performer is read as demonstrating a skill and not necessarily as communicating anything about an inner state or identity. This no doubt derives from the long tradition of transvestite theatre in Japan. As discussed in chapter 2, due to government concerns over the mixing of prostitution and acting in the 'women's kabuki' of the early seventeenth century, women were banned from the stage and women's roles came to be played by adult male female-impersonators (*onnagata*), a tradition which has been maintained until today (Shively 1968). Although many of these *onnagata* were sought after as sexual partners by other men, there is evidence that they were also popular as sexual partners among women (Leupp 1995). Indeed, the role of *onnagata* in Japan's tightly regulated and highly traditional kabuki theatre is often inherited and is passed down from father to son who takes on the dynastic name inherited from generations back.

In the Taisho period (1912–25), an all-woman theatre revue, known as the Takarazuka, was founded near Osaka, in which women play all the roles including those of men. The female male-role players (*otokoyaku*, literally 'male-role') are much more popular among women fans than their female-role counterparts and often appear on television chat shows as 'talents.' Takarazuka *otokoyaku*, like their female-role peers (*musumeyaku*, literally 'daughter-role'), are not allowed to get married while employed by the revue and have often been associated with homosexual scandals (Robertson 1998). However neither the *onnagata* nor *otokoyaku's* professionally transgendered personae can be simplistically read as indicative of any specific sexual orientation.

Another issue complicating the simplistic conflation of cross-dressing with same-sex desire is the large number of 'image clubs' (*imekura*) catering to straight men who want to dress as women (*josō suru*). There are two kinds of clubs, one type simply provides costumes, wigs, make-up and the advice of a professional beautician to help men to create the most attractive feminine persona. In these clubs, the cross-dressed men can adopt a feminine appearance and name and relax in a bar and sing karaoke with other cross-dressed men. Some allow the men to go out on the street and visit other bars and entertainment areas while cross-dressed in the club's clothes. The other type of club allows men to have sexual relations with the club's biological women while cross-dressed. This is referred to as *rezupurei* (lesbian-play)[8] and usually involves the division into butch (*tachi*) and femme (*neko*) roles where the client takes the passive role and is variously harassed, even to the extent of being anally dildoed by the club's employees (Altbooks 1998: 172). The binary homo/hetero division of sexual relations which focuses solely upon the genitals involved in sexual interactions is clearly unsuitable for categorising this kind of cross-dressed and transgendered situation. The existence of such clubs and the media attention given to them further complicates the issue of cross-dressing and its relationship to same-sex desire.

Hence, it is not surprising to find that Japanese people generally do not regard the flamboyant Mikawa Ken'ichi as 'gay.' Mikawa is not unique, Japan's modern entertainment world has many transvestite stars such as Maruyama Akihiro who, in Fukasaku Kinji's *Black Lizard* (1968), easily passes for a woman and commonly appears today on chat shows and in advertisements, and Peter, star of *Funeral Parade of Roses* (Matsumoto Toshio 1968) who is now a popular television chat-show host(ess), who similarly passes. Other stars make no attempt to 'pass' including Mikawa who rarely completely cross-dresses (*josō*), preferring to wear flamboyant jackets, jewellery and make-up. There are also many pop stars who employ transgender elements in their personae but who do not attempt to pass as women. Predominantly transgendered groups (where the men have long dyed hair, heavy make-up and wear 'feminine' if not actually women's clothes include *GLAY*, *La 'crima Christi*, *Mirage*, and *L'Arc en Ciel*. Other stars, such as IZAM (*see* Plate 17) of the group *SHAZNA* and Mana of *Malice Mizer* cross-dress and can actually 'pass' although their gender performance (language, etc.) is masculine.

I saw a television concert featuring all the bands mentioned above and was struck by the number of boys in the audience who had obviously styled themselves on their favourite transgendered performer. Many IZAM-inspired boys could have passed as women. The female compere who was interviewing these boys described them as 'stylish' (*kakkō ii*) and 'beautiful' (*kirei*). Some of these boys were also playing with gender in their names, choosing deliberately obscure names such as GiGi. There were also girls who had adopted aspects of their male idol's dress and make-up leading to the interesting situation of women impersonating men impersonating women, a modern parallel to the way in which kabuki *onnagata* were often trend setters for female fashion in the Tokugawa period (Dalby 1993: 275). There seem to me to be clear parallels between the transgender performance of many of these teen idols and the *bishōnen* (beautiful youth) characters in women's comics described in the next chapter. It could be argued that these boys have styled themselves to look like the beautiful boys ubiquitous in women's comics in an attempt to be more popular with young women. Thus real boys are attempting to style themselves in accordance with the fantasized boys in women's comics, an example of women's consumer culture actually affecting male stylisation. This situation is an illustration of how complex the interrelationship between gender performance and sexuality in Japanese popular culture can be.

Above, I have described a number of situations in which gender ambivalence is not simply tolerated but actually admired. However, they all take place in the context or frame of the entertainment world which has long been characterised by its fascination with cross-dressing and transvestism. As Hatano and Shimazaki suggest:

> The roles in both Kabuki and Takarazuka Opera have come to be viewed as a performance, something one sees only on the stage. Accordingly, occurrences in these fictitious worlds are not always so easily tolerated in the real world. A 'drag queen' appearing on television, for example, lives in 'television land,' a world from which most people feel detached (1997: 823).

As I point out in chapter 7 when I look at the life stories of my informants, many of whom were bullied at school for failing to successfully embody 'masculine' gender, gender ambiguity may be prized when it is displayed by a television star, but it is often despised when it occurs in a colleague or neighbour.

Gender nonconformism can be expressed in various ways including clothing and language, the latter being clearly divided into masculine and feminine usage. A female presenter like Wada Akiko, who chooses not to use hyper-feminine polite language (*sonkeigo*) but instead speaks in a plain form, even without the use of masculine pronouns and articles, is already straying into the domain of masculine speech. Similarly, gay men who wish to perform a feminine role (in Japanese, *onēsan*, or 'big sister') can do so simply by switching to a female-coded speech pattern. The film-critics and panel stars, Osugi and Piiko[9], do not cross-dress at all, but use hyper-feminine *onēsan kotoba* (literally 'big-sister speech') which marks them as transgendered. Thus, there are varying types and degrees of transgenderism in the Japanese entertainment world and seeing a man in a dress does not necessarily signify same-sex desire (as in the case of IZAM who has dated a number of high profile female stars). However, when Japanese people think of homosexuality, they do tend to think of a man in a dress, or a hyper-feminine man who uses 'sister speech' as will be discussed later.

The connection between cross-dressing, gender nonconformity and sexual orientation or identity is seldom spelled out on Japanese television and even when an individual is presented as an *okama* on a television show, no necessary connection is made between the man's gender nonconformism and his sexual preference. This is clear in the *Terebi Tōkyō* programme *Spirittsu* which regularly features *bikkuri goto* (surprising things/incidents) which are shown on video in front of a live audience and then commented on by a panel of personalities. On 12 December 1997 the programme featured a man who was a farmer by day and an *okama* by night. The man, referred to as *okama-san* and the diminutive *okama-chan* was shown working on the farm then going out shopping for women's clothes, getting made up and going to his night job as a hostess in an *okama* bar. He was described as a *shizenha okama* (natural-group *okama*) which presumably refers to his primary job as a farmer, or could refer to the fact that he lived in the countryside whereas *okama* are normally expected to live in the city due to their supposed connection with the entertainment business. In this programme, no reference was made to the man's sexual preference. The 'surprising thing' was his conflation of two apparently conflicting jobs: those of farmer and cross-dressed hostess.

This lack of reference to sexual practice is in no way due to censorship or to any reticence that Japanese media might have about discussing sexual topics. Other researchers have amply illustrated that Japanese comics (Buckley 1991; Allison 1996), magazines and tabloid newspapers (Hardacre 1997), animated cartoons and television shows (Abramson & Hayashi 1984; Bornoff 1991) are saturated with representations and discussions of sex. Nor is it to do with any reticence on the part of television stations about causing possible offense to homosexual viewers as this would require an acknowledgement in Japanese society that there existed such a minority group which needed to be respected. The sexual relationships of *okama* are not represented for two reasons: firstly, they are stereotypical figures whose personalities are outlined only with a few crude brush strokes, they are not real people and cannot therefore be represented as fully rounded individuals with sex lives, but, perhaps more importantly, the characterisation of the *okama* as a transvestite man whose preferred sexual act is to be the passive recipient of anal penetration makes it impossible to represent his partner. The obvious partner of an *okama* man is a 'straight' man (in Japanese, the usual words used to describe the concept of 'straight' are the English loan-word *nōmaru* ['normal'], or its Japanese equivalent, *futsū)*. Of course such a representation would be impossible as no 'normal' man would find an *okama* attractive. Valentine comments:

> In media portrayals, *okama* look like fakes, trying to be women but noticably failing ... Not really men, not really women, they are moreover, not really sexual. They are defined in terms of gender rather than sexuality (1997a: 103).

These stereotypical, partial representations of gender-nonconformist men in the Japanese media impact upon the lives of many Japanese homosexual men, particularly during the period when they are first becoming aware of their own same-sex attraction. Many of the homosexual men interviewed by Yajima (1997) say that their first intimation that a 'gay world' existed came from chat shows and documentaries focusing upon the *okama* stereotype. Some were left with the impression that same-sex desire necessarily required cross-dressing or that the only way they could 'be themselves' in Japanese society was to work in a transvestite bar. A male-to-female transgender individual interviewed in the newspaper *Tōkyō shimbun* (10, 11, 12 December 1997) recounts how s/he dropped out of high-school because of bullying and fled to Tokyo with the intention of 'finding sympathetic friends by working in a "new half" bar,' only to find that rather than being a safe space in which s/he could be him/herself, s/he was required to perform in a degrading manner for the entertainment of the straight patrons. S/he gave up the job because 'the work of the new-half is like that of a performer who makes patrons laugh'[10]. Similarly the individual identified as an *onabe* in the *Da Vinci* article discussed in the introduction also recalls the 'excitement' s/he felt when s/he saw a television show introducing a 'new-half show pub.' Commenting '[I thought] this is all there is [for me],' s/he visited the pub and started to work part-time there. It was in the pub that s/he met his/her 'girlfriend' (identified in the article as a *nyūhāfu*, or a male-to-female transsexual, who was also working there).

The media conflation of homosexuality with transgenderism has led to the popular idea that gay people are easily recognisable (and therefore rare, as such individuals are seldom encountered). When I spoke to students at Senshu university where I was studying for three months in 1998 and told them that I was researching gender in Japan and that I would like to interview some homosexual Japanese, they were very surprised. They were also surprised when I asked if they knew any homosexual people at the university I might approach. I asked over twenty students and not one admitted knowing any homosexual people. Most people had no idea how I might contact homosexual Japanese people but some suggested that I might go to an *okama* bar in Shinjuku. Of course no one knew the exact address of such a bar but I was told that if I just went to Shinjuku one night I would probably see people who 'looked like that' (*sō mieru hito*). I wondered how Shinjuku had become identified in the Japanese imagination as a hangout for 'people who look like that,' as well as what 'that' signified. Shinjuku's prominence as a site for sexual deviants was confirmed later when I came across an advert for the theme park Toshimaen in the entertainment magazine *Pia* (*see* Plate 1). The advertisement shows a transvestite/transsexual (*nyūhāfu*) admiring his/her nails with the theme park in the background. The caption reads 'I came from Shinjuku' (*atashi shinjuku kara kita no*). The speaker is linguistically marked as feminine by the use of the feminine first-person pronoun *atashi* as well as the sentence final particle *no* which indicates a female speaker. It is significant that the figure of the transvestite is used to advertise a theme park, a place of family entertainment, and shows how such figures are associated with humour and entertainment and are considered harmless.

Although it is true that Shinjuku Ni-chome has hundreds of gay bars, only a tiny fraction of them cater to cross-dressers. In fact Japanese men who cross-dress, like the man featured in the *Spirittsu* programme, often work in the entertainment world in *okama* bars where the clientele is straight. These bars are not situated in Shinjuku, but located in other mainstream entertainment districts in Tokyo like Roppongi and Shibuya. Thus, if I had gone to an *okama* bar I would have been very unlikely to meet any gay men or lesbians, although I would have met men, known in Japanese as *okama*, *nyūhāfu* and *misutā redii* (Mr Lady), who may or may not have, in addition to their cross-dressing, identified as 'gay.'

Representations of homosexual men as transgendered in popular print media

When homosexual men are represented in the Japanese media, even when not actually cross-dressed or transgendered they are still often marked as transgressing into the feminine domain in other ways. An article in the tabloid magazine *FOCUS* (1 April 1998), reporting the 'homo-play' (*homopurei*) and drug abuse of an official in the Finance Ministry is ambivalent about how to treat him. The article asserts that he was well-mannered, hard working and betrayed no strange behaviour, while simultaneously upholding that he was soft (*yawarakakute*) and effeminate (*joseippokatta*) and had a liking for extremely cute things (*zuibun kawaii mono*). A photograph of one of these cute things, a chicken-shaped tissue-box cover is reproduced along with a photo of the drugs and syringes for which he was arrested as though both were equal symbols of crime. Also, much is made of the fact that 'he was not yet married,' a clear sign of deviance in a middle-aged man; as Valentine comments 'to be unmarried is a form of disability. Not to be paired up is clearly odd' (1997a: 99). An otherwise gentle and retiring Japanese man is suddenly 'understood' as perverse in the light of his sexual acts, a colleague stating 'when I think about his tastes (*shumi*), it all makes sense,' causing characteristics which are common of many Japanese men to suddenly be highlighted and given etiological significance.

This approximation of homosexual man with woman/woman's realm is extremely pervasive and at times seems a little forced. For example, in the comic series *Tetsujin ganma* (The iron man, Yamamoto Yasuhito 1995), the hero, Teruo, is sexually harassed by his boss (*see* Plate 13). In the case of sexual harassment, it would normally be the harassed (subordinate) partner who is effeminated by the power differentials at play. However, in the case of same-sex harassment, it is the harasser (the homosexual) who is effeminated. This is done in two ways, firstly, the boss's name is 'Kamasu' which incorporates the '*kama*' of *okama* and thus serves as a linguistic marker associating him with the effeminate stereotype. Secondly, he is linked with the world of women by means of a flashback immediately preceding the harassment scene. In this flashback, Teruo remembers watching a girl swing a hoop around her hips, he concludes 'hips are important for women' (1995: vol.9). In the next scene, we see the boss from behind as he is practising golf in his office: swinging his hips, thus directly linking him with the preceding image of the girl playing hoop and the statement 'hips are important for women' (and therefore for *okama* who are woman-like).

The idea that a man's homosexuality is indelibly marked on his body and personality is clear from a book which helps women 'check out' their partners (*chekku auto shite*) for any homoerotic tendencies.

Written by Nomura Sachiyo (1995), the wife of one of Japan's top baseball coaches and a famous television *tarento* in her own right, the book *Anata otoko no kantei dekimasuka? chekkupointo wa 17 ka sho* (Can you judge men: 17 check points) includes a chapter on how to spot homosexuals. The chapter is entitled 'You should suspect a man who likes to be neat of being homosexual' (*Otoko no kirei-zuki wa homo wo utagae*) and firmly locates the same-sex desiring man in the female realm. She says that men who cross-dress (*josō*) should clearly be suspected of being gay (though she does qualify this, suggesting that some heterosexual men just like to dress up) (1995: 135). However, men who are overly interested in their masculine appearance are also suspect. She says that many gay men are 'narcissists' (*narushisuto*) and 'go to the gym in order to get a masculine, sexy body' (1995: 137). They are also overly conscious of their appearance and their clothes are never in the least dirty or messy. They also smell different, always using perfumed items. She confidently asserts that 'homosexuals like perfume' and that there is a secret conspiracy between homosexuals who, all using the same perfume, can spot each other. At the time of writing, she suggests that this 'gay' (*homo muke*) perfume, is Christian Dior's 'Eau Sauvage' (1995: 138). Gay men are here marked as feminine by their obsession with the body, clothes and perfumes, which in their case is symptomatic of self-obsession.

If a woman is suspicious of her boyfriend based on his over-refined appearance, the next step is to check out his room (1995: 138). It is necessary to check for 'womanish things' (*onna no bubun*). These include lace curtains, chandeliers, rococo-style furniture and rose-patterned wallpaper[11]. The boyfriend should also be asked to prepare a meal and the manner in which he cooks brought under scrutiny to see if he 'cooks in a feminine manner' (*onna no yōna tsukurikata*) (1995: 139). Also, his room shouldn't be too tidy. If it is, he may be a homosexual; although one has to be careful on this point as another woman friend of his may be cleaning the room for him. She concludes that 'as you'd expect, homosexuals are somehow feminine' (*homo wa yahari doko to naku joseiteki*) (1995: 140).

However, after carrying out the above checks and coming to the conclusion that one's boyfriend is homosexual, the relationship does not have to be abandoned but 'started (over)' (*kaishi suru*) (1995: 146). After all, it's nice for a woman to have a handsome male friend who talks good sense and likes to listen. Nomura clearly does not consider gay men to be bad or sick people, indeed she even recommends them as making excellent friends for women. Gay men are presented in a rather contradictory way: as being both self-obsessed (*narushisuto*) but also sympathetic listeners to women (which their heterosexual counterparts are presumably not). Even when not cross-dressed, their sexual preference is still manifest in their 'feminine' obsession with their appearance, interior decoration and cooking. They look different from straight men, smell different and cook differently too. Nomura's message is that gay men are everywhere, but the smart woman can spot them. Nomura's typification of gay men very much supports Valentine's suggestion that the domestic sphere is called upon for conceptualising homosexual men in Japan. He argues that 'a province thought appropriate to women is especially suitable for the identification of gay men, who are primarily conceived as transgressing gender boundaries' (1997a: 102). It is in this context then, that the cross-dressing farmer discussed earlier can be represented as a *bikkuri goto*, or 'surprising thing.' What is surprising is his conflation of two mutually opposing roles: those of transvestite and farmer. Had he been a hairdresser or a stay-at-home 'housewife,' his cross-dressing would not have been under-stood as surprising in this way.

The above examples have all been taken from popular print media where discussion of homosexuality is incidental. However, there are books and comics which take homosexuality as their main theme. Homosexual men in women's comics will be discussed at length in the next chapter; here I will just mention a few comic collections which deal primarily with homosexuality for humorous effect. In 1994, the Japanese gay rights group OCCUR (*akā*) published its first 'Gay report' (*Gei repōto*) which included the first large-scale questionnaire survey about gay life in Japan actually conducted by gay men themselves. This report is parodied by the manga artist Yamamoto Hideo in his *Okama Report* (1996) which is a collection of comics originally published in the weekly comic magazine *Young Sunday Comics*. That it was conceived as a parody is clear from a letter from OCCUR reproduced at the back of the compilation, complaining about the stereotypical portrayal of gay men in its pages. *Okama Report* shows similar confusion as to the significance of cross-dressing for sexual orientation as is apparent in television and other entertainment media. For example, in some of the stories in the 1996 edition, men cross-dress as women either to become more attractive to women (see the arguments in the next chapter as to why this is so) or in order to gain sexual access to women. In one scene, a cross-dressed man who has so far successfully passed as a woman is discovered to be a man during a company trip to a hot spring when he gets an erection in the women's bath. Not all the men in this comic series are cross-dressed however. One story involves a boy who is shown making love to a girl with a look of extreme perseverance on his face. The next page shows the sexual interaction as it appears in his fantasy: he is in fact making love to another boy. After the act is over, he lies awake repeating 'It's true that I love Miki (a girl's name).' Here, the boy is clearly 'homosexual' although he has been having sex with a girl. However, he is not cross-dressed. Yet, other men who *are* cross-dressed, are shown to be heterosexual; illustrating how complex is the interrelation of transgender, transsexuality, cross-dressing and homosexuality in Japanese popular media.

The letter from the gay rights organisation OCCUR, entitled 'On how to portray male homosexuals' (*Dansei dōseiaisha no kakare kata ni tsuite*) which is reproduced at the back of *Okama Report*, itself seems to conflate the terms *okama* and *dōseiaisha*. The group's use of the term *dōseiaisha* is significant, in that, as described in the introduction, it is a medical term which does not have wide currency. The use of this term is therefore an attempt to circumvent the associations that other, more common terms, such as *gei*, have with transvestism. As described above, however, many of the stories in the collection concern men who are clearly heterosexual who cross-dress in order to gain better access to female spaces such as the women's bath. The letter complains that male homosexuals (*dansei dō-seiaisha*) are treated as objects of humour (*warai mono*) but it is by no means clear that the characters in the stories are 'male homosexuals' or indeed, that it is their homosexuality *per se* which is being ridiculed.

There is also a genre of women's comics known as YAOI, the name being taken from the first part of the words *Yamanashi* (no climax, literally 'no mountain'), *Ochinashi* (pointless), *Iminashi* (meaningless). The writer and gay activist, Fushimi Noriaki defines *YAOI-zoku* (YAOI-group) as 'manga and animation characters aimed at women which parody homosexuals' (1991: 14). YAOI manga grew out of an underground movement of non-professional manga artists (many of them women) who used manga clubs and conventions to circulate their privately printed work (Kinsella 1998: 301) in the mid-1980s. However, YAOI are characterised by their parody of a number of mainstream comics such as the exaggerated masculinity of many men's manga characters and are as much a parody of the manga genre itself as of 'homosexuality.' Hence, Fushimi, like the members of OCCUR, seems to take offense at any humorous representation of homosexuality, irrespective of the context. This seems strange when the context is comic books where the treatment of all the characters is extremely parodic and exaggerated. Lunsing reports that 'in general ... gay informants liked the genre' (1997: 274) although he does mention a discussion in the magazine *Choisir* where one gay man attacked these comics for 'abusing male homosexuality for the sexual gratification of women' (1997: 274). Women admirers of the genre, however, argued that it was purely a fantasy genre and that fantasy should be free (1997: 274). Gay activists, therefore, do seem to veer towards essentialism when they identify the rather flexible image of the *okama* as he appears in YAOI manga, with 'male homosexuals.'

Another comic which uses the cross-dressed man as an object of humour is Nitta Tomoko's *Okama in the Office* (1997) which has the English headline 'UMI chan, his life as a woman' on the cover. This is a collection of comics originally serialised in *Manga Time Family*. Again, it is not clear whether Umi is sexually interested in men or women. However, on the one occasion when Umi comes to the office dressed as a man (although still with long hair and make-up), all his female co-workers immediately fall in love with him. The construction of the transgendered man as an erotic fantasy for women is another factor complicating the issue of homosexuality and transgenderism in Japanese culture and will be explored in the next chapter.

The treatment of homosexual men who 'pass'

So far, the images of homosexual men that have been considered are those that represent them as somehow transgendered. Although the overwhelming number of images of homosexual men represent them as transgendered or cross-dressed figures of fun, considered so harmless that they can be featured in comics directed at young people, or used to advertise places of family entertainment, on the few occasions when more gender-normative homosexual figures are presented, they are treated somewhat differently. The homosexual man who is transgendered and restricts himself to the entertainment world is tolerated, even appreciated. However, the homosexual man who 'passes' and turns up as your boss, your teacher, your neighbour or even your husband occasions a great deal of anxiety; he is a figure to be feared and or despised. As Valentine suggests 'outsiders who remain clearly outside do not pose the problem of marginality; it is within an insider context that their peculiarity is perceived' (1997a: 96). Hence, representations of homosexual men who have somehow insinuated themselves into 'ordinary' domains such as the office or the school, are often treated as figures of fear.

Because explicit representations of homosexual men other than the *okama* stereotype are so unusual on Japanese television, I never encountered any during the period of my fieldwork. However, I did see a number of television programmes which hinted at homosexual behaviour or attraction which was assessed in a negative way. One of these was broadcast on the *TBS terebi* channel on 12 December 1998. Entitled 'Life-consultancy special' *(Jinsei sōdan supesharu)*, it featured a number of re-enactments of difficult situations faced by viewers which were then commented on by a panel of talents who offered advice. One of these re-enactments was described as 'A loving son's crisis' *(Itoshii musuko no kiki)* and centred around the relationship between two male university students. The 'loving son' of the title had a best friend who often came round and shared meals with the family. However, the mother thought there was something strange about this friend as he behaved towards her son 'like a lover' *(koibito no yō)*. The one illustration of this given was when the friend requested some sellotape in order to remove fluff from the son's jacket, a request that the mother thought extremely strange. Some months later, after the son has moved out into his own apartment, the friend turns up at the mother's house looking for him. The staging of this scene can only be described as lurid: the boy's face, lit from underneath, seems eery and ghoul-like and his manner of speaking is clearly deranged. As he stands in the hallway, a call comes from the son warning his mother not to talk to this friend who has become a 'stalker' *(sutōkā)*. In this story the intimacy between the two young men is presented as strange. The normal, nice 'loving son' is contrasted with the weird, ghoul-like friend whose same-sex attraction ultimately leads to insanity.

Other negative references to more explicitly gay men are analysed by Valentine who was resident in Japan during 1990 and 1992–3. He argues that 'gay men are ... portrayed on Japanese television, but without sexual relations, and generally without sexuality' (1997b: 63). When reference *is* made to homosexual men's sexuality, it is met with either shock and horror or understood to be sad, pitiable and doomed to failure. He discusses an AIDS drama, *A Tale of Love between Him and Him*, which at least attempts a sympathetic treatment of the relationship between a younger and an older man. The love here is treated along the lines of the trope of 'forbidden love' which has a long history in Japan, as Valentine points out 'the love must be hidden and death is the solution' (1997b: 67). The young man conveniently dies before the relationship can be consummated, leaving the older man free to get on with his marriage. A less sympathetic relationship is presented in the movie *Section Chief Shima Kōsaku*, a film in which a male colleague declares his love for the hero Kōsaku. Not put off by the hero's obvious signs of rejection and disgust, the homosexual colleague attempts to blackmail him into giving in to his sexual predations. Of course, Kōsaku heroically resists and his blackmailer's attempts are thwarted, condemning him to a life of loneliness and frustration. The impossibility that male-male love might be requited or that two gender-normative men might come together in a kiss is also highlighted in a children's animation programme, *Young Master*, where elementary school boys are shown putting on a stage show. In one scene, two boys are shown attempting to steal a kiss from a princess, however, she slips away leaving the two boys in a long kiss with each other. The schoolboy audience is so incensed by this that they storm the stage and attack them (1997b: 67).

Lesbianism, too, although even less evident on Japanese television, is treated harshly when the lesbian figure leaves the frame of the entertainment world and turns up as an ordinary person. Ishino and Wakabayashi comment that 'lesbian characters ... are generally portrayed as tragic characters who try to seduce pretty women and fail' (1996: 100). One instance illustrating this, referred to by Valentine, concerned the unsympathetic portrayal of a lesbian student at a girls' school. In *High-school Teacher*, a temporary male teacher falls in love with a female student, a relationship which is treated sympathetically (after all, it is 'natural' for older men to be interested in young girls). Unfortunately, Mami, a female student who is represented as a stereotypical lesbian: short hair, powerful body, she is both sporty and a bully, becomes jealous of this relationship. She forces a kiss upon the unwilling girl and later falsely accuses the male teacher of rape and in a subsequent episode throws a bottle of acid at him (1997b: 59). In a curious inversion, in both this episode and the film *Section Chief Shima Kōsaku*, discussed above, the homosexual characters who might be supposed to themselves be the victims of homophobic attack, actually become the aggressors. In the 'real' world, homosexuals become the evil outsiders who attempt to pervert and destroy the happiness of those 'normal' people from whose ranks they have been banished because of their perverse desires.

However, it must be stressed that there are other, more positive representations of love between gay men in a number of movies and television dramas arising out of Japan's 'gay boom' which took place in the early-1990s as well as in the huge number of women's comics which deal with love between beautiful boys (*shōnen'ai*). Yet, as I will argue in the forthcoming chapters, these representations are primarily aimed at women and the image of the 'gay man' is still being manipulated and controlled. Gay men are not here represented as a threat to straight men, but as a friend to straight women. In many of these representations, it is straight men who are shown to be violent, manipulative and cruel. Indeed straight men become the perverse 'other' while gay men are reinscribed as women's best friends. Unfortunately, these images are just as much media fantasies as are the predatory homosexuals who stalk offices and schools.

Conclusion

It is clear from the material discussed above that many Japanese people have rather stereotypical ideas about homosexual men, considering their same-sex attraction to be necessarily effeminating. Thus, when I was told by students at Senshu university that Shinjuku Ni-chome was a place where I could find people who 'looked like that,' it was clear that the first image that came to mind when I asked about homosexual people (*dōseiaisha*) was the transgendered *okama*, a figure familiar from many television documentaries and panel shows. This image is not necessarily negative, for there are same-sex desiring men who wish to appear and act like women (just as there are straight transvestite men who also like to do this). The problem with the image is its ubiquity: it appears everywhere in Japan, in a variety of media, and gives young men who are just becoming aware of their same-sex attraction, a partial and distorted image of what this attraction means. This is a problem mentioned by many of the men interviewed by Yajima (1997), and was also brought up by my interviewees.

Representations of 'ordinary looking' homosexual men doing ordinary things and living ordinary lives are conspicuously absent in Japanese media. Farmers (or doctors or salarymen) are not shown living with their same-sex partners and quietly going about their daily lives, but are displayed as *bikkuri* (surprising) objects of humour for media consumption. It is true that any sexual component of cross-dressing is seldom referred to but this is largely because no attempt is made to flesh out these cross-dressed figures and represent them as real people living real lives. *Okama* are represented as humorous but ultimately sad and pathetic women *manqué* who try to act like or perform as women, but ultimately fail. Representations of sexually nonconformist Japanese women follow the male pattern but are rarer, so rare in fact that many of the Japanese people I spoke to were unable to give female equivalents for common male terms. When Japanese media do go beyond the constraints of the *okama* stereotype, the homosexual man ceases to be a friendly object of humour and is instead presented as a threat to other men, or as a sad and pathetic figure worthy of pity. The notion that two gender-normative men might find each other attractive and come together in a relationship much as men and women do is seldom entertained in mainstream media.

How then, do same-sex desiring men in Japan respond to this situation? As Valentine has stated:

> Negative stereotypes can work in three ways on those stereotyped: they may accept the representation as valid and adopt the negative self, attempting to conform to that image; they may accept the representations as valid and doubt the evidence of their own sexual orientation ... ; or they may reject the validity of the representation' (1997b: 74).

I found evidence both from my own interviewees as well as from the interviews collected by Yajima (1997) and from anecdotal evidence gained from books and articles written by gay men that homosexual men variously adopt all three strategies. However, by far the most common strategy is the latter: homosexual men generally reject the images they are offered by popular culture, acknowledging them as the products of fantasy, ignorance or prejudice. However, the very ubiquity of these images makes many homosexual men reluctant to 'come out' about their same-sex preference as those around them have only negative categories in which to place them. When a homosexual man comes out to colleagues, friends or family in Japan, he is very likely the first such person they will have met. Furthermore, there are no positive representations within popular culture which they can use to come to an understanding of their friend's, son's, or colleague's declaration. Thus a person who up to now has been considered to be a 'normal' member of the in-group (*uchi*) is suddenly 'othered' and becomes a member of the out-group (*soto*). It is for this reason that declarations of homosexuality are so often met with incomprehension, disbelief and silence, as I illustrate when I describe the life stories of my interviewees in chapter 7.

In the next chapter, I will look at another pervasive image framing homosexuality in Japanese popular culture, the love between 'beautiful youths' (*bishōnen*) in women's comics, which has also been criticised by homosexual men as providing an unrealistic and distorted image of same-sex love. These images not only impact upon young same-sex desiring youths who come into contact with them, but actually influence how Japanese women generally think about homosexuality, which in turn has implications for how homosexual men are treated.

Chapter 4

The Love between 'Beautiful Boys' in Women's Comics

Introduction

In the previous chapter, I argued that mainstream media tend to conflate homosexuality with gender nonconformism and that gay men are therefore frequently shown to be women *manqué*. So long as gay men (or rather *okama*) content themselves with their ascribed role as entertainers, they are accommodated, even appreciated. Yet, in some media representations when gay men turn up as friends or colleagues, they are received more coldly – often with fear and contempt. However, in this chapter and the next, I shall argue that this vision of the 'feminine man,' when consumed by a female audience, is received more positively. There are certain discourses in Japanese media either aimed at or produced by women which represent gay men (understood to be woman-like and therefore sympathetic to women and their problems) as preferable to straight men. I shall first look at the genre of boy-love (*shōnen'ai*) which exists in women's comic fiction.

Although the remarkable obsession with the love between boys (*shōnen'ai*) in manga fiction directed at young women (*shōjo*) in Japan has attracted a limited amount of attention in English, for example Aoyama (1988), Buckley (1991) and Allison (1996), the literature in Japanese is sparser. This is partly to do with the reluctance of academia in Japan to take both sexuality and popular culture seriously. As Lunsing (in press) states:

> Talking about sex in a personal and serious manner is largely prohibited by discourses concerning it. In general, sex is regarded as *asobi* (play) and not seen as an activity decent people discuss, including in academic contexts.

Also, popular culture, particularly that produced by and directed at women is not considered worthy of serious attention. Just as sex is considered to occupy a separate, recreational realm, the 'fantasy' world of comics is also dissociated from real life. Although I often quoted examples of the many comics which deal with homosexual themes when arguing that homosexuality actually has a large profile in Japanese culture, my Japanese friends and colleagues wanted to insist upon a sharp division between these fantasies and the 'real Japan.' It was as though there were no relationship between representation and reality. Yet, I was still left with the question as to why the love between beautiful young boys was marketed at and consumed by young women? There must surely be something about the real Japan which makes these images so fascinating and so successful. In this chapter, I attempt to theorise why Japanese women should be so interested in same-sex romance depicted in manga, despite its apparent absence in the real world. In order to do this, I first look at how heterosexual love is treated in the media generally, and in pornographic videos and manga directed at men. I then look at how the love between boys in women's comics differs from the love between men and women portrayed in more mainstream manga. Finally, I consider some responses from gay men themselves towards the same-sex love stories which are so apparent in women's comics.

The treatment of women's sexuality in media discourse

Japanese women are taught that their gender destines them for motherhood; Buckley says of the female body that it is 'inscribed as the motherbody, as an organ of the body politic'(1991: 179). Women who reject this association, for example those working in the twilight world of bars and clubs (*mizu shōbai*), are not considered respectable and tend to live in clearly defined locales and socialize primarily with other similarly employed women (Mock 1996). When Japanese women assert their rights to sexual expression unbounded by marriage or parenthood, they are often penalized in a way that men who do the same never are. Recent examples include the massive media attention surrounding young women (mostly high-school girls) who engage in 'compensated dating' (*enjo kōsai*) with older men from whom they receive money and presents. These girls and their aggressive use of their sexual appeal to get money and brand-name goods are attacked by the media, but their mostly middle-class, middle-aged clients remain unchallenged (*Newsweek*, 23 December 1996, p.14–18; Kawai 1997). Also, in the early-1990s the derogative term 'yellow cab' was invented in Japanese to describe 'loose' young women who were, like New York taxis, 'easy to get into, and out of' (McGregor 1996: 242)[12].

Kinsella also notes that the Japanese media are on the offensive against young women's expression of sexuality, pointing out 'a barrage of sexist stereotyping and insults – frequently propagated under the guise of media or academic social analysis' (1995: 250). The media are full of criticisms of 'selfish' women who supposedly target foreign men, older businessmen, or keep two or three boyfriends on the go, one to provide free meals on the town, one to provide a late-night taxi service (so-called *messhii-kun* and *asshii-kun*, Mr Meals and Mr Legs). Japanese women who sleep with foreign men are often demonized in the press as AIDS carriers, as if Japanese men who sleep with foreign women both abroad and in Japan's own sex trade were somehow immune (Ma 1996: 65). However, representations of women's increased consumption of sexual services has also been parallelled by an increase in men's consumption of images of women. As Skov and Moeran comment 'Japanese women's increasing independence goes hand in hand with their increasing sexualization, and this ambivalent process is closely linked to their consumption as well' (1995: 41). When women are shown as sexual consumers, they are stigmatised. However, men's consumption of erotic and at times violent and degrading images of women goes unchallenged.

Helen Hardacre (1997), in her recent study of discourses stigmatizing women who have had abortions, *Marketing the Menacing Fetus in Japan*, argues that there has been a marked rise in media interest in women's sexuality since the 1970s. This was a time when women, having won greater economic and social rights, were beginning to insist on their right to sexual self-expression. She argues that the aggressive *ribu* (women's liberation) movement was instrumental in achieving some liberalization of public attitudes towards women's sexuality, particularly premarital sex. The Japanese sociologist Ochiai Emiko, however, who lived through the first boom of the women's movement in the early-1970s, questions whether much was gained. She draws attention to the 'blatantly biased' treatment of the movement and its ideas in the media. The media used the common tactic, when male discourse attempts to contain feminist challenge, of reducing the arguments to the 'sexual' or dismissing the women activists as overly emotional and hysterical, referring to their arguments as 'red ranting' (red being associated with Communism but also being the colour associated with the feminine in Japan) (Ochiai 1996: 86). Ochiai argues that '[the media] automatically saw the movement in terms of sex, did not take it seriously, and accused its members of being unfeminine' (1996: 86). Ishino and Wakabayashi cite a particularly clear example of this kind of negative media bias towards women's issues. In 1981, the weekly magazine *Shukan bunshun* published an article on a lesbian social group named Fresh Green Club along side a pornographic picture which had nothing to do with the group. It also reduced the group's social identity to the sexual by printing the headline (a parody of Japan's three imperial 'sacred treasures'): 'Three sacred treasures for them are fingers, tongue and lips' (1996: 100).

Sandra Buckley also suggests that changes in attitudes towards female sexuality were 'superficial' and largely restricted to nonmarried women (1994: 178). She quotes a Japanese feminist as saying that even after the liberalization, women in Japan still lacked a language or a discourse in which they could articulate their own sexual needs and desires publicly:

> We have to be able to express our experience of our bodies and of reality to a lawyer, a policeman, a doctor, without any sense of shame ... Japanese women don't have a sense of freedom of expression, don't even have the words to express their experience, their desires, regardless of whether they are in a doctor's surgery, a lawyer's office or their marriage bed (cited in Buckley 1994: 178).

Hardacre argues that as women became more sexually aggressive, the media reacted negatively to their perceived sexual license and stressed only negative consequences (disease, unwanted pregnancy, abortion), creating the figure of the 'menacing fetus' which lay in wait for women who expressed themselves sexually outside marriage. She 'examines the development in tabloids of a symptomology and discourse of *mizuko kuyō* [religious rites for aborted fetuses], which since the mid-1970s has stigmatized – even demonized – the nonreproductive sexuality of young women' (1997: 14). She argues that from this time, the tabloid press has been full of images which picture 'women's degradation as a result of sex, a consequence from which men are immune, and of which women can never be free' (1997: 85). Some comics aimed at women also represent heterosexual sex as abusive; women who want sex outside marriage get what they deserve – they are used as sexual objects on the terms dictated by their male partners. Images of women tend to revolve around the services they provide for men: either mothers (providing children) or prostitutes (providing sexual 'relief'). It is difficult to find any images in popular culture which show women as sexually independent of men, or sexually in control (or at least equal) in their relations with men.

A brief look at the huge number of pornographic videos produced in Japan suggests that sex is not something Japanese women are expected to enjoy; as the journalist Richard McGregor points out, 'the two lines used by most AV [adult video] actresses are *yamate* [sic: *yamete*] (stop it), and *itai* (it hurts)' (1996: 245). This is not a recent trend, the film critic Donald Richie (1991), in an essay on pre-video Japanese porn movies, argues that 'the Japanese eroductions are about something other than the joys of sexual union ... [they are] about the denigration of women' (1991: 161). He goes on to catalogue a number of 'common' scenes where:

> Women must run naked through the fields or streets ... nude or near nude women are overtaken in rice paddies, knocked down, mauled and dirtied by their attackers; scenes where women are blackmailed or are in other ways compelled to giving themselves to various perversions, the most overwhelmingly common being: tied up, hung by wrists, savagely beaten, otherwise mistreated with sticks, lighted candles, and – odd, but, an eroduction favourite – long-handled shoe horns (1991: 161).

Richie compares these images of women with American porn where '[a woman's] only motivation is to have and give a good time' (1991:161). However, in the Japanese versions, '[w]oman must be denigrated and she must deserve to be' (1991:161). Richie puts this down to men's fear of impotence and the idea that 'women are evil ... sex is their instrument ... men are their prey' (1991: 168). Although Richie's reading of American pornography where the women are performing simply for the fun of it is somewhat optimistic, he does touch upon an element of anxiety which many Japanese men seem to feel in their sexual interactions with women and which has also been commented upon in literature (Napier 1990) and comics (Allison 1996) which will be discussed later.

The apparent discrepancy between men's freedom to dictate the sexual agenda and women's requirements to comply has not gone unnoticed among Japanese commentators on sexuality. The feminist Ueno Chizuko has written extensively on the commodification of women's bodies in Japanese popular culture, especially in her *Theatre Beneath the Skirt* where she argues that 'it is obvious that women's sexuality is being masculinised' (1992: 122). Male writers, too, such as the sex-education researcher and writer Yamamoto Naohide, have argued that male and female sexuality are unequally valued in Japanese society. He points out that even male and female genitalia are differently valued from childhood, the penis being affectionately referred to as o-chinchin, a term which is often used in the mass media, but that the equivalent female term for the vagina, o-manko, is considered obscene and is often represented by 'xxxx' when written, making it unmentionable (1997: 25). The idea that women's sexual organs are dirty probably derives from the view that women's menses, in folk-religion known as the 'red pollution' (akafujō) (Namihira 1987: 68), meant that they were unclean during this period. Consequently, women were traditionally banned from entering holy sites, or dangerous areas such as bridge or tunnel construction sites for fear that they would pollute them and invite disaster. This stigma has not been entirely overcome, even today. Hardacre (1997) points out that effective contraception is severely compromised in Japan because of women's unwillingness to talk about their menses and the workings of their sexual organs with their partners, or even to handle them (apparently tampons and diaphragms are unpopular in Japan for this reason). Yamamoto (1997: 25) blames sex education in schools for failing to address these issues and encourage young boys and girls to investigate the workings of their own bodies in an atmosphere free from stigma. However, this problem is far more pervasive than just faulty or absent sex education.

Representations of women in men's comics

As John Lent points out 'the hugeness of the Japanese comic art industry has no parallel in the world' (1989: 230) and sex, especially violent and intrusive sex, is commonly represented in Japanese comics of all kinds, particularly those written for the male market. Anne Allison's *Permitted and Prohibited Desires* (1996), is the most extensive discussion of sex in Japanese comics in English; she comments 'sexuality is heavily imbricated with violence in Japanese comics' (1996: 71). Masculinity in men's comics is variously represented but there are no figures who approximate the beautiful youths (bishōnen) of women's writing. Men in men's comics are usually hyper-masculine figures who are highly competitive and aggressive. Allison describes them as being 'drawn with harsh features – few smiles, gruff expressions, meanness around their eyes' (1996: 64). These men who 'both look and act like brutes'(1996: 64) have short hair and exaggerated muscles, quite the opposite of the bishōnen who usually have long hair, long limbs and few muscles. Of course straight men are sexually active and sexually aggressive; Allison says that 'the sexual aims that are dominant in *ero manga* [erotic manga] and dominantly male are seeing, possessing, penetrating and hurting' (1996: 64).

Censorship requires that the penis cannot be drawn, so it is instead symbolised by phallic objects such as baseball bats, beer bottles, swords, knives and even trains! Because the actual depiction of genitalia is forbidden, interest is generated in other ways, most commonly by the inclusion of violence. Men in general are presented as obsessed with sex, constantly on the look-out for it, and physically endangered if they don't get it. Allison remarks that:

> Male behaviour is brutish and narcissistic, driven by extreme emotions that find expression in acts of violence ... almost everything about males is jagged. Their faces are chiselled and nasty; their bodies are laden (and interfused with) machinery and object parts; their language is sparse and incomplete. And most important, they attack, expressing their desires through aggression (1996: 73).

Women are represented as compliant with men's sexual needs and as inviting sexual domination: 'sex, typically, is something that is done to them' (1996: 62).

I spent a day looking through the Hong Kong University Japanese Department's collection of manga (over 300 volumes) looking at the way heterosexual sex was treated. I found plenty of examples of violence used against women, some of which I quote below, but very few interactions which could be described as 'equal.' In Yanagisawa Kimio's (1997) *Iro otoko iro onna* (Randy man, randy woman), a man in the midst of sex says 'For the first time, I've stopped being a man and become a male animal' (*watashi wa iya ore wa hajimete otoko de naku osu ni natta*). His language here is interesting, shifting from the polite gender-neutral first-person pronoun *watashi*, to the vulgar, exclusively male first-person pronoun, *ore*. In another scene in the same comic, a different man, who has been unable to have sex with his wife for weeks because her sister is staying in the next room (divided only by paper doors), is represented as becoming increasingly animal-like and in one scene actually grows animal incisors and begins to snort like a bull. His penis is pictured as an independent entity (rather like the daily manga story about the adventures of a penis in the tabloid newspaper *Gendai supōtsu* [Today's sports]). In another scene, as he becomes increasingly sex-obsessed, his head actually becomes a penis. In Hatanaka Jun's manga about a high school boy, *Ryōta* (1997), a woman teacher is shown being persistently spied on, and sexually harassed during a school trip to a hot spring. However, she actually enjoys the harassment, at one point saying, 'I want to cause anger (*okoraretai*), be treated violently (*ranbō ni atsukawaretai*) and insulted (*bujoku saretai*) by men' before drinking from a bottle of beer that she has inserted between the thighs of a male student in a simulation of fellatio. He quickly substitutes his penis and after he has come in her mouth, she says 'You shafted your teacher's throat, you'll be expelled for this you bastard.' Fortunately for the student, next morning she seems to have forgotten about the expulsion, commenting 'I slept so well. I was drunk last night and I can't remember anything that happened.'

When not depicted as sexually aggressive, men are shown to be rather sad and pathetic creatures who need their egos taken care of by women who do this through providing sex. As in Aogi Yūji's *Naniwa kin'yūdō* (Osaka's money trade) (1992) where the sad little salaryman who has just masturbated with a pornographic magazine in his small, messy room says 'I want a wife' and Yamamoto Yasuhito's *Iron Man* (1995), where the husband, Teruo, asks his wife to suckle him from her breast as she does the children. The latter comic is significant in its conflation of the figures of wife and mother; Teruo stands in a similar relation of dependence to his wife as do his children to their mother. She is always there for him and is a much sought after refuge from the hardships of everyday life as a salaryman. Although never sexually aggressive or precocious herself, his wife is always sexually available to Teruo, and sex is her gift to him: a means to lessen his tension. The artist focuses upon her huge breasts which are large, not because they are the sexually fetishised breasts of the prostitute or AV girl, but because they are overflowing with mother's milk. It is this 'idealization of the mother' which Ochiai Emiko considers to be 'the most powerful of the stereotypes which are internalized by and constrain women' (1996: 95).

Married sex life is often presented as routine as in *Iro otoko iro onna*, cited above, where a husband comments 'suddenly we stopped kissing and it seems there's something missing ... ' Sometimes it is described as unpleasant as in *Iron Man*, where a colleague confides to Teruo that he can no longer have sex with his wife since she became a mother as he regards her vagina as a birth channel. This latter image suggests that when 'woman' is seen as 'mother' she becomes desexualised. Hardacre (1997) suggests that women are broadly split into two categories: the unmarried and the married, but it is only the former who are constructed as sexually desirable. As Allison also argues 'because males are encouraged to pursue forms of sexual recreation outside the home, the home and marriage remain grounded in notions of duty and gendered role expectation that are more stable than the far less stable ones of romance or sexual compatability' (1996: 47). Although it may be questioned whether men are actually 'encouraged' to look for sex outside the home, and if so, by whom, this is an important observation which I will consider further when I discuss the meanings attached to marriage in modern Japan in the next chapter.

Heterosexual sex, then, is rarely presented as an equitable exchange in men's manga, mainly because the men are either aggressive super-heroes or miserable failures. In the first case, sex is a commodity men take from women and in the latter case it is a commodity women bestow on men. Erotic manga which are aimed at a female audience are no different. Allison comments that 'women are the targets for manga violence even in comics aimed at women' (1996: 78). The comparatively recent genre of erotic comics aimed at women, termed 'ladies comics,' does not depart from tropes established in men's comics: 'the pages are filled with stories and images of sadomasochism, forced enemas, anal insertion of various objects and substances, fellatio, paedophilia, bondage, homosexuality, masturbation, arousal, kissing, and nakedness' (1996: 155). Rarely, in either genre, is there a sense of mutual exchange which is common in the *shōnen'ai* stories. Heterosexual sex rarely takes place in the context of a relationship, nor does it lead to a relationship, Allison comments that 'sex acts are momentary and superficial, engaged as much (if not more) to break someone down than to achieve orgasmic release, and they rarely result in enduring unions' (1996: 72). This is very different from many of the sexual relationships depicted in *shōnen'ai* fiction which are represented as both loving and enduring. When they end, it is usually tragically; not through the infidelity of one of the partners, but through the cruel and intrusive demands of an uncompromising outside world.

The 'love between boys' in women's comics

Given the violence and denigration that female figures receive at the hands of men in a wide variety of popular media, one would expect in media created and consumed by women to discover a more equitable or romantic vision of love between the sexes. However, women's comic fiction in particular is full of images of (predominantly male) homosexuality. In fact, the most pervasive images of male homo-sexuality outside the pages of the gay press exist in young women's comics (shōjo manga)[13]. This may, in part, account for the fact that young women in Japan are statistically the most accepting of homosexuality. The results of a survey published in the Asahi newspaper on 1 January 1998, show that in response to the question 'Do you agree or disagree with the statement that homosexuality is one way of loving' (ai no arikata)? 28 per cent of respondents overall assented whereas 65 per cent disagreed. However, more than half of all women below the age of thirty five supported the statement, a figure that the article refers to as 'of deep interest.' Young women's interest in, and support of male homosexuality is indeed of great interest and in this and the following chapter, I will explore the significance of this interest and suggest reasons why young women in particular should be so attracted to images of male homosexuality.

Manga directed at a female audience appeared in the early-1950s but at that time were written by men, it was not until the late-1960s that women authors began to be published. At first, these women writers followed familiar tropes which were already well established (a female protagonist follows the thorny path of love, ending either in a happy union or tragedy) (Buckley 1991: 170). However, the early-1970s saw a significant departure from this theme when these comics began to deal with male homosexuality, particularly the love between young boys, (shōnen'ai). Aoyama (1988) puts this interest down to the genre's need to find new images and ideas to replace the 'worn-out image of femininity.' She notes that, 'a pretty girl waiting for a handsome prince is boring, a pretty boy meeting another pretty boy is interesting' (1988: 194). However, another decade has passed since Aoyama made her analysis and there is no sign of the genre's interest in the love between boys waning. On the contrary, the genre has expanded onto the Internet which provides a new, interactive forum where girls and women who consume this material can participate in specialised shōnen'ai clubs and discussions[14]. Although the women writers who first featured images of homosexuality in their work may have been looking for new themes and ideas, the genre has now taken on a life of its own and its popularity cannot, after nearly thirty years, still be ascribed to its innovation. Despite initial scepticism on the part of publishing companies with regard to the viability of boy-love stories, the role these publishers now play in creating a market for this kind of fiction cannot be overemphasized. In Japan, the appeal of homosexual love interests to a female audience is so great that, as the journalist Richard McGregor argues, 'people have discovered these days they can make money out of it' (1996: 229). The publishing houses, as well as the manga writers themselves, then, have vested interests in stimulating the demand for this kind of fiction.

There are so many titles that fall under the *shōnen'ai* category, some of them running into as many as twenty volumes that it is difficult to make generalisations as there will always be some titles which escape categorisation. However, having looked at a considerable number of these comics and consulted the literature in English which discusses them, including Aoyama (1988), Buckley (1991), Allison (1996) and Kinsella (1998), I will make a few general observations about the type of representations they contain and suggest how these representations affect how some Japanese women view homosexuality outside of comic pages.

Firstly, the genre is characterised by its anti-realism. The stories are usually set in an ill-defined 'other' place (often Europe or America), in another historical period (more often the past but sometimes the future) and often deal with boys who are also somehow 'other,' being aristocrats, historical figures, vampires, angels or even aliens. All the boys do, however, have something in common: they are always beautiful, depicted with the big eyes and flowing hair which characterises female figures in men's comics. In fact, the boys are very androgynous and it is difficult for someone not familiar with the illustrative tropes of the genre to work out the sex of the figures. Ten years ago, it was possible for Aoyama to comment that although the stories were often set in 'other' countries situated in North America or Europe, none of the characters were troubled by the issue of 'gay identity' that is so much a part of the western discourse of sexual rights. As Aoyama stated 'none of the residents of the idealized world feels guilty about his being a homosexual, or has to seek his identity' (1988: 196). These earlier comics were pre-political, existing in a world untouched by sexual or gender politics. The genre was one of pure romance where like attracts like and the natural lover of a beautiful boy is the mirror image of himself. However, this emphasis upon romance at the expense of social realism now needs to be qualified. More recent works such as Ragawa Marimo's *New York New York* (1997–8) (*see* Plate 6) deal with issues such as homophobia, coming out, sexual-abuse and rape, in a location (modern-day New York) which, although still idealised, attempts to refer to the very real social problems in which same-sex desire is grounded. Yet the melodrama of the story and the extremely sentimental treatment of the lovers works against a realistic interpretation of the narrative. The inside cover describes (in English) the relationship between the two young lovers, Mel and Kain:

> They had to go through several misunderstandings, before, gradually, they found that they love each other strongly. Soon after, they decided to live together. After the struggle with the prejudice against homosexuality, blessed by Kain's parents, they held a wedding in a gay church. In the midst of their sweet newly-married life, however, Mel suddenly disappeared ...

The story goes on to describe how Mel was abducted by a serial killer who only attacks beautiful blond boys who remind him of his dead younger brother. Much of volume three is taken up with Kain's search for the (naturally beautiful) serial killer in the company of an equally beautiful (female) FBI agent.

The *B-boy* comic series published by Biburos also prefers more realistic situations: often a Japanese high school, but the 'otherness' of the stories and situations is underlined by the extensive use of foreign-language borrowings (in *katakana*) which would not be immediately intelligible to most readers. Examples include, *Platonic Dance, Street Guerilla, Bodyguard, Miss Guardian, Le Due Personne, Easy Boys (Ecstatic!)* and *Be my Baby*. Also the plots are still rather unlikely. For example, few Japanese boys celebrate graduation by french-kissing their peers as in 'I wanna be something' (*Dōnika naritai*) (Uchida Kazuna, *B-boy*, December 1994) (*see* Plate 4); or have sex with their art teacher and maths teacher simultaneously, as in 'I want to kiss rude and loose' (*Rūdona* kiss *wo rūzu ni shitai*) (Takahiro Fujisaki, *B-Boy*, December 1994).

One of the first writers to take up homosexual themes in her work, Hagio Moto, said in an interview in *Eureka* 1981, that when considering a story about same-sex love, she was unsure whether to situate it in a boys' or a girls' school. She finally decided on a boys' school because 'I found the plan about the girls' school to be gloomy and disgusting ... Take a kissing scene, for instance ... as sticky as fermented soybeans' (cited in Aoyama 1988: 189). It is possible that Hagio made this decision in order to avoid homophobic reactions from her female readers who might have found the idea of girls kissing disgusting but would have found boys kissing somehow safer (just as

some straight men appreciate lesbian eroticism). One of Summerhawk
et al.'s lesbian informants describes just such a negative reaction to
lesbianism when she asked her female school friends why they enjoyed
comics depicting love between handsome boys. They replied that 'they
depict "such beautiful things" that didn't exist in reality' (1998: 138).
When she asked 'Why aren't there any about love between girls?' her
friends replied 'Love between girls is disgusting!' (1998: 138).
However, the genre has now expanded to include representations of
love and even sex between girls, aimed at young women, as in *EG:
onna no ko no himitsu ren'ai monogatari* (EG: girls' secret love
stories, 1994) (*see* Plate 5); although there are not as many titles as
those dealing with boys. For instance, Biburos comics had (in 1994)
only five anthologies of stories about beautiful young girls (*bishōjo
ansorojii*) whereas it had seventeen about boys.

The fact that representations of same-sex love between women are
still far fewer than those between men, leads Buckley to comment that
'on the whole it remains true that tolerance of male homosexuality is
greater than of lesbians' (1994: 174). There are a number of reasons
why this is so. Until recently, the terms *rezu* and *rezubian* appeared
primarily in male pornography describing women who had sex with
women, not for their own enjoyment, but for the gratification of a
male gaze. As Ishino and Wakabayashi comment 'lesbian-themed
pornography made by and for heterosexual men has had a great
influence on popular perceptions of lesbians' (1996: 100). As
mentioned earlier, the term *rezupurei* (lesbian play) refers not to
two women but to a biological woman and a cross-dressed man, or to
two cross-dressed men engaged in a sexual interaction. Furthermore,
as Allison's comment cited above suggests, there is the strong idea that
sex is something 'done' to women by men. So, not surprisingly, a
female informant mentioned to me that she found the idea of girl-love
(*shōjo ai*) 'a little strange' because it was unclear who should 'take the
lead.' 'Taking the lead' (*riido wo suru*) occurs often in discussions of
sex, it always being understood that the 'man' (or the partner playing
the 'masculine' role) will take control. Even in the relationship
described in the *Da Vinchi* article discussed in the introduction,
between a *nyūhāfu* and an *onabe*, the interviewer is very interested in
who takes the lead in their sexual interactions. It is, of course, the
individual identified as an *onabe* (in the context of the article, best
understood as a female-to-male transsexual) despite the fact that s/he
doesn't have a penis whereas his/her partner (identified as a *nyūhāfu*, a
male-to-female transsexual) does. Here is another clear example of

what Judith Butler has termed 'gender performativity,' wherein gender performance can overrule or occlude biological sex.

Buckley argues that it was women writers who first depicted sex in the now ubiquitous 'bed scene' (*beddo shiin*) (1996: 171), the first such scene to pass the censors appearing in Ikeda Riyoko's *Rose of Versailles* (1972–4). This is a story of cross-dressing and mistaken identity. Buckley states that the story 'plays endlessly with gender identity and the relationship between that identity and sexuality, disrupting the myth of biology as destiny. Gender is mobile, not fixed in this story' (1996: 172). Significantly, the story was taken up by the all-woman drama troupe, the Takarazuka, and was 'a phenomenal success ... the most popular girl's comic ever staged by the Takarazuka' (Buruma 1984: 118). In the stage play, the heroine is a girl who is brought up and passes as a boy so that she can serve in the army. She plays a significant part in the French revolution, finally being killed by a cannonball while storming the Bastille. As she is taken up to heaven on a chariot, surrounded by clouds of dry ice, the chorus sing:

> In the flashing golden light
> The guardsman's uniform burns red
> Fair hair waving, she takes the reins of the chariot.
> Ah, those blue eyes, ah, the waving fair hair
> (cited in Buruma 1984: 121).

Buruma refers to the sense of *akogare* or 'yearning' which many Takarazuka fans say they feel with regard to the actresses on the stage. He says 'it is used for people, places and ideals that seem impossibly far away' (1984: 121). This is also emphasised in Jennifer Robertson's work on the Takarazuka theatre which she states was conceived as a 'dreamworld (*yume no sekai*) "a place where dreams are made and sold" according to the Revue's advertisements' (1998: 71). The Takarazuka male-role player (*otokoyaku*) is thus an analogous figure to the *bishōnen*, not man, not woman: 'the player of men's roles can be seen as an exemplary female who can negotiate successfully both genders, and their attendant roles, without being constrained by either' (Robertson 1998: 82). In Japanese society, where gender roles are rigidly fixed, popular culture aimed at women provides a safe space in which the normally non-negotiable regimen of gender can be subverted and overturned. It is no surprise, then, that women, whose sexuality is seriously restrained by its association in the popular imagination with either the sex trade or motherhood, should find these fantasies so attractive and be so involved in both their production and consumption[15].

Another manga cross-over can be found in the movie *1999 nen no natsu yasumi* (Summer vacation 1999; Kaneko Shūsuke 1988). The English write-up of this film says it is 'a provocative and lushly photographed tale of budding sexuality and the loss of innocence that owes more to French cinema than that of Japanese film making' (Murray 1994: 464). However, the most direct influence upon the film is clearly *shōnen'ai* manga. Firstly, the plot in which a new student strongly resembling a dead friend joins four students who are left behind at their isolated boarding school during the summer vacation, is very close to the famous comic *Jūichi gatsu no jimunajiamu* (November gymnasium) by Hagio Moto (1971)[16]. In this comic, the long-lost twin brother of a dead school friend becomes involved in a love triangle at a public school much like the one in the movie. Most significantly, however, the androgynous status of the heroes/heroines is underlined by having female actors play the roles of the boys. This creates a curious ambivalence as the girls are playing boys loving boys. Here the fantasy of a girl becoming a boy so that she may love another boy has been fulfilled, and yet all the 'boys' are really 'girls,' so is the movie really about lesbian love, which, so far, has received far less exposure in popular culture than love between men? The cinematography makes constant references to the comic genre, giving the location an intensely eery and otherworldly feel and claustrophobically focusing upon the inner conflicts of the boys/girls. Although too early to be counted as one of the 'gay boom' movies of the early-1990s, *Summer Vacation* is significant in that it illustrates how the representations of male homosexuality in women's manga have broken out of the comic genre and found a wider audience where the associations between gender-play, same-sex love, androgyny, emotionality and otherworldliness are played upon.

Bishōnen do not just appear in women's comics but have crossed over into a variety of media; in fact *bishōnen* are perhaps *the* masculine ideal in all media directed at women. The influence of the beautiful-youth archetype upon masculine stylisation is particularly clear in the boy bands that appeal to women. As mentioned in the preceding chapter many boy bands integrate transgender features into their stage personae, usually long, dyed hair, heavy make-up, and flamboyant clothing. The most extreme example of this trend is IZAM (*see* Plate 17) of the band *SHAZNA* who is used in television and magazine advertisements to sell cosmetics to women. IZAM could easily pass as a woman, so immaculate is his female appearance, and his choice of name, IZAM, is another example of gender non-specific names being used as a site of gender play/disruption. An article about IZAM in the men's magazine *BRUTUS* (1 August 1998) states that he is 'not a simple transvestite' but that 'surpassing sexuality (*sekushuariti wo chōetsu shite*) he embodies the beauty of both sexes.' Described as a *shōjo Arisu* (girl Alice), he is linked with Lewis Caroll's famous character and her adventures which take place in a 'wonderland.'

Almost as famous as IZAM and equally, if not more, beautiful, is Mana of the band *Malice Mizer*. Like IZAM, his name denies gender ascription, and he always appears cross-dressed and heavily made up: hair in long blond curls and dressed in black lace and taffeta reminiscent of a genteel Victorian femininity. He is interviewed in a *Da Vinchi* article (March 1999) where his 'otherness' is highlighted in the headline 'The angels who choose their sex' (*Sei wo erabu tenshi*). Unlike the women who idolise Mana and consume his band's music and products, Mana himself lives in the entertainment world and is free to 'choose' his gender. As he says in the interview 'It's absolutely not the case that I want to become a woman ... it's a matter of personality ... although I was born a man and am recognised by society as a man ... I know there is also a woman inside me who transcends the time (*jidai wo koete*) ... and I want to recognise the woman that is also inside me.' Mana has a constant desire to 'transcend' and 'go beyond' both social and temporal gender restrictions, mentioning his interest in Virginia Woolf's novel *Orlando* about an immortal Elizabethan courtier who changes gender as s/he passes through time. He says 'I want to travel freely through both the past and the future.' It is clear that Mana has very much styled himself along the lines of the androgynous youths in women's comics who move effortlessly through 'other' times and places experiencing a malleability of gender role impossible in the here and now.

Yet another performer who integrated transgender elements into his persona was Hide (Matsumoto Hideto) of the group *X Japan* who committed suicide in May 1998. Apparently, 'Hide's death produced scenes of grief and hysteria not witnessed for a music star since the war' (*Asiaweek*, 22 May 1998, p. 40). Sixty girls fainted during the funeral procession and had to be taken to hospital, and 200 were treated for minor injuries. Many of the girls interviewed said that Hide and his music helped them to live. Watching his funeral on television was an interesting experience. High above the altar on which had been piled a huge array of white chrysanthemums, stood

Hide's photograph. Normally, the deceased would be solemnly portrayed in a dark tie and jacket, however, Hide was pictured with shocking pink hair done up in a Mohican, and wearing a skin-tight pink body suit. There was not a single person with undyed hair in the funeral parlour. One member of Hide's band sang Hide's most famous song, the English chorus of which goes 'forever love, forever dream'. As he stood with his back turned to the audience to hide the tears streaming down his face, his voice cracking with emotion, a huge crowd of mainly female fans outside screamed themselves sick in a bacchanalian frenzy of grief. Hide is yet another example of Japanese girls, in particular, idolising neither man nor woman but an integration of the two in a transvestite star.

The 1997 year-end *Red and White Song Contest*, mentioned in chapter 3, featured many boy bands in the men's team who clearly displayed transgender attributes. The style of many of these boys' clothing and hair was distinctly nineteenth-century European aristo-cratic, a period much favoured by *shōnen'ai* manga writers. These boy bands are of a different order entirely from popular western boy bands such as *The Back Street Boys* or *Boyzone* whose members are of course beautiful, but in a recognisably masculine manner; they most certainly do not wear make-up or cross-dress. However, to the untrained eye, some Japanese boy-band members display the same kind of androgyny which makes it difficult to ascribe gender to many of the *bishōnen* heroes. These boy-band members are thus yet another example of androgyny as perhaps the ideal gender, a trend which has long been part of Japanese tradition. For example, Hatano and Shimazaki (1997: 767–8) argue that 'gender definitions in Japan can transcend the anatomical; masculine and feminine attributes can fade or fuse through conventions.' They cite the *daijōsai* enthronement ceremony where the emperor becomes an incarnation of the goddess Amaterasu, along with the long history of gender reversal in the Japanese entertainment world.

The above discussion of *shōnen'ai* fiction has focused upon romance, however, there are also frequent depictions of aggressive sex where the beautiful youths are positioned as victims. Aoyama suggests that sex which takes place in 'a violent context' seems to be 'an act of revenge' on the part of women readers who now 'become a spectator rather than a prey' (1988: 196) but she does not cite examples supporting this and I have encountered no such scenes which would support this interpretation. Firstly, the *bishōnen* are not really 'men' but rather androgynous figures (not simply in the way they look but in their sensibilities). Also, the young men are frequently situated in sexual interactions which position them as 'female.' For example, in *New York New York*, Mel is the beautiful victim of childhood sexual abuse. He escapes from home, where he has been repeatedly humiliated and abused by his step-father, only to become a street prostitute. He is 'saved' from life on the street by a married client who later dumps him for fear that his wife will find out. Rejected, Mel attempts to commit suicide, but is stopped in time. He becomes the lover of a policeman, Kain, and his life seems to be back on track until he is kidnapped by a masked attacker (who turns out to be Kain's police partner who is secretly in love with Kain himself). All these situations of sexual subjugation are modelled upon roles traditionally fulfilled by female victims. The reader is clearly supposed to identify with the youth, who, as victim, is placed in a subordinate (read, feminine) position. Also, in Hagio Moto's *Zankokuna kami ga shihai suru* (A cruel god reigns; 1993) (*see* Plate 7), a young boy is sexually abused by his stepfather in scenes of increasing violence and sadism, but cannot tell his emotionally unstable mother for fear of destroying her dream of a happy marriage. In this story, both the boy and the mother are the victims of exploitative adult male sexuality.

Women's comics as a site of gender resistance

It is clear that the images of masculinity endorsed by many women in Japan are at variance both with those representations of 'real men' so apparent in media directed at men as well as in how real men actually behave; in fact the *bishōnen* resist being read as 'masculine.' Firstly, they transgress to the feminine in both their beauty and in their sensibilities which are seen as romantic and pure. Also, in falling in love with each other, they are side stepping the political divide between men and women and the reproductive demands of the family system. The *bishōnen* can be read as a figure of resistance: both to the notion that biology is destiny and to the correlation between biology and gender role. Women readers do not just vicariously participate in the *bishōnen* world but identify with the androgynous figures, not just as ideal lovers or partners, but in a sense as their ideal selves. Like the Takarazuka male-role players (*otokoyaku*) who can 'successfully negotiate both genders ... without being constrained by either' (Robertson 1998: 82), the *bishōnen* have both 'feminine' sensibilities and the freedom to live and act as men. Within patriarchy, which assigns very strict roles to women according to their supposed capacities, the androgynous youth is one way in which the female reader can picture herself as separate from the sexist roles assigned to her by the family system. Aoyama mentions comics where female characters 'wish to be a male homosexual in order to love a beautiful boy' (1988: 191).

Significantly, statistics published in the *Asahi* newspaper survey on 'the changing shape of love between men and women' (1 January 1998, p.24) suggest that a sizeable number of women, in fantasy at least, would like to be men. In reply to the question 'If you were to be reborn, would you prefer to be a man or a woman?' 32 per cent of women said they would prefer to be men as opposed to just 8 per cent of men who would prefer to be women, leading the writer to suggest that Japan is 'probably still a man's society'. It is important to remember that the concept of 'sex change' is not new to Japanese culture and precedes the development of medical sex-change operations by hundreds of years. Due to Buddhist influence, there exists the idea that karma inherited from a previous life not only determines the sex of one's present life but can also affect one's present gender performance. This has been a minor theme in literature since at least the Heian-period (794–1185) novel *Torikaebaya monogatari* (If only I could change them) which is about a pair of transgendered siblings. Jennifer Robertson (1998: 85) draws interesting parallels between the Buddhist doctrine of *henshin* (bodily change), where bodhisattvas are able to change both body and sex in order to better help suffering beings, eighteenth-century kabuki discourses of *henshin* explaining how the *onnagata* or female-role performer actually becomes 'Woman' on stage and animated cartoons popular from the 1960s where characters can change at will into more powerful forms (*henshin dorama*) or so-called 'morph dramas.' It is significant that Mana, of the band *Malice Mizer*, refers to Buddhist notions of rebirth to explain his desire to cross-dress in his present life; as he puts it, 'to recognise the woman that is also inside me.'

Another factor which may influence some women to fantasize themselves as men is that, as outlined earlier, women's sexuality is circumscribed by anxieties about pregnancy[17], so if women love these boys as women, they are liable to end up pregnant or loving them as wives, neither of which bear much romance in Japan. Only a boy who loves a boy (or a girl who loves a girl) is truly free in Japanese society to love beyond the constraining roles imposed by the marriage and family system. Something of the psychology at work here can be gleaned from an excerpt from a Takarazuka fan club magazine published in 1955. The article tries to explain why a young girl might become fixated on a male-role player (*otokoyaku*):

> She thought about how if she actually got together with a male, she would become trapped in a feudal household system, and if she got together with a female student, the relationship might not work out. If a woman chooses same-sex love, and if she happens to be infatuated with an *otokoyaku*, then her female partner should be dressed 'as if' she were actually male but more handsome and more refined (cited in Robertson 1998: 185).

Japanese women's attraction to *bishōnen* seems to be similar to the strong feelings directed towards female male-role actors. Both are fantasy figures which, as such, cannot disappoint. The *otokoyaku* acts 'as if' she were male but is in fact female, able to provide the kind of woman-oriented romance that patriarchally socialised biological men cannot. The *bishōnen*, although actually male, acts 'as if' he were female, displaying the beauty, emotionality and vulnerability often associated with female gender. Both are 'more handsome and more refined' than any biological male could ever be.

Buruma argues that Japanese girls do not want to be boys; what they really want is to be sexless 'because they realize that becoming an adult woman means playing a subservient role in life' (1984: 118). Treat (1995: 281) also argues that the *shōjo* readers 'constitute their own gender, neither male not female but something importantly detached from the productive economy of heterosexual production.' This may explain why the heroes of *shōnen'ai* comics are both ageless and androgynous; they are of a different order of being *entirely* from the boys presented in manga directed at men, making it easier for women to identify with them as idealised models. Kinsella (1998: 300) also regards the *bishōnen*, although biologically male, to be 'in essence ... ideal types combining favored masculine qualities with favored feminine qualities.' Buruma supports this reading when he contrasts the heroes in Japanese women's comics with those in western comics: 'although girls' comics in the West are full of impossibly beautiful young men ... they are still unmistakably men ... In Japan ... they are more ambivalent, and sometimes get each other' (1984: 124–5). He goes on to say that they are 'a faraway romantic ideal ... *Bishōnen* are treated in a similar way to vampires or creatures from outer space. Outcasts all, they are the pure, eternally young victims of adult corruption' (1984: 127). The journalist, Richard McGregor, also stresses women's comics' role in 'dreamily transporting their readers far away from their conformist everyday lives' where, he suggests, 'even wimpy men are threats' (1996: 229). It is for this reason, then, that images of male homosexuality are so popular among Japanese women, not simply in women's comics but also in novels, theatre and film. The lesbian author and activist Sarah Schulman, for instance, when invited to attend a gay film festival in Tokyo in 1992, was extremely surprised to find that the venue was a popular shopping mall and that 'the audience was eighty percent straight women' (1994: 245).

Japan's most preeminent *shōjo* writer, Yoshimoto Banana, also plays with transsexuality and androgyny in her novel *Kitchen*. Eriko/ Yuji, the transsexual father/mother of the heroine's boyfriend is presented in terms similar to the beautiful and fantastic youths of *shōjo* manga. The description of Eriko sounds like a Takarazuka *otokoyaku*:

> This was his mother? Dumbfounded, I couldn't take my eyes off her. Hair that rustled like silk to her shoulders; the deep sparkle of her long, narrow eyes; well-formed lips, a nose with a high, straight bridge – the whole of her gave off a marvellous light that seemed to vibrate with life force. *She didn't look human* (1993: 11) (emphasis mine; transl. Megan Backus).

Images of androgynous youths, cross-dressed and transgendered men and women are apparent in a wide range of women's media. Why should these representations prove so popular and so enduring? John Fiske, an analyst of popular culture, argues that:

> If the cultural commodities or texts do not contain resources out of which people can make their own meanings of their social relationships and identities, they will be rejected and will fail in the marketplace. They will not be made popular (1989a: 2).

These transgendered images are popular, then, not because of any inherent interest or attraction attributable to homosexuality but because these idealised homosexual figures can support meanings and feelings that real men consistently disappoint. It is for this reason that *bishōnen* are popular among women in Japan, even lesbian women, as this comment from one of Summerhawk et al.'s lesbian interviewees makes clear:

> [In the early-1970s] comics by women writers began coming out that depicted love between boys. The characters they drew were

beautiful boys who loved each other, with such shapely and delicate bodies that they didn't appear to be male. It was easy for me to project my feelings onto the characters in these stories (1998: 24).

The beautiful youths in women's fiction, then, are not like real men, nor are they like actual gay men. They are popular because, like the Takarazuka *otokoyaku*, they 'perform' masculinity in a manner deemed attractive by women. These comics say nothing about how gender is, but about how it ideally should be: negotiable, malleable, a site of play. In the figures of the *bishōnen* and *otokoyaku*, biological sex is overlooked and gender becomes a *performance* which, when acted out in fantasy, is free of the restrictions which impose certain gender traits on male and female bodies. Hence, through reading these comics, women are, in fantasy at least, resisting the hegemonising demands of a gender regime which brutally insists upon the performance of strict gender roles based upon biology, overlooking both predisposition and preference.

The discourse of 'boy love' in women's comics therefore has similar 'rhetorical effects' to other discourses prevalent in Japanese women's media. As Karen Kelsky (1999; and work in progress) has argued, the interest that many Japanese women's magazines show in 'internationalism' and the way in which they contrast the (supposedly) progressive attitudes of foreign (white) men with the 'backward' attitudes of Japanese men, are examples of how women's media produce narratives which implicitly criticise the native by eulogizing a foreign 'other.' Kelsky cites examples of 'the discourse of internationalism' in women's media which 'allow women to challenge hierarchies of the native over the foreign, of male over female, of the nation over the world, and construct an alternative reality under which all that had been maligned is now revered, all that had been revered now rejected' (1999: 238). My reading of women's *shōnen'ai* manga suggests that in these texts, women are indeed constructing an alternative reality in which heteronormativity and the reproductive demands of the family system are overthrown by homosexuality. In this discourse, 'the homosexual,' a despised or at best redundant figure in terms of the patriarchal family system, becomes 'revered,' held up as a mirror reflecting back all those things that women most desire but that straight men are considered unable to deliver.

Shōnen'ai comics are predominantly written by and for women. However, the author's name is another site in which gender identity is resisted. Many manga writers write under one or several pen-names and it is impossible to know whether a male-gendered name signifies a male writer or a female-gendered name a female writer. Many of the names chosen are deliberately obscure, not simply about gender identity, but also contain coded references. Examples from the *B-boy* special edition discussed above include Motoni Modoru (which could be read as 'return to the origin'), and Maki Sayaka (made up of the characters 'demon' *maki*, and 'sand-night-flower,' *sa-ya-ka*). Another example, from the girl-love (*shōjo ai*) genre (*EG* [1994], mentioned above) is the name Kusamakura Tabito which can be translated as 'grass-pillow traveller'. The author of *New York New York*, discussed above, has the pen name of Ragawa Marimo. 'Mari' is written with characters commonly found in women's names, but the 'mo' character, when written separately, is pronounced 'Shigeru' which is always a man's name. By combining characters associated with both men's and women's names, the author makes it impossible for the reader to assign a gender to him/herself. These writers, of obscure gender, do not attempt to provide social-realist critiques of contemporary Japanese gender stratification, rather, the homosexual relationships they describe are simply a fantasy context for Japanese women to love without reference to reproduction. Buruma comments that 'the young girl's dream is to go as far away as possible, sexually, emotionally, geographically, from everyday reality' (1984: 121). The women's comic genre is characterised by everything that Japanese society is not: here gender is fluid, characterised by androgyny and mobility, as Buckley says 'normative or naturalizing narrative structures give way to narratives that follow a fantasy trajectory beyond the boundaries of dominant sexual identification and practice' (1996: 191).

As mentioned previously, the novelist Yoshimoto Banana, whose name also defies gender ascription, has created characters in her fiction who display the same fluidity with regard to gender. In *Kitchen*, Yuichi Tanabe's father Yuji/Eriko decides, upon the death of his wife, to become a woman: 'After my real mother died, Eriko quit her job, gathered me up, and asked herself, "What do I want to do now?" What she decided was "Become a woman"' (1993: 14). As Treat comments 'in the Tanabe home … the genders of male and female – seem distinctly rehearsed' (1995: 289). In Yoshimoto's short story *Moonlight Shadow*, Hiiragi, a high-school boy, decides to dress in his dead girlfriend's sailor suit; rather than alienating him from his school friends, he finds that 'all the girls are crazy about me, it must be

because, wearing a skirt, perhaps they think I understand them'
(1993: 120). In Japan, women's fiction is a site for gender play and
transformation; 'homosexuality' has become a commodity consumed
by women. In Japan, homosexuality is not necessarily an anxiety-
inducing 'other' but, for some women at least, it has become their
most desired other.

It is possible to see in the fascination with the love between boys in
women's comics a wider trend commented upon by Kinsella (1995)
who argues that the 'cute culture' so prominent among young women,
and now spreading to young men, is not an infantilistic refusal to
grow up but a calculated strategy of resistance against the conformist
demands of adult society. Just as *bishōnen*, like Peter Pan, never seem
to age, and no matter how much they are hurt or abused by adult
society, never lose their purity, so too do *shōjo* readers, in fantasy at
least, preserve their integrity. Despite the daily disappointments they
face in their real interactions with parents, teachers, bosses,
boyfriends and husbands, through *shōnen'ai* fiction, they can access
an ideal realm where the sharp insistence upon the correlation
between biology, gender and gender performance can be transcended.
In this ideal world biology is *not* destiny.

Gay men's responses to women's comics

As mentioned earlier, realistic representations of sex were first
pioneered in women's comics in the early-1970s and the sex portrayed
was predominantly homosexual (Buckley 1991: 173). At this time, the
women's comic *June* became the best selling of all women's comics, its
sales helped by a crossover market of gay men[18]. *June*, describing
itself as 'the discrimination-free comic' has come to acknowledge that
it also has a gay fan base and now runs articles on AIDS, and has a
homosexual problem page (Buckley 1991: 174). When a young
woman reads an issue of *June*, she is therefore aware of participating
in an activity shared, not just by other young women, but also by a
substantial number of gay men. However, the representations of gay
love and gay sex in these magazines are still far from the reality
experienced by the vast majority of gay men in Japan. The gay readers
of *June* are conscious of the fact that the magazine deals in fantasy,
not reality. As Kamata, interviewed by Yajima (1997: 97) points out,
although he began to read magazines like *June* at the recommendation
of his female colleagues, he was disappointed because 'they were a
fantasy, they didn't explain my physical desires.' This is because

although *June*'s comics often feature graphic homosexual sex, the stories very much follow the well-worn trope of the 'other.' For example, the *June* comic series *Rasuto zōn* (Last zone) (Akizuki Koh & Nakata Aki), published in 1997 as a special edition, features beautiful long-haired warrior youths who only take a break from fighting each other in order to be fellated and anally dildoed by their equally beautiful (but older) lovers. Similarly, the characters in Tamaki Yuri's *PARTNERS* (1993) are also hardly the boy-next-door type. This comic includes detailed descriptions of New York's SM scene including body-piercing and fisting. However, all the men in the story are young and beautiful: when not fist fucking each other they are dressing up in tuxedos and going to dinner parties in luxuriously appointed apartments.

Some gay men report that their first awareness of homosexuality came through reading girls' comics as children. Tanaka, interviewed by Yajima (1997: 176) says that he did not consider homosexuality to be perverse (*hentai*) but taken-for-granted (*atarimae*) because he was so familiar with it as an image in girls' comics. He says he got the impression that it was 'an unforgivable but beautiful relationship.' Another of Yajima's informants, Fukuda, discusses the troubling effect images of beautiful young men in women's comics had upon him as he became aware of his own same-sex desires. He says that he first became aware of the possibility of love between men when he began to read comics like *June* in the final grade of junior school and that through reading these comics, he became aware that he himself was 'homosexual' (*jibun no koto wo 'dōseiai' to ninshiki shite ita*) (1997: 307). However, he considers these comics to have had a bad influence upon him because they only represented beautiful youths who 'must be cute and pretty.' Because he was big for his age and did not have a cute face, he felt uneasy about his future, wondering 'what will become of me?' (1997: 307). Due to the influence of women's comics, he felt that 'being gay meant being a smart and beautiful member of the elite' until he came across a gay magazine in his first year of high school and realized that this was not, in fact, the case (1997: 311). Nishino Kōji (1993), the author of a gay-themed novel entitled *When I Meet You in Shinjuku Ni-chome* written to coincide with the early-1990s gay boom, said in an interview in the first issue of the gay magazine *Badi* (1994: 52) that he was motivated in part to write the novel drawing upon his extensive personal experience of the Shinjuku gay scene in order to combat the fantasies about gay life published in women's comics. He says that although there is material like *June* which caters to women who like gays, 'there still isn't anything written by gay men about real gay life.'

Conclusion

It is ironic that in one of the most extensive fantasy genres created and consumed by women, that of the love of beautiful boys in manga fiction, women are almost entirely absent. This is not unusual in postwar Japanese popular culture however, as Susan Napier has pointed out. In her book on *The Fantastic in Modern Japanese Literature* (1990) she includes a chapter entitled 'Woman lost: the dead, damaged, or absent female in postwar fantasy' where she charts a paradigm shift in the treatment of women in Japanese literature which took place after the war where 'women are no longer caretakers but objects of prey, only acceptable as victims upon which to enact male rage' (1990: 53). The male ego, rendered so fragile now that women have encroached upon all the areas of life that were once the sole domain of men: the realm of education, the workplace and even the sexual market-place, sees itself as under attack. Napier comments that in literary portrayals, 'male characters are shown as damaged and angry' (1990: 57) and women 'are frequently seen as agents of entrapment or humiliation' (1990: 56), resulting in a situation where 'women seem to have become increasingly Other, unreachable, even demonic' (1990: 57). She sees a profound feeling of separation and discontinuity as existing between the sexes, arguing that:

> In the works examined in this chapter, by male and female writers, all forms of love, from maternal to sexual, seem to become grotesque parodies of themselves, emphasizing the lack of connection between human beings (1990: 59).

Napier does not analyse manga fiction. If she had, she would have found that many of the themes characterising literary representations of the relationship between the sexes are also common in manga featuring stories about men and women. However, she would surely have noticed that the same-sex love affairs described in women's comic fiction manage to sidestep the many pitfalls that seem to be inherent in heterosexual relationships. In *shōnen'ai* fiction, the homosocial love, what the popular psychologist Doi Takeo refers to as *dōseiai kanjō* (same-sex-love feelings) (1985: 134), manage to circumvent the negative associations which are attached to hetero-sexual love stories. *Shōnen'ai* stories represent an ideal world of romance which is as much a utopia as is the world of heterosexual sex a dystopia.

When Napier suggests that 'the fantasies of both men and women can no longer envision any sort of connection or social community' (1990: 90) she is only right to the extent that she applies this statement to representations of relationships *between* the sexes. Same-sex love, however, manages to sidestep all these difficulties and present a picture of love which is pure and unsullied by the political relations which exist between men and women. As the female Japanese translator of American gay author Edmund White pointed out in conversation with Sarah Schulman: 'images of male homo-sexuality are the only picture we have of men loving someone else as an equal' (Schulman 1994: 245). Ironically, women as participants are largely excluded from the most popular genre of romantic stories created by Japanese women themselves. If it is only in fantasy that Japanese women can live a sexual life outside of reproductive concerns and avoid the stigma of the *mizu shōbai* (entertainment trade), then, as Buckley asks 'is it strange that schoolgirls are so attracted to a fantasy world of nonreproductive bodies, as remarkably non-Japanese as they are nongendered, moving across a backdrop of a nonspecific landscape that is nowhere, or more specifically, that is anywhere that is not Japan?' (1991: 179).

It would seem that in terms dictated by popular culture, women are trapped between a rock and a hard place. On one side, unreproductive sexual practice outside marriage is represented as semi-prostitution (recall the 'compensated' high school girls and the ever-ready 'yellow cabs'), the results of which are damaged morals as well as damaged bodies. However, 'licensed' sexuality which takes place within marriage leads to a wife becoming a mother whereupon she is desexualised (and some would argue de-individualised), metamor-phosing into the despised *obatarian* (old dowd) or the feared *mama-gon* (mother-monster). Even when women, as wives and mothers, are represented as sexual, it is a sexuality which exists entirely in relation to their husbands. They exist to provide their husbands with sex just as they do food, as part of their general role of nurturer. Given these constraints on women's sexuality, it is then, perhaps no surprise that in comics written for women, the love that is celebrated is the love between young boys. It is only in this context that love can be free of the 'violence and harassment' that Buckley sees as 'mechanisms for the containment and management of women's bodies and sexuality' (1994: 176). I see a parallel here with the problems many western feminists have faced in attempting to produce genres of erotica and pornography which cater to women. It has been argued that female sexuality has necessarily been structured in terms of male desire and that women's attempts to reinvent pornography are simply reinscribing female desire in male terms. The comparative lack of homophobia among Japanese women[19] has, however, enabled the development of an erotic fantasy genre which sidesteps the pervasive political divides involved in heterosexual representations by focusing upon love between beautiful young men. These 'men' (or rather youths/boys) are not really gendered as male but are shown as more feminine both in sensibility and in the situations within which they are inscribed. It must therefore be questioned whether these representations have anything to do with gay men. More likely, they represent the concerns and fantasies of the women who avidly produce and consume them. The love between boys in Japanese women's comics therefore has more to say about the limitations of heterosexual relations and the negative constraints on female sexuality in contemporary Japanese society than about the real situation of same-sex desiring men.

Chapter 5

Gay Men as Women's Best Friends and Ideal Marriage Partners

Introduction

The construction of gay men as feminine in both their looks and their sensibilities in women's comics is largely accepted at face value in other media directed at women. For example, one of the *CREA* (February 1991) articles which sparked the gay boom in 1991 is entitled 'Women who aim at spending a pleasurable life with gays.' The article assumes throughout that gay men are radically different from their straight counterparts. Echoing similar sentiments to Nomura Sachiyo, subheadings state that 'Women who have gay friends basically like ... splendour (*gōka*) and refinement (*yūga*).' The article goes on to stress that friendships with gay men involve an intimacy that is impossible with straight men, one woman stating that 'When we snuggle up together, it's not in the least unpleasant (*iyarashii*), it feels like petting a cat.' This latter comment betrays two important assumptions, the first being that straight men have a difficulty dissociating intimacy from sexuality (snuggling up to a straight man would become 'unpleasant') and that gay men, like pets, enjoy this kind of intimacy. The article further suggests that having to constantly compete with men on unequal terms causes many women in Japan to feel exhausted (*tsukareru*) but that a gay partner can 'relieve this exhaustion.' Hence, unlike the patriarchal 'other' against which women have to battle in order to win social space for female subjectivity, gay men are women's allies, described as nurturing women in much the same way that women are expected to nurture men. The comforting nature of gay men is a commonly occurring theme in this discourse, as will be seen later.

So far I have suggested that women's idealised depictions of gay men comes from the common assumption that they are woman-like. I have argued that the image of the feminine male is positively received by women for two main reasons: firstly, the feminine man is not a dangerous enemy but a comforting friend, and secondly, women identify with the feminine man who possesses all the attractive features associated with female gender while able to move with the freedom associated with male sex. When women fantasize ideal men, these representations contradict in every way the 'real' men depicted in men's media. In this chapter, I look at a variety of media discourses taken from magazines, movies and books which go one step further and actually present gay men as women's ideal partners. In order to understand how this construction is possible, it is necessary to first look at the various meanings structuring the marital relationship in present-day Japan

The contested meaning of marriage in modern Japan

The nature of marriage and the family in Japan has been analysed by western and Japanese researchers including sociologists, anthropologists and psychologists. It has been argued by many western researchers including Hendry (1981), Dalby (1985), Buckley (1991), Brinton (1992), Allison (1996), Jolivet (1997) and Robertson (1998) and as well as Japanese writers such as Iwao (1993), Mori Yōko (1994), Takada (1994) and Ueno (1997) that the various meanings surrounding marriage in Japan are structured in terms other than those of 'romantic love.' That marriage and romantic love are considered to be separate has been clearly vocalised in Japanese culture since the Tokugawa period and is still frequently heard today. An NHK family drama which I viewed in Japan in March 1998 contained just such a discussion arising from a young bride's refusal to go through with the marriage ceremony when she discovered her prospective husband was still seeing his previous girlfriend (whom he really loved but who was an unsuitable marriage partner). The popular short-story writer and essayist Mori Yōko also discusses a (fictive) case in her article, *The Fish she Let Get Away Was Big* which was first published in the women's magazine *AnAn* in 1991 (reproduced in Ashby 1994).

In this story, Mori's fictive bride, Yumi, dumps her student-days boyfriend despite his amiable personality and good looks because he is 'a drop-out from the social-advancement course' (1994: 6) which means he will never attain the high social position expected by both herself and her family. Instead, she marries, through an arranged marriage (*omiai*), a man 'who was like the image she had drawn in her imagination.' Unfortunately, although successful at work, he has no hobbies and no conversation, 'on the few occasions he was at home, he lay about the house in his pajamas just watching television' (1994: 6). Trapped in a loveless marriage, she cannot even escape from the home by working part-time, as her husband's social position is such that this would reflect badly on him. Instead she has a baby, but her husband is too involved in his social-advancement course to pay her or the child any attention. When she hears that her ex-boyfriend has emigrated to Australia and now runs a cattle ranch, she is both fascinated and appalled by 'such a rash life plan' (1994: 6). Having chosen stability, she now realizes that 'stability is a synonym for boredom' (1994: 6).

Mori's character Yumi is a typical member of what feminist sociologist, Ueno Chizuko calls the *Hanakozoku* (*Hanako* is a middle/ upper-middle class lifestyle magazine aimed at single Japanese women). Like many members of her class, Yumi's primary goal in marriage is to achieve financial stability and the public face of a *fujin*, or woman married to a professional man. As Ueno comments:

> Japanese couples get married for the institution and not out of romantic love. The *Hanakozoku* go into marriage with very low expectations of romantic or sexual satisfaction. They choose the institution of marriage because of the material advantages it offers them. They secure their lives financially and socially with a good match. That is not to say that they give up their sexual desire. There is no question of this. They simply don't pursue that desire within marriage (1997: 285).

The picture of married life which Mori draws in her brief article is not uncommon. It includes many of the features outlined by the sociologist Iwao Sumiko in her book *The Japanese Woman* (1993). She argues that there are broad differences in expectation between American and Japanese couples with regard to marriage, but that these expectations are shifting as new generations of Japanese women come of age who have been affected by increasingly liberal ideas regarding their education and career potential. Broadly speaking, Iwao says that 'Americans expect much more from a marriage than do the Japanese' (1993: 69). These higher expectations are almost entirely to do with the affective and companionate aspects of the marriage bond. For example, she quotes from a survey of Japanese and American attitudes towards marriage conducted by Roper and Dentsu in 1990 which shows similarities between the two cultures regarding practical issues such as 'financial security' which 66 per cent of Japanese women and 63 per cent of American women rate as 'very important.' However, striking differences appear over more 'affective' issues such as 'having a good sexual relationship' (Japanese women, 38 per cent; American women, 72 per cent), 'keeping romance alive' (Japanese women, 29 per cent; American women, 78 per cent), and, very significantly, 'sexual fidelity on the part of spouse' (Japanese women, 46 per cent; American women, 85 per cent). This data suggests that Mori's fictive bride is not alone in prioritising such factors as financial stability and family background when choosing a husband. However, Iwao suggests that women's attitudes and ideas about their place and role in the family and society are changing more rapidly than those of men and that a growing number, especially of younger women, are feeling constrained by the limitations imposed upon them by the role play necessary to be a 'good wife and wise mother' (*ryōsaikembo*) – a role which was previously uncontested in their grandparents' generation. Reasons for this include increased educational and career opportunities for women. Women are marrying later (the average age for women was 25.8 in 1990, one year later than the average ten years earlier [Iwao 1993: 60]) which means that they will have had more work experience and more 'life experience' generally, including number of sexual partners.

Although Japanese women are entering marriage later and with greater expectations, the vast majority are still getting married (95 per cent of Japanese people are married by the time they reach 40 [Jolivet 1997: 40]). In a comparison with the marriage practices of American women, Brinton (1992) found that the vast majority of Japanese women marry 'on schedule' and are assisted in finding a suitable match by 'stakeholders' such as parents and employers who feel that they have an investment in the future of the individual (in the case of employers, temporary female workers are often viewed as a marriage pool for the permanent male staff). She also found that Japanese women, after marriage, tended to follow a more homogeneous life path than did American women, consisting of giving birth to children soon after marriage and then returning to the labour market part-time after the last child reaches school age. There seems to be little incentive in Japan for either men or women to delay marriage, partly because, as Walter Edwards states in his book on Japanese wedding ceremonies, 'the failure to [get married] carries the severe implications of immaturity and lack of moral responsibility' (1989: 124). Yet, the popularity of marriage as an institution should not be read as an indication that Japanese people especially *want* to get married. As

Muriel Jolivet who lives and works in Tokyo has argued, 'of all the young people of the industrialized nations, the Japanese are those who are the least enthusiastic about getting married' (1997: 39). As I argue later when I look at the life stories of some Japanese homosexual men, many clearly understand marriage as an obligation to their parents and society which they cannot fulfill. Those homosexual men who give in to social pressure and decide to marry are not dissimilar to many Japanese women who similarly give up their own individual hopes and aspirations in order to settle down with a suitable partner. Lunsing (*in press*) makes this connection clear by grouping together the problems that gay men, lesbians and feminist women all have with the institution of marriage and its central place in Japanese society.

The comparative lack of emphasis in Japanese marriages upon affective elements, particularly 'romantic love,' is related to the practice, traditional among the samurai and richer merchants, of arranged marriages. The purpose of these marriages was to cement bonds between two families of similar background and to provide a suitable environment for the raising of the next generation, the first son of which would be destined to inherit the property or business and carry on the family name. Something of this way of thinking still remains in the practice of *omiai* marriages where the couple are introduced to each other by a go-between, usually a family friend of the older generation, or even a boss. The go-between is careful to only introduce couples he or she thinks will be mutually acceptable, and the *omiai* itself is usually preceded by the exchange of photographs and resumes. *Omiai* marriages are sometimes a last resort for professional men and women who have been too busy with their careers to devote time to relationships with the other sex. Women from good families who only want to marry high-status career men such as doctors and lawyers may also resort to *omiai* which are now organised by elite dating agencies. Interestingly, both the 'gay boom' movies, discussed below, feature prominent *omiai* scenes organised by concerned parents who decide to act on their (gay) sons' behalf to find them a marriage partner. These scenes work to great comic effect, especially in *Kira kira hikaru* (Matsuoka George 1992), when Mutsuki's father-in-law, having discovered that he is gay, angrily challenges him saying 'there was no mention of this on your resume!'

Although the *omiai* is far from extinct, the sex-education researcher and writer Asai Haruo, has argued that this traditional way of thinking has been superseded by a new discourse of romantic love (*ren'ai*) which he terms an 'ideology' (*ideorogii*). He says that of all the marriages that were contracted in 1990, 83 per cent were 'love marriages' (ren'ai kekkon) and only 15 per cent were 'arranged marriages' (miai kekkon). He suggests that according to the new ideology, only those marriages contracted for love are real (hon mono) and that 'love equals marriage equals childbirth' (1997: 181). Although couples are now pressured into love marriages, he argues that this is dangerous because for many men 'love' (ren'ai) is just something done for the sake of sex and as an entry to marriage. The period of love lasts, for many men, only up to the marriage ceremony or childbirth and that after this event, the 'real state' (jissai) of the relationship is that the couple become 'mother' and 'father' (1997: 181). Asai argues that many men are incapable of playing the love game and terms them 'love shy' (ren'ai shaiman), and points to the rising number of men in their thirties who remain unmarried as well as to the rise in the number of men who remain unmarried throughout their lives (1997: 182).

Hatano and Shimazaki (1997: 817) also note that Japanese men, particularly older men, 'tend to avoid the rather uneasy attempts to build a love-oriented heterosexual relationship' and point out that many men feel that they are being critically appraised by women. They say that 'marriage is not an easy life event for young and middle-aged Japanese men these days' and cite a 1991 Asahi newspaper poll which found that '60 per cent of Japanese women consider Japanese men unreliable.' It is not surprising that some men feel insecure when interacting with women, for, as Karen Kelsky (1999; and work in progress) has pointed out women's media in Japan are characterised by a 'discourse of internationalism' which positions Japanese men as 'backward' in relation to their supposedly more progressive western peers. In this discourse, the attitudes of Japanese men are presented as a 'problem' not simply for Japanese women but for the progress of the Japanese nation as a whole.

Karen Ma (1996) in her book analysing multi-cultural marriages in Japan, cites the negative image that many Japanese women have about Japanese men as the prime factor motivating some women to aggressively seek out relationships with foreign (European or American) men. She notes how young women have more time and money available for such things as socialising, study and travel, and consequently often have more expanded and international outlooks than their male peers. Many Japanese men feel they cannot compete with women in terms of this kind of sophistication, causing them to become shy and withdrawn in their company. As will be argued below, men's attitudes towards marriage seem to be changing more slowly than those of women, and the discourse of romantic love which is pushed before marriage and then suddenly dropped, leads to many women experiencing disappointment in their married lives.

The wedding industry in Japan is immense and aggressively projects the wedding ceremony as the pinnacle of a couple's life in advertising which is impossible to escape as it appears in magazines, newspapers, television, and even on buses and trains. One advertisement which I saw for a 'wedding package' exclaimed that 'the wedding ceremony is a couple's stage' (*kekkon shiki wa futari no sutēji*). It is in the wedding ceremony, which is directed much like a theatrical performance, that most Japanese people experience their 'fifteen-minutes of fame.' However, after such an immense run up, the reality of married life is sadly deflating for many couples (as one Japanese woman expressed to me, for most couples, marriage's real stage is a 2–DK [apartment with two rooms and a dining-kitchen] somewhere like Saitama [a prefecture neigbouring Tokyo which contains many bed-towns]). Ueno points out that although Japan adopted certain aspects of the western discourse of romantic love, it never adopted the 'couple culture' (1987: 82, note 15) by which she means that after marriage, husbands and wives do not appear much as a 'couple' outside of the home, participating instead in segregated social lives. The dating, driving, gift-exchanging, wining and dining and travelling that has been much commoditised in the run up to the marriage ceremony, after marriage rapidly fades away for most couples. As Jolivet points out, young women's enthusiasm to get as much out of their pre-married lives as possible is realistic 'given that their honeymoon is usually the last time they go on a luxury trip' (1997: 39).

The Japanese psychologist, Doi Takeo (1985) discusses the culture shock he experienced while visiting America in the 1960s. He was astonished by the 'emphasis laid in America, unlike traditional custom in Japan, upon contact between the sexes not only after marriage but before it' (1985: 135). He was surprised at the extent to which married couples participated in a shared social life, mixing with work colleagues, and even including their children. He remarks that in America, 'the relationship between a married couple, or between lovers, is always given preference' over 'social contact with members of the same sex' (1985: 135). However, he does recognise that Japan is changing more towards the American model of integration between the sexes. Yet Japan still retains strong homosocial divisions which work against a married couple sharing a social life. Men are still required to spend a large amount of time socializing with their (predominantly male, more so as they ascend the corporate ladder) colleagues after work and women's social life still revolves around the home and the PTA, both of which, as they include the care of children, are gendered as female spaces.

Doi's observation is also largely borne out by Hatfield and Rapson's (1996) cross-cultural analysis of love and sex. They emphasise the way in which different cultural constructions of self influence the ways in which individuals seek out and express intimacy. They claim that in America, where many middle-class people value individuality, uniqueness and independence, individuals tend to experience themselves as separate selves and seek intimacy in a sexual union with a lover. However, in Asian societies where the culture stresses interdependency, conformity and responding to the needs of others, and where self is understood in relation to the ancestors and the family, individuals tend to seek out intimacy with parents and kin rather than sexual partners. In Japan, where family bonds as well as homosocial bonds established at school and in the company remain strong, it is not uncommon to find couples sacrificing their time together to fulfill obligations to both family and colleagues.

Another factor that limits the amount of time Japanese couples have to socialise together is the very great demand that society makes upon the time and energy of both men and women which leaves them little free time for relaxation. Long commutes and regular overtime work mean that many husbands spend little time at home. Weekends, too, may be encroached upon by the demands of 'business golf' and other work-related social activities. This means that many men are too exhausted to participate in family life and are apt to regard such 'family service' (*kazoku sābisu*) as a burden (Jolivet 1997: 63). Wives, too, returning to part-time work after an initial period of child rearing, are busy caring for their home and children as well as bringing in much needed extra income to put towards expensive mortgage and education fees. Thus, husband and wife are not so much a couple as a team, both working hard in their separate roles to make the family function successfully. Edwards argues that 'Japanese notions of gender make marriage necessary because individuals – both men and women – are always incomplete; their deficiencies, more-over, are complementary. Men need women to manage both their money and their domestic lives. Women need men to provide economic security and proper representation for the family in the public domain' (1989: 123).

Married life, then, is not much romanticised in Japanese culture and as described above, Japanese women in particular, increasingly feel themselves to be disadvantaged by the role play that marriage inevitably involves. An increasing number of Japanese women seem to expect more from marriage, especially emotional and sexual satisfaction. The 1983 *More Report on Female Sexuality* reported that 70 per cent of the women between ages thirteen and sixty surveyed, felt 'sexually unsatisfied' (cited in Hatano and Shimazaki 1997: 819). Although extra-marital sex for husbands has long been catered for and tolerated in Japanese society, there is now evidence that an increased 'adultery boom' (*furin būmu*) is taking place among married women who are no longer willing to tolerate the double standard. Takada comments that '*furin's* new popularity may ... signal lowered expectations of the institution of marriage itself' (1994: 202) but, in the case of women, surely the opposite is true. Husbands have always had the opportunity to indulge themselves in Japan's widespread sex industry, the *mizu shōbai* (literally, water trade) and now their wives, no longer willing to tolerate their husband's lack of attention, are looking to other men for satisfaction.

Part of the commentary on the *furin* boom was a programme that I saw while in Japan in January 1998. The programme, shown on TBS, was entitled 'Tonight's revelation: for the first time a questionnaire reveals the real state of Japanese women, have you already slipped?' The programme revealed the results of a questionnaire administered to 5,000 women. It was discovered that these women had an average number of four partners before marriage. Eleven per cent had had an extra-marital affair and 22 per cent wanted to. Twenty one of the women interviewed revealed that the fathers of their children were not their husband's, but their lover's. This programme was obviously sensationalising the topic but even if its figures are unreliable, the fact that it occupied a prime viewing space (eight p.m.) suggests that *furin* is a topic which is of interest to many Japanese people. An even more interesting statistic was produced by a 1986 survey conducted by the Prime Minister's Office into the social background of female sex workers: it was discovered that 10 per cent of 680 sex workers arrested by the police were housewives (cited in Hatano and Shimazaki 1997: 820), suggesting that some housewives would prefer to earn high incomes in the sex industry rather than join their neighbours on the poorly paid supermarket checkout.

It is clear, then, that marriage in Japan has traditionally been seen as a kind of work team where the husband and wife work on behalf of the family as a whole in their respective jobs. Love, emotional sharing and eroticism have not been prioritised in this construction and sexual and romantic satisfaction have not been considered priorities, particularly for women. As Buckley states 'If marital sex is defined as a primarily reproductive function and the *okusan* [wife] occupies the motherbody space in relation to both her children and her spouse, then there is little room for sexual desire in the domestic sphere' (1991: 190). Women continue to marry 'neither for love nor as an expression of their sexuality but rather, as is common knowledge, to survive economically' (Robertson 1998: 145). However, a new understanding of marriage, what in the west has been termed 'the companionate model' (Stone 1977) is increasing. It seems that women are, on the whole, developing increased expectations in this area more rapidly than men. Ochiai Emiko puts this down partly to the influence of the women's movement which challenged the previous under-standing of marriage based on clearly delineated gender roles. She argues that 'In advocating sex as communication, arguably women's lib was seeking the full realization of one of the ideals of the modern family, namely the union of the sexes through true love and sex' (1996: 101). However, when women fantasize their 'ideal partners' as they do in the *bishōnen* of women's manga, the transvestite members of boy bands and in the *otokoyaku* of the Takarazuka theatre, their ideal men depart rather radically from the stereotypical representa-tions of mainstream masculinity. As a Japanese female translator of American gay fiction pointed out to lesbian activist Sarah Schulman: 'Japanese women are changing very quickly ... But Japanese men are not catching up. For us, images of male homosexuality are the only picture we have of men loving someone else as an equal. It is the kind of love we want to have' (Schulman 1994: 245). It is for this reason that gay men, who are understood to be woman-like and therefore more sympathetic to women and their problems, are sometimes represented as a woman's ideal partner, as I describe below.

Gay men as women's ideal partners in *Okoge* and *Twinkle*

Even before the scandal surrounding Olympic athlete Arimori Yūko and her 'gay' American husband broke in March 1998, there was considerable discussion in Japan about so-called 'counterfeit mar-riages' (*gisō kekkon*) which are also referred to as 'camouflage' and

'sexless' marriages (*kamofurāji/sekkusu nashi no kekkon*).The media
interest in this phenomenon was sparked by the 'gay boom' (*gei
būmu*) in the early-1990s during which gay-themed movies, books,
articles and television shows became popular. The effect of the gay
boom upon the perception of same-sex desiring people in Japan has
been discussed in English by Lunsing (1997) and Valentine (1997a),
and in Japanese by Itō (1996) and Kiyohara (1994), among others.
Rather than presenting a more balanced and realistic picture of the
diversity which exists among same-sex desiring individuals (as also
exists between other-sex, or both-sex desiring individuals), the gay
boom seems to have disseminated more broadly a narrow range of
stereotypes. In this chapter, I shall look at some texts which discuss
the issue of homosexual men and marriage, some of which present gay
men as a woman's best friend and her ideal marriage partner. I shall
start with a discussion of two of the most popular 'gay boom' movies
both of which, in different ways, present gay men as women's ideal
marriage partners.

Okoge (Takehiro Murata 1992) is one of the movies capitalising
on the 'gay boom' which swept Japanese media in the early-1990s.
Unlike *Summer Vacation 1999* (discussed in the previous chapter),
Okoge does not deal with the love between boys, but with that
between two men, Tochi, a forty-something salaryman and Goh, a
twenty-something self-employed artisan. However, the story is clearly
pitched at a female audience. The key character in the movie is neither
of the gay men, but Sayoko, a young woman who does voice-overs for
animated films. She sees Tochi and Goh kissing at the beach and finds
the scene irresistibly attractive, later commenting that 'it was
beautiful, your kiss.' The victim of childhood sexual abuse, Sayoko
can only feel safe when in the company of gay men. During a picnic,
she is shown lying down next to the two lovers as they make out,
exclaiming 'Such happiness!' She also listens to the two men make
love in the next room; this scene is then juxtaposed with a dream in
which she remembers the sexual abuse she received at the hands of her
step-father. Here, heterosexuality is the 'anxiety-inducing other'
whereas same-sex love is more romantic, more emotional and
somehow more 'safe;' as Sayoko tells the gay men, 'with you I feel
at ease.' The gay men spend a lot of time at Sayoko's apartment where
they do the cooking. The warmth of this surrogate family is
juxtaposed with the empty formalism of the relationship between
Tochi and his vindictive, neurotic wife, and the harsh manner in
which Goh's mother is treated by her eldest son and his wife. When

she is hospitalised, it is Goh, not the women of his family, who takes care of her. His sister-in-law comments, 'a normal man would never act like this, it's a good thing for us he's gay.' Ironically, although Goh is considered unfilial by his mother for failing to get married, it is he, not his brother or sister-in-law, who becomes the care-giver when his mother falls ill.

Heterosexuality is further 'othered' when Sayoko is raped by a straight man she meets in a gay bar. She has already been warned by the bartender that the man is straight because he is wearing a vulgar necktie and cufflinks, something a gay man would never do. She becomes pregnant and both mother and child are abused by the father, thus reinforcing the association between heterosexuality and abuse. Finally she runs away to an *okama* bar, pursued by yakuza loan sharks. The drag queens stage a battle with the loan sharks, rescue mother and baby and lend her money. The final scene shows Sayoko, Goh and the baby walking through Tokyo's preeminent gay area, Shinjuku Ni-chome, surrounded by drag queens, butch clones and gay foreigners: the gay 'other' has been naturalised. Goh and Sayoko have become a 'real' family in which sentiment takes precedent over the performance of roles.

Okoge means the burnt rice which sticks on the bottom of the rice pot (*okama*) and is a derogatory term meaning something like 'fag-hag.' Sayoko is shown as being compelled towards gay men because she associates straight men with sexual abuse. There are no sympathetic straight characters in the movie, Tochi's co-workers are shown to be narrow-minded and vindictive, their solution to the AIDS pandemic being to 'round up all homosexuals, douse them in kerosene and burn them alive.' Goh's elder brother mistreats his mother, and when she is left in the care of his sister-in-law, she develops bed sores which Goh then cures. Sayoko is raped both by her step-father and by her 'lover' and pursued by vindictive loan-sharks. The drag queens become her surrogate family, offering both material and emotional support. Gay men are represented as more human, more emotionally responsive, more caring, more socially responsible, in fact altogether preferable to their straight counterparts. In *Okoge*, gay men are represented as a girl's best friends.

Goh has much in common with the image of the 'feminine man' as he appears in other media directed at women. He is a handbag designer, working from home, where he has taken in and cares for his ailing mother. When visiting Sayoko's apartment, it is he who does the shopping and the cooking, giving Sayoko tips on how to cook and make a meal out of the leftovers. Also, he displays the sensitivity and emotionality commonly associated with female figures as he is shown becoming irrational and hysterical at the breakup of his relationship with Tochi. He is the 'passive' partner in relation to his older lover and sex, typically, is something 'done' to him by Tochi in that the movie's one (rather graphic) sex scene shows Goh being anally penetrated as he passively reclines on the bed. More importantly, however, Goh is shown to be an ideal parent, actively playing with and interacting with the son both he and Sayoko are to bring up together. Tochi comments that Goh has achieved 'every gay man's dream' in that he has established a loving family, but without the sex. When Sayoko tells him that she doesn't mind if he seeks another male lover, he refuses, sublimating his sexuality into love for his family, much as women are expected to do.

Shōko, the main character in *Kira kira hikaru* (Twinkle; Matsuoka George 1992) is a young woman prone to alcoholism and depression. She is told by a doctor that marriage will 'cure' her malaise and is subjected to a series of *omiai* meetings by her concerned parents. It is only when Mutsuki, a prospective groom, tells her that he prefers men, that she agrees to marry him. This movie is more psychologically complex than *Okoge*. Both Shōko and Mutsuki suffer from depression caused by the constraining effects of Japanese society and its emphasis on conformity. It is Shōko, however, who is shown to have the bigger heart. She tries to get Mutsuki back together with his lover, Kon, which he refuses to do because he wants to keep up appearances, she tells him 'you are narrow minded.' A complex relationship develops between the three characters as they try to find a compromise between their feelings (*ninjō*) and their obligations to family and society (*giri*). The oppressive nature of the latter is highlighted by a family conference which is called when Mutsuki is 'outed' to his in-laws. Both sets of parents talk over the couple, trading viciously polite insults: 'you didn't mention your son was gay on his resume,' 'well, you didn't tell us your daughter was an alcoholic.' The parents want them to divorce but the couple wants to continue as they are. It becomes clear that Shōko loves Mutsuki, and after a final crisis, it becomes clear that Mutsuki has also come to love Shōko. After a surreal scene in which the three go through a dark night of the soul, the movie is noncommittal about their future together. The overall theme of the movie contrasts the genuine feelings of the central characters with the empty formalism of their parents (the idea that marriage per se will 'cure' any social non-conformity).

Like Sayoko in *Okoge*, Shōko is a 'new woman,' she has her own career, is financially independent and resists pressure to get married; but she pays a price – depression leading to alcoholism. Also like Sayoko, the only way for her to maintain her independence within marriage is to marry a gay man. *Kira kira hikaru* is realistic about the pressures that this involves, not only external pressure to perform the roles of husband and wife and thereby keep up appearances, but also the psychological pressure which comes from trying to create a relationship outside of role play. The film's ending is not as upbeat as that of *Okoge*, but we are left with the impression that the three characters, driven to the brink of destruction, have discovered the inner resources necessary to negotiate their survival in a hostile environment.

Sayoko is abused by the men in a sexist society, Shōko is patronised by them. Both break out by allying themselves with society's despised other: gay men. In a curious inversion, gay men are here inscribed as the positive term in the homo/hetero binary, they are the genuine object, the real thing, women's best friends in the battle to win social space for female subjectivity.

Real and counterfeit marriage

Sparked by the scandal surrounding the Olympic athlete Arimori Yūko and her supposedly 'gay' American husband, the popular weekly magazine, *SPA* (18 March 1998), known for its sensationalist coverage, published an article with the title 'The reason why gays choose to marry women and women choose to marry gays' in which some interesting issues are raised with regard to the nature of homosexuality, marriage and inter-sex relationships. The article begins by problematising marriages between women and 'gays' (*gei*), terming them 'counterfeit' (*gisō*), while also acknowledging that some women consciously marry gay men. The subheadings suggest two reasons why: firstly, some gay men want to have a household and children (*katei ya kodomo*), and secondly, some women consider marriage to gay men to be 'more convenient' *(tsugō ga ii)* than to 'ordinary men' *(futsū no otoko)*. An inset picture displays the 'marriage corner' personal ads from *Barazoku*, a gay magazine, and states that 'there are a large number of ads addressed to gays from women including lesbians (*rezu*).'

One man interviewed says that most people's image of a counterfeit marriage is that between a gay man and a lesbian who appear as a couple in form only and after a few years divorce so that they can tell colleagues and relatives that they had been married but it didn't work out. However, the article stresses that not all marriages between gay men and gay and straight women are 'sexless' (*dorai*), arguing that the meaning of 'sex' should be expanded to include intimate (not necessarily penetrative) physical contact. Recently, there has been an increase in the number of women who want to have 'friendship' (*yūjō*) marriages with gay men. A forty-eight-year-old gay man who two years ago married a woman who understood his sexual orientation is quoted as saying 'we maintain a good partnership which will last longer than one just based on sex.'

The article points out that Japanese society is changing and it is no longer the case that people have to marry against their wishes. So why are some gay men choosing to marry women? One man, who has been living in a sexless partnership with a woman for the last four years says, 'we appear as more of a couple than most couples. I trust my partner more than anybody else and can talk about anything with her. I feel that this person is my partner above all other men and women. I love her as a human being. So I think it's a good thing for gay men to marry women.' Another man comments 'marriage and romantic love (*ren'ai*) are different things. Marriage is about inspiration (*insupirē-shon*). If it's the one, there's no problem living together. It's the same whether it's a man or a woman.'

The article also points out that many gay men have a longing for a family which is stronger than their desire for romantic love and sex. One man comments 'the meaning of marriage is to establish a stable family, sex is just an added extra. I want to have a family more than sex.' However, the desire to have children without the sex does present problems as another man says 'my image of marriage is walking about town with my kids. I want to have kids without the sex but I don't want to adopt because they won't be bound to me by blood.'

There are clear advantages for gay men and lesbian women who choose to marry in order to ease social pressure. However, what reasons do 'ordinary women' (*futsū no josei*) have for forming such partnerships? One twenty-nine-year-old 'straight woman' (*sutorēto no josei*) writes in the inset *Barazoku* marriage column, 'I'm thinking of marrying a gay man. I am healthy and financially independent. I would like to live together and have children if possible. I'm waiting for replies from sincere people who live in the city.' But, the article asks, what do straight women expect from gay men? There seem to be a variety of expectations. One woman thinks that gay men are more 'calm' (*yasuragi*) and 'comforting' (*iyashi*) than straight men (*nonke*). Other women mention wanting to marry men who will share the housework: 'the gay men I know are all domestic. I don't expect my husband to do all the housework but men who can do housework are attractive. If you need sex, then I don't mind if you get a lover just for that.' The article suggests that 'the fact that straight men are considered to lack these qualities is a point for reflection.' However, just as intriguing is the question not discussed in the article of why gay men in particular are considered to have them – an issue that I discuss further below.

Other reasons are given as to why some women want a gay man as a marriage partner, one woman says 'the easiest explanation is that I don't like sex.' She adds that some straight men, even if they realize their partners don't enjoy sex, only think of themselves and constantly request it. So when one considers that a marriage is a partnership for life, the 'best partner' (*besuto pātonā*) is a gay man. She comments that marriage is necessary in order for a man to advance in his career and preserve his public image, so marriage with a gay man involves more give and take. As far as children are concerned, it is always possible to have artificial insemination and, anyway, she thinks that 'cloning is a better way to have children because you can guarantee there will be no strange blood.' This woman's ideal partner is an 'auntie-like' (*obasanppoi*) older man who would like to take care of her. A gay who harmonizes the best aspects of a man and a woman would be ideal. The article concludes that it is not the case that gay men are 'using' women but that, on the contrary, women are using gay men.

An inset mini article by a gay free writer states that 'of course it would be better if men could marry each other.' However, 'marriage between gays and women is one test which shows the marriage system is being reconsidered.' He argues that the traditional marriage system is breaking down and people are beginning to think more in terms of domestic partnerships (*domesuttiku pātonāshippu*). The days when men supported women are over; women now demand economic and sexual independence. Straight men and women are now fighting each other through the legal system. If heterosexist (*hetero chūshin*) marriages break up then it is necessary to have a new kind of marriage system. He argues that this is not just about a change in the law or a problem with human sexuality, but about being able to choose as a partner the person one most loves. This means that marriage needs to be thought about in terms other than sex. Sex should not be thought of as just putting a penis into a vagina but should be understood more broadly to include the deep affection that can be felt between gays and women. Even without sex, marriages between gays and women are still meaningful. He concludes that now is a time when love surpasses sex (*sekkusu wo koeta, ren'ai no jidai*) when people come to consider marriage partners.

This article is interesting both because of the issues it chooses to discuss and those it ignores. It accepts at face value the idea that gay men represent some kind of androgynous intermediary between the sexes, uniting the best of male and female. Gay men are presented as being more caring, feeling, giving and responsible than their heterosexual counterparts. What is more they also take responsibility for household chores. Straight men are said to only be interested in sex, whereas gays and women are more interested in human relationships and feelings. Thus, a marriage between a gay man and a woman can be seen as more authentic, even without the sex, than that between a woman and a straight man.

Why are women who marry gay men 'trendy'?

The negative, if somewhat fatalistic attitude many Japanese women hold towards marriage has been outlined earlier, as has the romantic interest many women have in homosexual love stories. The journalist Richard McGregor makes a connection between the two when he quotes a source saying that the reason for women's interest in gay stories is that 'girls look at their marriage prospects and it doesn't look attractive ... Men are very serious, even threatening ... That's why almost anything homosexual can get an all-female audience' (1996: 229). However, not all women who say they want to marry gay men do so because they perceive gay men as more romantic partners than straight men. In *Homotaimu* (Homo time), a sensationalist expose of the gay world written by a gay-porn photographer (Kiyohara 1994), there is a chapter entitled 'Are women who marry gay men trendy?' (*Homo to kekkon suru onna ga torendi?*). None of the cases he discusses from his personal experience are based upon the supposed empathy and understanding which exists between straight women and gay men. In his view, marriage, which is considered by most people to be 'half business' (*hanbun bizinesu*), is undertaken by these people for reasons of convenience only. Firstly, he suggests that straight men in Japan have an extremely negative image. One woman married to a gay male model says of straight men, 'no matter how smart or attractive he may have been as a bachelor, he soon becomes middle-aged (*ojisan ni natte shimatte*) and leaving everything up to his wife, lies around on the sofa drinking beer and watching television' (1994: 125). This is the stereotypical portrait of husband as *sodai gomi* (bulky garbage) which lies around and clutters up the home (Takada 1994: 293). Another common saying relating to husbands is 'The best husband is a healthy one who is never home' (*teishu wa genki de rusu ga yoi*), suggesting that husbands are appreciated as breadwinners, not lovers. Kiyohara suggests that many women find the prospect of taking care of a man distinctly unappealing. Instead, the same woman comments 'I want to live my life doing what I like, I hate being dependent on a man. Only a gay man could probably fit in with my expectations' (1994: 125). This couple, the eldest son and daughter of their respective families, were being pressured into marriage. They had known each other since childhood and got on well and finally agreed to a convenience marriage. The marriage made their social lives much smoother.

The pressure that many Japanese people feel to get married should not be underestimated. This pressure is not felt equally by all but falls particularly upon eldest children where property is involved. Hendry (1981) found that 'traditional' ideas about the centrality of marriage were still strong in rural Japanese communities in the 1970s. She emphasises that in Japan marriage was traditionally understood as a deal between two families, negotiated primarily for ensuring the continuation of the family unit *(ie)* and its property or profession by providing descendants. She concludes that marriage is 'a fundamental institution [which] offers resistance to the sweeping tide of change' (Hendry 1981: 239). Although the rise of an enormous urban middle class for whom the transfer of property is not an issue has removed this specific pressure from many people, individuals (particularly men) who are on fast-track careers feel constrained to marry in order to appear 'normal' and be accepted for promotion. Marriage is expected in Japan 'because everyone gets married' (Kiyohara 1994: 127) and it is the final step into a fully adult and responsible state. Marriage is an essential step on what Mori Yōko terms the 'course for future social advancement' (Mori 1994: 6). Marriage normalises a person by integrating him or her into Japanese society. As Kiyohara states 'all one needs to do to appear normal is get married' (1994: 127). There is something suspicious, even deviant about a middle-aged professional who remains unmarried as was discussed in chapter 3 in relation to the Finance Ministry homosexual scandal reported in the magazine *FOCUS*. Indeed, the man at the centre of the scandal was identified as a member of the non-career group (*non kyaria gumi*) partly on the basis of his suspicious single status. Thus, many men, whether gay or straight must 'kill their selves' (Kiyohara 1994: 128) and get married. The personal sacrifices involved in getting married differ between gay and straight men only in degree, a gay man finding it harsher to share 'the same roof with a strange woman' (Kiyohara 1994: 128).

A further concern voiced by Kiyohara affecting both men and women is the way in which after marriage, men's and women's roles change and they become *ojisan* and *obasan*. These terms translate as 'uncle' and 'aunt' but are difficult to render into English. Kinship terms are used more widely in Japanese than in English as terms of address, particularly when talking to children. Children will refer to older children and to young adults as *oniisan* and *onēsan*, older-brother and older-sister. Once a person has married, they then become *ojisan* and *obasan*, uncle and aunt. However, these terms have recently developed negative connotations, particularly for women who are often termed *obatarian* (from *obasan* and the English word 'battalion'). Depictions of *obatarian* are common in magazines and manga, they are represented as middle-aged, dumpy women with bad perms and big glasses who are shown aggressively competing with each other for bargain items and train seats. They commonly terrorize their husbands and children, often metamorphosing into the *mama-gon*, or 'mother demons' who spy on their children to make sure they are doing their homework or lurk around in the hallway waiting for their drunken husbands to return. Kiyohara suggests that many women resist this 'obatarianisation' process which overtakes them after marriage. Hardacre, in her study of discourses surrounding abortion in Japan, has also written about this transformation from 'unmarried or childless woman' which she says is 'characterized as maximally sexually desirable and autonomous' to the status of a mother which is 'marked by the assumption of a desexualised appearance' (1997: 53), particularly during maternity which she argues 'represents a "death" of desire and desirability'. Wives are desexualised because sexual desirability in Japan has traditionally been projected onto women of the entertainment industry. This is supported by the American anthropologist Liza Dalby who writes in her ethnography of a geisha house, 'Geisha embody precisely those aspects of femininity that are absent from, or only incidental to the role of wife,' noting among other things, 'sensuous appeal' (1985: 171).

Given that marriage and the maternity which soon follows represent the end of a woman's perceived desirability, it is not surprising, as Kiyohara says, that 'some women who do not want to turn into "*obasan*" after marriage think about marrying gay men' because gay men are less likely to turn into *ojisan* and expect all the role playing which goes with it (1994: 126). The concept of role or performance (*engi*) is crucial here, as he suggests that many Japanese people feel uncomfortable with the restrictions that these roles impose on them. He points out that there are no magazines in Japan that cater to 'women' who happen to be married, they instead cater to 'married women' (1994: 126). Magazines exist which are directed at single women, mothers, wives, *obasan* etc. but not at women who just happen to be also married. He says 'Japanese women cease to be *women* when they marry' (1994: 126). As outlined in the previous chapter, the roles of wife and mother are often conflated in popular culture leading to the end of a woman's experience of sexuality independent from her husband, and sometimes to the end of all sexual experience.

Ueno Chizuko quotes one theorist as saying that in Japan 'Neither men nor women are sleeping with the opposite sex, they are sleeping with a system' (1992: 140). This system scripts sexual interactions between men and women in terms of wider social discourses which reflect the basic imbalance of power between men as a group and women as a group. As Ochiai argues,

> The coerciveness of unequal power relations is present even in sex. Moreover, the male-female dynamics of power revolving around sexuality are not simply personal dynamics: they are embedded in the sexual mores common to society as a whole (1996: 91).

Hence, despite the quality of individual relationships between spouses, men and women as husbands and wives are networked into a wider system of gendered relationships which seriously constrain the amount of freedom they have to negotiate their roles. Thus, it is not surprising that some women resist this transformation from 'woman' to *obasan* by marrying a gay man who is himself attempting to thwart the system. This is easy to understand in Japan where marriage is not structured primarily in terms of romantic love but is commonly regarded, as Kiyohara points out, as 'half business' (*hanbun bizinesu*) and at times 'all business' (*zembu bizinesu*) (1994: 127).

This 'business model' is also endorsed by Fushimi Noriaki whose book *Private Gay Life* (1991) was an important contribution to

Japan's 'gay boom.' He argues that 'even if a man is gay, I think it is fine for him to live with a woman as part of a "mutual reproduction project" (*saiseisan purojekuto*)' (1991: 17). He defines this 'mutual reproduction project' as 'a partnership based on the possibility of working together to give birth to and bring up a child' (1991: 17). He says that although he personally dislikes the marriage system, everybody is different, and for those gay men who want children, then it is fine for them to marry because 'love and sex life are different' (1991: 17). In his book, Fushimi gives a bleak analysis of the current state of marriage and women's rights in Japan which many women would probably identify with. He says that after university gradua-tion, for many young women 'the dream is over' (1991: 94) and that their most important job is to 'sell themselves at as high a price as possible on the marriage market' (1991: 94). He says that straight men are only interested in sex and that 'you can't tell a man's true feelings until immediately after he has ejaculated' (1991: 94). His advice to 'smart women' is to 'become feminist' (1991: 94). Fushimi is an important figure in the discourse linking women with gay men in the struggle against supposed patriarchal oppressors. Gay men and women are somehow 'smarter' than straight men and can therefore manipulate patriarchal institutions for their own advantage.

Women who choose to marry gay men are 'trendy,' then, because they exemplify the values of the new 'me-first' generation. They want the stability and assurance that comes with conforming to social expectations while at the same time maintaining the erotic and financial independence they enjoyed as 'unmarried aristocrats.' As with the male model and his wife, they act as a couple when in the public eye but are cautious not to intrude upon each other's private life (Kiyohara 1994: 126). Marriage to a gay man is thus one way in which a woman in Japanese society can continue to enjoy the recently won benefits of greater economic and erotic independence past her late twenties. Yet the question still remains unanswered as to the extent to which gay men really do differ from their straight counterparts in their performance of gender roles both within and outside marriage.

Are gay men really women's best friends?

Recently, there have been a number of publications written by gay men which address a female audience. *Kairaku no gijutsu* (The art of pleasure) by Fushimi Noriaki (1997) is a collection of discussions with the bisexual author Saito Ayako aimed at clarifying the different ways in which men and women achieve sexual pleasure. Topics covered include the penis, the vagina, anal sex, SM, orgies and pornography, both Saito and Fushimi arguing that sexual pleasure needs to be reconfigured outside the traditional stereotypes of the male 'active' and female 'passive' roles. Another book by Fushimi, *Sūpārabu* (Super love; 1998b) stresses the common interests which exist between gay men and straight women. Fushimi gives tips, from a male standpoint, on what men really think and feel, what kind of men to avoid, and advises women how to see through men's lies, what to do when they find their boyfriends are cheating on them, etc. Fushimi offers advice to women from a gay man's standpoint on how to deal with straight men in a manner similar to Nomura Sachiyo (1995), discussed in chapter 3, who gives women tips on how to find out and deal with men who are really gay.

However, Fushimi has a political agenda absent in Nomura's text. In the foreword to his book he suggests that the whole field of cross-sex relationships needs to be reimagined. For example, he questions whether women should always follow the man's lead in sex, whether after marriage a woman's role should really be to stay in the home and raise children and a man's role should be to work outside to raise money. He claims to have a special vantage point since he 'was born with a gay sexuality (*gei to iu sekushuariti ni umaretsuita*)' (1998b: 3) which meant that despite the pressure he felt from others (*seken*) he had to think critically about his own lifestyle (1998b: 4). He argues that instead of thinking 'I was born a man, so I should act in this way; or I was born a woman so I should act in that way,' people should think 'I am myself (*boku dakara*), so I want to be this kind of man; or I am myself (*watashi dakara*) so I want to become this kind of woman' (1998b: 4). Fushimi sees gay men and straight women to be at the forefront of this re-envisaging of gender roles, based not upon rules (*rūru*) but upon individuality (*jibunrashisa*). He argues 'men are slow to change and should hurry up' and that 'gay men and women who are being themselves should join hands, let's make a paradise' (1998b: 5). He claims that his book is aimed at developing friendship (*yūjō*) between women and gay men. Gay men have much to offer straight women, for they are man enough to understand straight men and be able to give women inside information on men's real feelings, but they are also born with a different sexuality from straight men which gives them a special vantage point on social customs, enabling them to be more individual than their conformist straight counterparts. However, despite the common interests which some women feel exist between themselves and gay men, and which gay men such as Fushimi suggest should exist between gay men and women, a look at representations of women in gay media suggests that many gay men share the same view of women which characterises the straight male world.

Many homosexual men, whether they approximate to the transgendered images prevalent on Japanese television or not, do not feel particularly sympathetic towards women. In fact misogyny, common in many all-male situations, is quite apparent in the Japanese gay world, directed both against biological women and against men who dress or behave too effeminately. For example, a panel discussion about gay-themed movies in the gay magazine *Badi*, asks why 70 per cent of the audience for these pictures is made up of women. One headline states that 'I/we hate young women who like to look at "gay things"' (*'homo mono' wo mitagaru wakai onnatachi wa daikirai*). Osugi, a movie critic and media talent who uses camp speech, says that many women go to gay movies, or hang around gay bars just to peep at gay men and that he feels like a spectacle all the time. However, he comments that men do not do this. Fushimi also complains about *okoge* whom he defines as 'girls who hang around gays in the Shinjuku Ni-chome area' (1991: 24). He says that girls like this who cause trouble for gay men are performing a kind of sexual harassment (*onna no sekuhara*) (1991: 24). Furthermore, many gay websites contain messages which state that women are forbidden to enter (*josei no kata no nyūshitsu wo okotowari shimasu*). On the whole, gay men do not regard the invasion of gay space by heterosexual tourists, either male or female, particularly favourably and do not seem to feel the same empathy for straight women as some women do for them. They feel that women cannot understand gay feelings and only want to mix with gays out of curiosity.

As is discussed in chapter 6, gay venues which admit women (either lesbian or straight) are rare in Japan. This extends even to AIDS events. For example, I attended a fundraising show for Voice for Gay Friends, an AIDS action group, in a public hall in Tokyo in December 1998. The tickets stated 'entrance limited to men' (*nyūjō dansei ni kagirimasu*) which seemed odd in that some of the performers were biological women as well as men dressed as women. After each performance, the performers left the stage to join the audience. However, the lesbian members of the lesbian-and-gay Square Dance team 'Edo 8s' hung around near the back of the hall, obviously not sure if they were welcome to stay around or not. When I asked one of the organisers about this policy, he said that it was designed to prevent straight women who liked to hang around gay men coming to the performance and perhaps recognising a co-worker on the stage or in the audience, thus inadvertently outing him. Some men I spoke to thought this absurd, whereas others seemed to feel that it was a real threat.

Many of the life stories of homosexual men collected by Yajima (1997) contain negative allusions to women. One man recalls how he began to feel a strong dislike of women during junior high school. He used to resent the women he saw having sex with men in heterosexual pornography and would masturbate while blocking out their faces (Yajima 1997: 94). Later, when he began to cross-dress (josō) he was extremely shocked to find that this made him very attractive to some women (1997: 106); however, the attraction was not mutual. Another man comments that 'Basically, I don't like women. It's not just the problem with sex, but I can't get to like their mannerisms and way of speaking' (1997: 83). Some men also recall their first sexual experiences, often with women hired for the purpose. Rather than the sharing of mutual sympathies, what these men report as most satisfying in these encounters is being able to command or being commanded to perform sexual services. One man mentions that what felt good in his interactions with a prostitute was 'being ordered to lick her feet' (1997: 119). In fact, although many of the men interviewed by Yajima mention that they first came out to female colleagues, relatives or friends, few of them report intimate relationships with women.

Japanese homosexual men also lack a sense of connection with same-sex desiring women. This is reflected in the fact that there is no nationally distributed magazine or newspaper similar to the American *Advocate* or Britain's *Gay Times* which addresses itself to the wider lesbian, gay, bisexual and transgender community. Also, venues which cater to both gay men and gay women are rare and there is little social interaction among them. The vast majority of gay bars have a door policy which restricts entry to men only and this makes it difficult for gay men and lesbians to go out together in public and discuss issues freely in a supportive environment. Furthermore, Buckley has noted that 'Gay men's organisations are often criticized ... as being bound to very traditional notions of the feminine and female sexuality' (1994: 174) suggesting that simply being homosexual does not necessarily mean a man will have more liberal views about women and their capabilities than those held by most straight men. This point is nicely expressed by the Chinese-Australian gay activist Tony Ayres who writes that 'it was in a gay bar that I learnt, contrary to my university demagogy, that being gay did not give a person privileged insight or an ideological commonality with other lives and oppressions' (1999: 89).

The gay press contains many negative images of women, particularly women who are seen as being in competition for the same sexual partners as gay men. These women often include the wives of men who would rather be having sex with other men. One such story occurs in the manga entitled 'Let me have your father' (*Otaku no otōsan wo boku ni kudasai*) in *Barazoku* (1994, vol.6, 213–228). Here, the wife and her mother are represented as spoiled, brash, hysterical, vindictive and manipulative. The mother blames the daughter for her lack of control over her handsome husband, saying that she should have condescended to love a man who was 'short, fat, bald' implying that such a man would be easily manipulated; however, 'being loved by a handsome man for ever is something that only happens in the world of girl's fiction.' When the father is sent to talk to his son-in-law about his daughter's complaints about their sex life (or lack of it), the son-in-law seduces him and the two men bond together against the manipulative women in their lives.

Another comic, reproduced in Kiyohara (1994: 223–235), targets the spoilt 'princess' (*ojōsama*). Here, a rich boy is dating an *ojōsama* simply because she is a rich girl from a family approved of by his parents. However, he secretly desires the boorish sake-delivery boy who is despised by the girl for his common origins. The girl becomes jealous of the attention her boyfriend pays to the delivery boy, especially when the boy is invited to join them on a cruise. She tells him not to bother them any more because he is getting in the way of their relationship, to which he replies 'I've also slept with him!' The comic ends with her shocked profile and the English words 'What's happened to ... ?' The *ojōsama* is a type often targeted in gay fiction. She is shown to be spoilt, selfish, manipulative and cruel, attempting to entrap eligible men in order to establish her own social position. As the girl in this story says about her boyfriend, 'He's tall, gentle, handsome. His grandfather's rich, his father's a successful man in America, he drives a silver porsche ... he's a pure-hearted, top-quality boy ... if only I can establish our relationship, he'll marry me!' In the gay press, women are hardly represented as sympathetic marriage partners, even for straight men.

Negative attitudes towards 'family values' are also displayed in Murano Inuhiko's (1996) *Gakuran tengoku 2* (Tumultous heaven 2) which contains the comic *Sora iro no tamashii* (Sky-blue spirit). In this war-time story, a young boy falls in love with a senior student *(sempai)* who is soon called off to war. The older boy makes a statuette of himself which he gives to the young boy as a keepsake until his return. Predictably, the older youth is killed during battle, but his younger lover cannot forget him, and preserves the statue as a memorial to his dead friend. Many years later the man, now married, has a child who unfortunately breaks the statuette. Transported into a rage, the man beats his child in front of the shocked eyes of his wife. Shown as disinterested in both wife and child, the man becomes increasingly reclusive and cold towards them. He finally rejects his grown-up son who turns to him for fatherly advice. One day, now an old man, he revisits the site of the stream where he once consummated his love with the dead soldier. Shocked, he sees his lover waving to him from the other side of the bank. The final scene shows the old man's body lying dead in the field while his youthful spirit soars into the sky locked in the embrace of his lover. Because 'family values' in Japan are constructed in terms other than romantic love, the sympathy in this story is for the same-sex lovers and not for the neglected wife and child. Here, the husband's faithful commitment to his dead lover is seen as purer and more romantic than the mundane ritual that is married life.

Gay men's changing response to marriage

Although the *SPA* article discussed earlier in the chapter is ostensibly arguing for a new definition of marriage which transcends sex and focuses upon intimacy and shared feelings (which gay men are understood to be more capable of than their heterosexual counterparts), the majority of men cited stress their longing for a household *(katei)* and not a partnership. Many of these men see their future closely bound up with the *role* of father/husband in a family which is clearly stronger than their concept of an individual relationship with their spouse. As one man comments 'my image of marriage is walking about town with my kids.' Here, being publicly seen acting the role of father/husband is the desired end of the marriage process. Voller (1986) quotes a gay Japanese man as saying, 'Marriage for many Japanese men is a matter of necessity, of realising that they are ageing, have reached the right age for marriage. After the wedding, the woman becomes a *mother* and the man becomes a *father*, and they live together for the sake of their babies.' In this construction, marriage is primarily about role play and the issue of sexual attraction or sexual orientation is sidelined. This is very much the traditional understanding of the marriage relationship held by both men and women born before the 1960s baby boom. However, as discussed above, new 'romantic' or 'companionate' models of marriage are increasingly being adopted by younger people, meaning that no one univocal stance is held by all homosexual men on the topic of marriage. The following personal communication is interesting in this regard. The writer, a man in his late twenties (the optimum age for marriage), wrote:

At present I'm wondering about getting married to a woman. Although I don't have a partner who wants to marry me, when I think about my parents and social standing etc. of course I think I want to get married. But, even if I do get married, I don't think my sexual interests will change. When I bring up this kind of topic with my gay friends, they often say such things as 'it would be a shame for your partner.' But it's not that I want to have a fake marriage (*gisō kekkon*); I'm confident that I can treasure (*daiji ni shite*) and love (*ai suru*) my female partner. But it would be unreasonable to stop dating (*tsuki ai*) guys completely. So, today, I'm emotionally confused about various things.

This response is interesting in that it integrates two different aspects of marriage: the social and the affective. This man wants to get married in order to please his parents and secure his place in society, but he also believes that he can love and treasure his partner. This indicates that it is no easy thing to discern discrete motives in why people marry. Their reasons are complex and it is artificial to insist on too clear a distinction between social and affective pressures. This point will be discussed later when I look at the attitudes towards marriage held by my interviewees in chapter 8.

A look at the problem pages on Japanese gay Internet websites shows that the 'marriage problem' (*kekkon mondai*) is a cause of considerable stress for many gay men, especially those who have passed the age of thirty at which point outside pressure to hurry up and find a partner intensifies. As outlined earlier in this chapter, when and if to get married is not generally understood to be the sole decision of the individual involved. Rather, as Brinton (1992) suggests, other people, both family and employers who see themselves as 'stakeholders' in the future of the individual may feel as though they should get involved in the decision making process. It is this communal nature of marriage preparation which seems to cause the greatest distress to some gay men. For example, a letter from a thirty-year-old gay man submitted to the gay activist Itō Satoru's homepage *Sukotan* explains that what distresses him most about the marriage problem is the difficult position he has put his parents in *vis à vis* the community (*seken*). Although he has told his parents that 'I will find [a wife] myself,' his parents are constantly having to decline offers of introductions (*miai no hanashi*) from relatives and acquaintances. He states that 'I feel I am acting in an unforgivable (*sumanai*) way towards my parents.' He feels so guilty that he is reluctant to go home (literally 'the doorstep has gotten high') and only spends one night with his parents even at New Year and Obon (summer festival). Many men seem reluctant to disappoint their parents by refusing outright to discuss the possibility of marriage or meet with prospective partners. For example, one of Ōhama's informants (Ōhama 1994) a thirty-two-year-old salaryman says 'lately I feel obligated to see someone at least as an act of kindness for my parents' sake ... I think I should at least see someone my parents introduce me to.'

Itō's response to this problem is to ask the question 'For whose sake do you get married? Your own or your parents?' He goes on to argue that gay men should 'live more selfishly' because 'your life will be extinguished if you live it only for the sake of your parents.' This is typical of Itō who has published a number of books (Itō 1994; 1996), some with feminist writers (Itō and Ochiai 1998), in which the discourse of 'individuality' (*jibunrashisa*) is highlighted. However, it is one thing for Itō, a gay activist who famously lives with his male lover and his own disabled mother, to stress the need for an individual to take personal responsibility for his own life, and quite another for a regular salaryman from a provincial town who is closely tied into the local family and community. As Lunsing (*in press*) has pointed out, a major problem afflicting gay men such as the above letter writer is that asserting oneself as gay means that one cannot live a mainstream lifestyle (which invariably involves getting married and having children). He cites the case of a man who actively sought out sex with other men but declared that he could not be 'homosexual' because he was supposed to return to the countryside to take on his parents' farm which would inevitably involve getting married. It is therefore no easy matter for many gay men to extricate their lives from other 'stakeholders' who have an investment in their future solely on concerns of being more 'individual.'

Lunsing (*in press*) notes that 'within gay circles much animosity exists around the theme of marriage.' There is a split between older men in their forties and fifties who are more likely to be married as they were born in a generation when nearly everybody got married because there were no other conceivable life paths, and younger gay men in their twenties for whom the pressure to marry is less, both because they are still young and also because Japanese society is slightly less insistent upon the necessity to marry. As I have argued earlier, the 'romantic love' model of marriage is becoming increasingly accepted in Japan, especially by younger people, irrespective of their sexual orientation. This means that younger gay men are necessarily critical of older men who are married because, according to their constructions of what marriage *should be*, the older men are being duplicitous and deceitful. However, older men, whose construction of marriage is closer to the traditional 'business model' do not necessarily see their roles as husbands and fathers as false.

There are four types of marriage between gay men and women among Lunsing's interview sample. The first he terms 'marriage of convenience' in which both parties agree to get married solely to ease social pressure from family and friends (*seken*); these couples often live apart, or agree upon a time period after which they will divorce. He comments that these are 'not very common.' The second type is the 'friendship marriage' in which the wife knows about the husband's homosexual preference. Some women choose this kind of marriage because it gives them the security and social advantages of the married status while releasing them from unwelcome sexual advances and giving them more bargaining power in negotiating roles. The relationship between Shōko and Mutsuki in *Kira kira hikaru*, discussed above, best fits this model. The third model is that of 'deceptive husbands' where a man marries without telling his wife about his homosexual preference. Lunsing describes such cases as 'much more common.' However, these men do not necessarily use their marriage as a cover while they have affairs with other men (which are difficult to organise without the exchange of phone numbers and a regular venue to meet up), more common is the situation in which these men do not have sex at all. This is obviously unsatisfactory for both partners in the relationship. The final type discerned by Lunsing is 'latent homosexuality' where men marry while not yet fully aware of or accepting of their homosexual preference. Men in this category often speak of themselves as 'bisexual' stating that they feel different kinds of love for their wives and their male partners, stressing the love or empathy they feel for their wives (*aijō*) and the more romantic attraction they feel for men (*ren'ai*).

Lunsing is right to problematise the assumption that 'homosexual men cannot have sex with women' and that a gay man who is successful in having sex with his wife must 'really' be bisexual. The frequency and ability to have sex with a woman differs among 'gay' men just as it does among 'straight' men. Just because a man has sex with a woman does not necessarily mark that interaction as 'heterosexual,' because it is impossible to access the fantasies of the man (or woman, for that matter) who may well be fantasizing an interaction quite other than the one that is taking place. Many of the homosexual men interviewed by Yajima, and some of those interviewed by myself, had had their first sexual experiences with women, either with school or university girlfriends, or with women from the entertainment world. However, they did not consider these experiences to have made them 'bisexual.' If, as I have argued, 'gay identity' is less developed in Japan, gay men are less inclined to rule out the possibility of having sex with women. Given that the importance of a good sex life within marriage is less stressed in Japan generally, this adds support to the idea that homosexual men do not necessarily understand themselves to be disqualified from marriage solely on the basis of their same-sex preference. Thus, I agree with Lunsing when he suggests that:

> What is different in Japan [from North America and northern Europe] is that there are also marriages in which the man recognizes his homosexual desire, which is accepted by the wife, or in which the man does not have many qualms about hiding his homosexual desire from his wife. In North America, northern Europe and Australia such constructions appear to be less feasible due to the importance attached to the contents of marital relationships, due to heterosexual couples being expected to present themselves as lovers (in press).

One twenty-seven-year-old gay man writes in to Itō Satoru's Internet problem page that although he experiences no sexual desire towards women, he does not want to give up the possibility of marriage entirely. After all, he comments, 'for a man and woman to get married, form a household (*katei*) and bring up children, is the greatest happiness.' He says that he is afraid that 'solely because of my sexual desire (*seiyoku no tame dake*) I must live alone without getting married.' This kind of response towards marriage was also commonly reported among Lunsing's gay informants. Lunsing noted that 'sexual preference [was] generally not seen as a feature that determine[d] one's personhood more than partially' (1997: 285) and therefore some Japanese gay men do not regard their homosexual desires as representing a necessary barrier to marriage. Interestingly, this man rejects pressure from others (*mawari*) as the main reason for getting married, saying instead that 'family (*kazoku*) is a wonderful thing ... after all.' Once again, this man is not interested in forming a partnership with any particular woman but instead sees marriage as a project designed to achieve a household/family through the production of children. He values the *institution* of the family to such an extent that even his total lack of sexual interest in women is not necessarily seen as an obstacle to marriage. The way in which the man cited above discusses marriage is common among gay men in Japan where it is marriage as an institution which is prized; that marriage can also be a partnership or relationship between two people who are 'in love' is seldom entertained.

However, the above construction is not limited to gay men in particular but is prevalent among men in general. In Japan, there is widespread tolerance of extra-marital affairs by husbands and I do not see any great difference between a man who is 'really' gay having sexual relations with other men in cruising grounds or host bars, and straight men who pick up prostitutes or visit soapland on their way home on Friday nights. Many marriages become sexless as is evidenced in the large amount of literature (directed at women) discussing this as well as recent media attention to the topic and soap dramas and movies focusing on the problems caused by lack of sex in a marriage (discussed in *Newsweek*, 23 December 1996, p.18). Reasons suggested in the literature include the fact that both partners (husbands especially) are likely to be physically and emotionally exhausted by the pressures of work and commuting; the roles of wife and mother are traditionally desexualised in Japanese culture encouraging a husband to seek other women as sexual partners and contraception in Japan is unreliable (primarily condoms and the rhythm method) thus making sex for many women an anxious experience.

Yet, as discussed earlier, more and more young people are developing heightened expectations about their lifestyle as well as of their life partners. Japanese constructions of marriage, too, are moving increasingly towards the western 'companionate model.'

Japanese women, in particular, are becoming less satisfied with husbands who simply fulfill the role of husband and father and are more likely to insist upon a relationship founded upon love and desire. Younger gay men, too, are also likely to see the old role-play model of marriage as intolerable as they seek relationships in their lives which conform to the new 'ideology' dictating that they must live with the one they love.

Conclusion

In all the representations of homosexual men discussed so far in Japanese popular culture, there is a basic agreement about the nature of same-sex desire: it somehow 'feminizes' a man. This desire is read as necessarily expressing itself through the body and personality: even going to the gym in pursuit of a perfect, masculine body is somehow 'feminine' as it is unnatural for a man to be too concerned with physical appearance. Personal effects, too, speak about a man's sexuality whether they be chandeliers or chicken-shaped tissue-box covers. Also gay men are overly conscious about 'interior decoration.' What's more, they dress better, smell better, cook better and keep house better than straight men. Unlike straight men, they can be placed in feminine situations and thereby sympathise with female subject positions: they can be sexually abused, raped, discriminated against on the basis of their sexuality; indeed all the negative treatment dealt out to women by a patriarchal system, can also be dealt out to gay men. They therefore make better friends for women because, despite their narcissism, they are more genuine, emotional, sympathetic and understanding. They are also more capable of loving and caring relationships, because, unlike straight men, they are not afraid to express their emotions. Such men sound like ideal partners; unfortunately the above characteristics seem to be thought incompatible with sexual interest in women.

That this lack of sexual interest is not seen as an insurmountable problem by some gay men and straight women, is, however, an indicator supporting the rather low priority sexual satisfaction within marriage is given. Even straight husbands are not always considered able to provide their wives with adequate sexual satisfaction for a number of reasons discussed above, both social and psychological. Some women seem to feel that marriage to a gay man would give them the financial stability and public face they desire along with emotional support and help with domestic tasks. The traditional tolerance of infidelity on the part of men (and increasingly, it would seem, women) would also grant them a degree of erotic independence in that their sexuality would not revolve around the demands of their husbands with all the accompanying worries of unwanted pregnancy: a lover would perhaps be more flexible about the use of contraception than would a husband.

The fact that some gay men and straight women resort to marriage ads in the gay press to find a partner suggests a rather pragmatic approach to the whole affair (like *omiai*, relying upon some intermediary to arrange a meeting rather than waiting simply to happen upon 'the right one'). The women, too, acknowledge the practicality of the affair, some commenting that because marriage is a necessary step for a man's social advancement he will be grateful to his wife for providing this and there will therefore be more give and take in the relationship than could be expected in a relationship with a straight man.

However, the above discussion does not really suggest that the nature of marriage in Japan is under interrogation at all. Whereas marriage was traditionally understood to be quite distinct from love (*ren'ai*) it was never constructed in terms of just sex either. It was rather the coming together of two families of suitable background, tied together in a network of mutual obligations and responsibilities, to provide a suitable environment for the upbringing of the next generation (Hendry 1981). Not much seems to have shifted. Men and women, even gay men and women, still see the family unit (*katei*) as a desirable social institution and the fact that in these relationships men may do more of the housework does little to question the perceived centrality of the mixed-sex couple with children. Indeed, there is considerable resistance in Japan to conceiving of 'the family' as anything other than a married mixed-sex couple with children. A panel discussion on the gay American film *Torch Song Trilogy* in the gay magazine *Badi* comments on the strangeness of American gays' desire for children. Under the headline 'In America where male couples can adopt and make a "family"' (*Otoko no kappuru ga yōshi wo tori 'kazoku' wo tsukuru Amerika*) the participants think that it is 'interesting' that American gays really seem to want children. As if a gay couple having a child was not strange enough they also comment on how 'it has even become a status symbol (*sutētasushimboru*) for single women to have kids' because in America having children is a matter of 'rights' (*shiminken*). This individualistic approach to marriage and children expressed in terms of an individual's 'right' to choose his or her own partner (irrespective of gender) and to produce or adopt children irrespective of marital status has arisen in Anglo-American and northern European societies due to the gay movement's development along lines similar to that of the American sixties civil rights movement (Adam 1987). However, this approach is foreign to Japan where decisions impacting upon family, workplace and society such as lifestyle choice are taken with regard to the individual's wider social network rather than based solely upon his or her preference.

Discussions of 'homosexual' issues in the Japanese press largely ignore the American-style discourse of individual rights. Of course, some of the commentators on the marriage debate add that it would be best if men and women could choose their partner irrespective of gender, but this observation is not pursued, presumably because it is too foreign an idea to have any hope of succeeding. Instead, the role of the mixed-sex marriage as the central Japanese social institution is affirmed. As Itō Satoru comments 'Japanese mass media are founded on the absolute values that man+woman+child=happy household' (Summerhawk et al. 1998: 90). In this discourse a same-sex marriage must be an oxymoron.

However, the meaning of marriage is variously negotiated. Marriage is presented both as a deep bond between two individuals which transcends such superficial concerns as sexual attraction (the companionate model), and as a purely business arrangement where each party simply performs a role in front of society while quietly getting on with their real (read private) life (the business model). The latter model also downplays the significance of sexual attraction between the partners. There is an ingrained conservativism displayed here which questions whether relationships between gays and women in Japan are really at the cutting edge of new ways of reinventing marriage. What is more likely is that in their disillusionment with the hand traditionally dealt them in marriage, some Japanese women are fantasizing a better relationship with an imagined 'other': the gay man who is not only cleaner, smarter, better dressed and more supportive than his heterosexual counterpart, but who can also wash the dishes.

Chapter 6

Images of Homosexuality in the Gay Media

Introduction

In the preceding chapters 3, 4 and 5, I discussed various representations of homosexual men which can be readily observed in mainstream Japanese popular media: the 'feminine' man, the beautiful youth and the girl's best friend. However, in this chapter, I want to look at the various representations of men which are on offer in media produced by or directed at same-sex desiring men themselves. These images are not, of course, necessarily any more realistic than those images of homosexual men produced for the consumption of women because, just as many women consume stories about homosexual men as romance, many homosexual men consume stories about other men as pornography. These pornographic images and narratives are designed to stimulate sexual response in the reader and are primarily consumed as aids in masturbation. Lunsing (1995) comments on the very common use of gay magazines as masturbatory aids and many of the informants interviewed by Yajima (1997) mention the important role gay pornography played in their sex lives before they made contact with a same-sex partner.

Just because a man experiences same-sex desire, it does not necessarily follow that he will purchase or otherwise consume the products of the gay media. When I spoke to H-san, an editor on the gay magazine *G-Man*, about the potential market in Japan for 'gay' products (magazines, books, videos etc.), he estimated that there were about 200,000 men who regularly involved themselves in Japan's gay community by visiting bars, saunas and gay bookstores and purchasing magazines and videos. This is obviously a very small number when compared with the number of men who can be expected to experience same-sex desire in a population of over 126 million[20]. In chapter 8, I outline reasons why many gay men in Japan choose not to involve themselves in the gay scene or to associate themselves with any of its products, mainly to do with concerns about secrecy and security. However, some of my informants also expressed feelings of alienation and dissociation from the 'typing' that goes on in the gay scene and the obsessively sexual focus of many of the gay media. It is therefore not possible to read the images of homosexual interaction in the gay media as any more true or representative of gay men in general than those images produced in the television world or in women's comics. However, it is interesting to investigate the images prevalent in gay media as they contradict in many ways the representations of gay men in the wider culture. If the main paradigm for understanding homosexuality in popular culture is that of transgenderism (a homosexual man is in some ways like a woman), in the gay media, the most prevalent image is that of the gay man as hyper-masculine and hyper-sexual.

Stereo-'typing' in the gay community

In the following sections I will look at some of the most commonly recurring fantasy images in pictures, comics and short-stories in the gay press and on the Internet as well as common themes in gay pornographic videos. As outlined in the introduction, Japan does not have any nationally distributed gay magazines or newspapers similar to those published in Europe or the US which focus more on 'lifestyle' or 'identity' issues. Many gay media exist, but they are pornographic in emphasis, primarily presenting homosexuality as an act, or series of acts; that is, homosexual identity, such that it exists, is constituted by participating in a series of genital interactions between men. Gay media do little to promote a sense of gay identity or lifestyle beyond the pursuit and enjoyment of sex. As Hatano and Shimazaki comment (1997: 821–2) 'Gay magazines ... and gay comics are sold everywhere, but like the many heterosexual erotic publications, their emphasis is more on titillation than information, and certainly not on sociopolitical activism.'

The absence of magazines targeting a wider lesbian, gay and bisexual audience or an even wider 'queer' community of other sexual non-conformists has important implications for the development of a 'gay identity' in Japan. The influence of the highly developed and sophisticated gay media focusing on a range of topics which exist in many western countries has recently been questioned by some queer theorists who argue that over-identifying with one's sexual orientation is limiting rather than liberating. In Australia, for instance, Offord and Cantrell (1999: 209–10) argue that gay and lesbian 'community newspapers' are made possible only through 'political conformity' to certain fixed and easily identifiable modes of *being* lesbian or *being* gay. They write that in lesbian and gay magazines:

> The resonance of conformity, expressed through fixed images, held together by a supra gay, lesbian or sexual identity, displaces, alienates or disowns the subject who is characterised by an understanding that he or she is composed of various and diverse elements (1999: 210).

They further comment that 'in a politics of conformity there is no space for ambiguity' (1999: 210). In the discussion of Japanese gay magazines which follows, it is clear that Japanese gay media have much more in common with Japanese straight men's manga and magazines than they do with western gay magazines. Just as straight men's media tend to define masculinity through a man's ability to perform sexually, so too do Japanese gay media. The sexual interactions and scenarios in both media tend to be situated in a 'fantasy' setting divorced from the realities of everyday life. Hence there is no very great difference between Japanese straight men's erotic magazines and gay men's magazines: both tend to emphasize the aggressive and often violent pursuit of sex with masturbatory intent and have little interest in any wider social issues.

Japanese gay pornography, like the gay scene generally, is very type-specific in that some magazines cater specifically for men who are interested in certain 'types' (*taipu*) of sexual partner whereas other, more general magazines, include type-specific stories and images in an attempt to provide something for everyone. Individuals who like certain 'types' are designated in Japanese by the suffix *sen* which derives from the term *senmon*, meaning 'speciality.' These include *gaisen*, who like foreigners; *naisen*, who like other Japanese; *debusen*, who like fat men; *fukesen*, who are young men after older lovers; *wakasen*, who are older guys seeking younger and *urisen* or hustlers. Other 'types' exist, designated by the suffix *kei* or 'group' such as *janiizukei* (Johnny's club) which refers to very cute guys such as the members of pop groups like Hikaru Genji or SMAP which are managed by 'Johnny' Kitagawa's production company and *gatenkei* or blue-collar workers. There are, of course, *supōtsuman* (sportsmen); *birudā* (bodybuilders); *kuma* (bears); 3K (referring to construction workers whose jobs include the three 'k' words–*kitsui* or 'harsh,' *kitanai* or 'dirty' and *kiken* or 'dangerous'); and *onēsan* ('big-sisters' or effeminate men). Other types are based on kinship terms[21] and roles and include *aniki/otōto* (big and little brother); and *otōsan/musuko* (father and son); as well as the more general *sempai/kōhai* (senior and junior). Other common type-related words are *tachi* which signifies a 'top man,' *otokomae* or 'butch' and *neko*, or 'bottom.'

These types which are clearly recognisable from gay magazines and pornographic videos are also clearly recognisable on the streets of Tokyo's pre-eminent gay area, Shinjuku Ni-chome. Bars dedicated to the various types and their admirers are common and mixed venues where it is possible to encounter a leatherman, a drag queen, and an equal mixture of young and older men are rare. For instance, the *Utopia* Internet page which features information about the gay scene in Tokyo warns the visitor against entering a bar before being sure what type it caters for, stating that because of space restrictions 'Japanese or not, [you] will be given a decisively cold shoulder if [you] occupy precious space.' It does go on to point out, though, that 'local venues that feature your "type" will welcome [you] to a cozy and secluded world where other patrons are pre-matched to your taste.' It was my experience that questions about my type were commonly asked whenever I met a new gay friend in Japan. Lunsing (*in press*) also confirms this, stating 'in almost all gay circles I participated in, discussion of what type of person one could love occurred regularly ... it appeared that most gay men had quite definite ideas of what their type is and usually practice agreed with this quite closely.'

However, strict segregation by type is beginning to change under the influence of such men as H-san, an editor of the gay magazine *G-Men* and an AIDS activist, who, although a macho 'bear' type himself has been trying to get a variety of homosexual people together for the purposes of socialising. Along with BuBu, a female sex worker living in the Kansai region, he has been organising get-togethers in rented premises in Shinjuku Ni-chome for all kinds of sexual groups. At one party in 1998, attended by eighty people, there were prostitutes (male and female), gays, lesbians, drag queens as well as some straight people. Although a bear, he himself appeared in semi-drag (wearing women's clothes behind but typical bear clothes in front). H-san was quite clear that for him the 'bear' type was a fantasy (specifically a sexual fantasy) figure that he did not want to be limited by in his personal interactions and he has been an important figure in the Ni-chome scene in providing mixed venues for men and women with different sexual interests such as the Rainbow Cafe, a coffee shop and meeting place which features a prominent bulletin board advertising events. He would particularly like to see increased visibility for women in the Ni-chome scene as he clearly feels a solidarity with all people, irrespective of their sexual orientation, who are marginalised in Japanese society through their refusal to abide by normative understandings of sex roles. Yet despite these efforts, typing remains strong in Japan's commercial gay scene.

Japanese gay magazines

I shall start by discussing Japanese gay magazines generally and then look at some of the recurrent fantasy themes which occur in them. I will then relate these themes to those present in the other main gay media: pornographic movies. This will be followed by a section which discusses what gay men say they are looking for in a partner in personal ads in gay magazines. I argue that 'typing' is also at work when men look for actual partners, just as it is when they engage with a fantasy partner through pornography. I also look at the various representations of same-sex sexuality in Japanese webpages on the Internet. I conclude that gay identity, such as it is fostered by these media, revolves primarily around participating in, albeit vicariously, a variety of same-sex genital interactions. Gay media in Japan do not, on the whole, address issues of lifestyle and tend to avoid discussion of homosexuality in terms of legal reform or human rights – issues which take up considerable space in gay media in Europe and the United States. Japanese gay Internet sites and magazines tend to be very mixed, juxtaposing erotica with information[22] and this mixing of genres thus makes it difficult to compare Japanese gay magazines with those in Europe, America or Australia which tend to be more specialised. Thus the American *Advocate*, the British *Gay Times* and the Australian gay newspaper *Sydney Star Observer*, although containing a few erotic pictures, are mainly news and lifestyle oriented whereas pornographic magazines such as *Honcho* or *Torso* focus more specifically upon erotic fantasy. Japan so far has no nationally distributed glossy magazines similar to the *Advocate* or *Gay Times* which, directed at gay men, lesbians and transgender individuals, focus on issues of gay identity, lifestyle and rights, although as I point out in the current chapter, such articles are occasionally sandwiched between the pornography in Japanese gay magazines. More importantly, although Japanese gay magazines do cater to 'types,' specialising in cute boys, macho men or older men etc., they do not appeal to particular age or social groups. There are no magazines such as the American *XY* which caters to middle-class gay teens. This magazine is extremely lifestyle oriented, stressing that 'being gay' resides in a positive self attitude which is expressed in taking good care of one's hair, skin, body, diet and clothes and is full of pictures of young, healthy, well-dressed and extremely beautiful young gay men with 'attitude' as well as a disposable income. Japanese gay magazines, then, tend to be targeted at certain 'types' of fantasy figures, i.e. 'Bears' (*G-Men*), 'Daddies' (*Samson*) and cute guys (*Badi*), rather than types of reader. Significantly, *Adon*, the one gay magazine which attempted to break out of the erotica mold and address issues to do with lifestyle and politics soon found itself in financial difficulties and eventually went out of business in 1996 (Lunsing 1998: 283).

At the time of writing, Japan has six major gay magazines published monthly and distributed nationwide. These are *Barazoku* (*The rose clan*), the oldest and second-best selling, first published in 1972. *Za gei*, the successor to *Za Ken*, first published in 1982, is the most political with the most explicit photos. *Sabu*, first published in 1983, is the most supportive of international relations. *Samson,* for those who like older, sturdier men was first published in 1984. Two more publications appeared in the early-1990s, *Badi*, which is now the best selling, and *G-Men,* which caters to 'macho' types. All the magazines have a similar format 21 x 15 cm and consist of about 500 pages and sell for around ¥1,500 ($12). The contents are also broadly similar, consisting of pornographic photos (censored), pornographic manga, video and book reviews, editorials and news sections, erotic and romantic short stories, personal ads and a large number of ads for bars, saunas, books, videos, accessories and services (occupying about one-third to half of all the pages). So far the only extensive discussion of this material in English is by Wim Lunsing (1995). He suggests that 'providing information, building a gay identity, and letting people know they are not alone are important functions of gay magazines' (1995: 74) which is largely borne out by the discussion below[23].

Lunsing estimates that about 150,000 copies of gay magazines are sold every month (1998: 283) but this does not give an accurate picture of the actual readership. The readership is likely to be far in excess of this figure in that many gay men share these magazines among their friends, copies are often left lying around in gay bars for customers to read, and there is a brisk second-hand market for gay magazines in many of Japan's second-hand bookstores where, even if a man is too embarrassed to buy them, he can at least read them in the anonymity of the store. So many of the gay men I spoke to, plus those interviewed by Yajima (1997) and other men whose life stories appear on the Internet, mention the impact that their first encounter with a gay magazine made upon them, that it is clear that these magazines play a very important role in the Japanese gay subculture.

As is clear from the life histories collected by Yajima (1997) and myself, discussed in chapter 7, one of the most important functions of the gay magazines is to help gay men network in the wider gay community. They do this by providing personal ad space so that men in isolated areas can arrange to meet others in their area, and they include information on cruising grounds (*hattenba*) across the country, as well as ads for gay saunas, bars and hotels in various locations. Readers are also invited to write in with observations, experiences, questions or problems and get advice from the staff. The publications have a 'community' feel about them and one or more are bought regularly by many gay men. Most of the informants interviewed by Yajima (1997) report coming across copies of these magazines in second-hand bookshops all over Japan. These book-shops seem to be well stocked with erotica of all kinds, maybe, as Lunsing *(in press)* comments, because many gay men off-load their gay magazine collections to second-hand shops when they get married or move back in with family or take a room mate. Also, I have found gay magazines in largish bookstores throughout Japan, and not just in designated 'pink' areas. The impact that these gay magazines have upon homosexual men who come across them for the first time cannot be underestimated. Although Yajima mentions several men for whom discovery of these magazines represented a turning point in their lives, the most startling story I heard came from my informant Jirō, who, finding a gay magazine in the rubbish outside his home at age twenty five, was suddenly precipitated into an awareness that he was gay (*see* Jirō's story in chapter 7). I have also come across interesting stories on the Internet which suggests that gay men in provincial areas cruise each other in second-hand bookstores by watching who gravitates towards the gay magazine section. A number of men report being picked up outside a bookstore after having spent time looking at the gay magazines; for some of these men it was reportedly the first time they had ever been propositioned.

I will take one issue, the April 1994 issue of *Barazoku*, and discuss the different sections and their contents to give a picture of the wide range of information and material included. The cover features a drawing of a cute young man (*bishōnen*) holding a teddy bear. The artist, Rune Naito, has a distinct style and all his covers feature cute, short-haired, well-built, dark skinned boys in a 'cute setting' (pictured with cats, dogs, toys, flowers etc.). The men/boys featured in the photos and manga are also generally of the young, cute but well-built type. They differ from the *bishōnen* of women's comics in that the figures are less stylised and androgynous; the cute boys in gay comics are obviously male figures as the prominent bulge in their trousers emphasizes. The magazine opens immediately to seven pages of full-colour pornographic pictures of men having sex. In this issue the first set of photos features 'soft' SM with the protagonists wearing black leather. The next scenario is a 3P scene (three people) featuring an oral/anal combination which is very common. All genitalia are blacked out with dark patches of varying opacity. Next is a manga about a young man's trip to Bali where he has some sexual adventures. This is followed by more colour pages entitled 'Men's Treasury' which contains 'scrap erotica' from the 'men's world' (*nansekai*). This includes a discussion of professional wrestling, a review of a Chippendale photo album, how to put on a *fundoshi* (Japanese loincloth), a review of an early twentieth-century erotic collection of boy pictures and an SM comic. Then follow more pornographic pictures, starting with a young boy who looks about fifteen (and is shown naked, looking cute and masturbating), another 3P scene and finally 'sportsman live' which shows candid-camera pictures of sportsmen training. There are now four pages of erotic poetry, followed by more naked pictures, this time of cute boys at the beach in jockstraps, cute boys covered in semen, and more 'sportsman live' pictures, this time of lifeguards with erections under their speedos. Finally, on page 54 comes the contents page, suggesting that the magazine is bought more on the basis of the boys in the pictures than the articles listed in the contents!

The main body of the magazine starts with an article about the television soap drama 'Classmates' (*Dōsōkai*) which featured Japan's first televised gay kiss in 1993. Information about the international gay scene is offered next in part two of a serial entitled 'New York gay information' which lists gay strip joints in New York, detailing addresses, show times and entrance fees. It also details bars which have 'dark rooms' and the kind of activities that the writer observed there.

Next, one page details 'homoerotic pick-ups' where readers write in with their experiences and another page called 'media watching' is for readers to comment on gay topics or themes they have seen in the media. There is one page devoted to cruise spot information (*hattenba jōhō*). A typical entry reads:

Kanazawa
This is a park where people rarely come. The toilet has one urinal and one stall. The stall has three holes in it from which you can see straight men's penises when they use the urinal. Recently, when I went to see what was going on, I heard a squelching sound coming from the stall. I was interested in seeing what kind of men were putting on so lively a performance so I hung around and saw two very satisfied-looking high-school boys in uniform come out. On other occasions I've seen university students sitting on the benches and masturbating as well as semen-stained porno books lying around. Evening is the most busy time. I'd like more young people to visit here!

The (twenty-seven-year-old 'Y club' [presumably 'young club']) writer is here performing a service in advertising a cruise-spot which may be of interest to men in the area and thereby increasing the number of men passing through which will also increase his chances of meeting a partner. Further opportunity for reader participation is given by 'This month's "Oh gosh!"' (*Kongetsu no korā!*) where readers write in with annoying experiences they had while out cruising.

Gay magazines' role as disseminators of information and advice is made clear by the next section which contains 'Forty-five embarrassing questions' and their answers. Questions are about sexual positions (particularly problems connected with anal sex), how to attract attention in a cruise spot, penis size, cause of homosexuality, how to act in a gay sauna etc. Ordinary magazines and newspapers for men often detail information on 'how to sex' and bookstores carry manga and more serious books about sexual technique. However, very basic questions about the etiquette and practice of homosexual sex are of course not covered in these sources nor are they mentioned during sex education at school (or covered in sex education manuals). Hence, the gay press is an important forum for discussing and sharing this information.

Following is information about a gay-friendly hot-spring, a monthly column discussing movies, 'pajama talk' featuring funny/erotic stories, 'Mr. M's dream collection' featuring a picture and discussion of the career of the 1940s film star Farley Granger, a brief discussion of 'traditional' SM practices, and a full-page advert for a gay novel. Next is a manga entitled 'SM builder,' about a young man who decides to go weight training and falls secretly in love with his trainer only to be tied up, have his pubic hair shaved, and then be raped by the gym's owner. He is then beaten up by his trainer who is himself in love with the owner.

There are then 54 pages of personal ads (777 in total) from all over Japan and also foreign countries. The following ad from Sapporo is typical:

> I am 160×58, 26 years old. I'm looking for friends or lovers with whom I can sing karaoke and go drinking . I'm waiting for letters from those the same age or younger. Put a photo and your telephone number in the envelope and I will definitely reply.

Nearly all the ads are in Japanese but a few are written in English either by Japanese seeking foreign partners or by foreigners who are looking for Japanese. However, many foreigners place ads in Japanese and some Japanese ads mention that foreigners are also welcome to reply. The following is a typical ad in English:

> I'm bored to death after work. Isn't there any way you can help me? Japanese ($165 \times 56 \times 34$) seeks a quite handsome American friend who is polite and Kyoto resident. I want to meet you and see what happens. Send me your letter with a picture and phone no.

After the ads section is a one-page short story followed by a 'looking for someone' page where readers can write in and try to contact lost friends or previous casual partners whose address they failed to get. This is followed by 'Boys' room' (*Shōnen no heya*) where boys write in with their problems and experiences and ask for help, advice and try to make friends. This is followed by a 'beautiful youth' (*bishōnen*) manga similar to the stories told in girls' magazines about the love between youths (*shōnen'ai*). Next come some short essays on a variety of topics connected with readers' own experiences of homosexual life, an essay by the publisher Itō Bungaku on the problems one can encounter when giving out one's telephone number to casual encounters, and a section where readers write in with their thoughts and experiences. There is a two-page spread, part of a long-running series about homosexuality in the Edo period (*Edo danshoku kō*, number 190). Next is a gay star-signs section, followed by a page where readers can contribute their own erotic pictures and then another erotic story entitled 'Wandering wrist' (*Samayō tekubi*). This is followed by another forum for readers to contribute their experiences, 'Readers' experience mini-collection.' Next is an erotic story about a young boy, 'My twelfth spring,' followed by an erotic story about a student being raped by his archery teacher.

Following next are 259 pages of ads headed 'Barazoku men's town guide.' As outlined above, the role of the gay press is important in bringing gay men together not simply for sex but for a wide range of social interaction. Approximately one-third of each magazine is devoted to ads for bars, saunas, hotels, video and book mail-order as well as chat rooms, and massage joints. The ads also recruit for part-time jobs (*arubaito*) usually for massage, models, host or escort services (*see* Plates 14 and 15). It is common knowledge in Japan that many women choose to work in the entertainment industry (*mizu shōbai*) and its sex offshoots because of the relatively free schedule and high hourly rates, and similar opportunities also exist for young men (commonly aged between 18 and 25—although age is less of an issue when special features such as 'huge penises' are required). This world was brought to the attention of the Japanese media by the novel *Yes, Yes, Yes* by Hiruma Hisao (1990; for English extracts *see* Stephen Miller 1996) and the movie *A Touch of Fever* (Hashiguchi Ryōsuke 1993) and is also discussed by the gay-porn photographer, Kiyohara Munetaki (1994), in his sensationalist expose of the gay subculture.

I will outline a few of the ads to suggest the variety of what is on offer in these pages. 'Gay nights' at major disco venues are advertised (few Japanese gay bars are large enough to permit dancing). There are a huge number of adverts for both domestic and foreign videos (with stills) covering the usual gay fantasy figures: sportsmen, builders (both bodybuilders and building site workers), 3P and orgies, SM, as well as more particular Japanese fantasies: yakuza, men in *fundoshi* (loin cloths), candid-camera shots of straight men masturbating *(nonke no onanii)*, and Shinto naked festivals (*hadaka matsuri*). Telephone sex is on offer, general and SM as well as 'normal talk line' (*nōmaru tōkurain*) for men to discuss things other than sex.

The ads offering sexual services are fairly explicit. For example, *Shōnentai* (Young boys' club) offers 'young boy's private room skin massage' (young boy's *koshitsu sukinmassāji*) at four different prices: 'flower' (*hana*) is ¥9,500 ($80) for 70 minutes; 'love' (*ai*) costs ¥11,000 ($90) for 90 minutes; 'dream' (*yume*) is ¥13,500 ($112) for two hours and the 'special' is a 3P service for ¥27,000 ($225). The club also sends boys out (*shutchō*). The club recruits for 'massage boys' who look like actors, who have beautiful appearances, as well as students, and sportsmen. Other clubs also offer differently priced 'courses' (*kōsu*). Some clubs specialise in such things as SM or in a certain type of host such as 'short-haired macho lads with big cocks' (*kyokon no tanpatsu yarō*). 'Shibuya Dicks' (*see* Plate 14) is one such club offering a delivery service specialising in well-endowed youths. There are also ads from men's clinics which specialise in circumcision and penis-lengthening operations[24]. The ads are almost entirely sex related and feature none of the 'gay lifestyle' ads common in foreign gay publications which offer such things as travel services, cosmetics, deodorants, clothes, sports equipment, health foods and vitamins, and books and videos of a non-erotic nature.

Fantasy figures in gay magazines

Barazoku is a useful magazine for discussing the variety of fantasy figures produced in the gay press for erotic enjoyment because it is the most general of gay magazines and tries to include a little of something for everybody. Thus many of the familiar types occur regularly in its photo, comic, and short-story sections. In the June 1994 edition, the father/son (*otōsan/musuko*) fantasy is graphically depicted in the manga 'Let me have your father' (*Otaku no otōsan wo boku ni kudasai*) where a son-in-law seduces his wife's father. There is a *bishōnen* (beautiful youth) comic entitled 'Let's kiss under the dazzling sky' (*Mabushii sora ni* kiss *shiyō*). The short stories include one about a 'sportsman,' in this case a rugby player; two middle-school boys who have their first sexual encounter together; and a story entitled 'Cute lollipop' which identifies itself as a story about young-boy love (*shōnen'ai shōsetsu*) and describes an adult man's infatuation with a junior-school boy. The April 1994 issue has a comic entitled 'SM builder' featuring the body-builder type as well as a comic story in a style similar to that of girls' comic stories about boy love, entitled 'A story of naive young boy love' (*Junjō shōnen'ai monogatari*). The stories include a sportsman, this time an archery instructor, and a story about a young boy's sexual awakening entitled 'My twelfth spring' (*Jūnisai no haru*). The April 1998 issue has a comic about sex in a student dormitory and stories about young boys, including 'My lover is twelve years old,' and another story about hunks on the beach. The photos in the June 1994 edition are predominantly of slim, handsome young men in their early twenties, but other editions show a wider range of types. For example, the April 1998 edition shows older men with beards as well as cute, hairless youths and, unusually, it also has four pages of foreign men, both Caucasian and black. The April 1994 edition has masked men in an SM fantasy setting, and a very young-looking boy with no body hair as well as generally cute-looking young guys.

The magazine *Badi* is similar to *Barazoku* in its inclusion of a wide variety of types and scenarios and according to H-san, mentioned earlier, who used to work on its editorial team, it is currently Japan's most popular gay magazine with a circulation of around 30,000. However, other gay publications are more specialised and cater to a niche market such as *Samson* which specialises in older, well-built men. *G-Men* is a publication devoted to rough trade and the June 1998 edition bills itself as a *Gatenkei* special. *Gaten* is difficult to translate, but according to my Japanese informants conjures up images of self-reliant, capable, strong men such as builders and plumbers to whom dirty, difficult tasks can be left[25]. This is borne out by the photo collection which features men in a variety of labourer uniforms, including building site, mechanic, and railway engineer workers. The pornographic photos feature older, sturdier men, with an emphasis on body hair. Even the younger models have beards (though not very successful ones). Tattoos are also common, as are *fundoshi* (loincloths). The older, hairy, well-built (even fat) men are referred to as *kuma*, or bears. The types in all these publications are generally not mixed, in that bears have sex with bears and cute guys with cute guys. Although the photos in *G-Men* abide by the censorship laws which forbid both pubic hair and genitalia, the comic pictures are more graphic than those of *Barazoku*, the penis being drawn in graphic detail. The comics themselves are more relentlessly sexual, taking less time to establish character and mood before getting into the sex scenes. The sex is also always of the hard variety, as in the comic strip 'Pride' which features face fucking, ass fucking and SM. *Sabu* is also a magazine dedicated to the harder end of sexual fantasy, often featuring short-haired, well-built, hairy men with a strong emphasis on bondage and SM. Neither *G-Men* nor *Sabu* feature stories about young boys or beautiful youths. None of the magazines I looked at (with the exception of a few stories in *Barazoku*) contain stories or comics similar to those found in women's comics about love between young men although stories in which an older man/boy sexually initiates a much younger boy are quite common.

The fantasy figures produced in the gay press are always clearly identifiable types who engage in sexual interactions in common, well-defined situations such as the gym, the building site, the locker room, the beach and the classroom. Like all pornography, they are scripted to create an escalating sense of sexual arousal which ends, sometimes in the final frame or sentence, with ejaculation. These stories are of course short and it is necessary to pack a lot of erotic details in to them at the expense of more 'romantic' scene setting. However, even in longer manga series which are sometimes published separately, there is more emphasis upon sex than there is on building an enduring relationship. One example of this is the manga *Naburi mono* (Laughing-stock) by Tagame Gengoroh (1994), originally serialised in *G-Men*, where a wrestler who has refused. a gangland boss's advances is kidnapped, tortured and subjected to relentless sexual abuse. One of his yakuza torturers finds himself attracted to the wrestler, eventually freeing and going into hiding with him. The two fall in love and have sex. Unfortunately the yakuza, who has broken his oath of allegiance to his boss, is faced either with life on the run or suicide. So, in order to preserve his honour and that of his new lover, he douses them both in petrol and they die in flames together. This is a *giri/ninjō* (duty/feeling) theme common in Japanese literature which typically ends in suicide. However, the 'love story' simply serves as a context for graphic, violent sex sessions and is thinly developed.

The hard-sex magazines generally spend less effort in building up a character or scene before getting down to the serious business of sex. However, *Barazoku* does contain some well-crafted stories which might be better described as erotic rather than pornographic. Some of its writers are, in fact, established authors such as Nishino Kōji, the author of *When I Meet You in Shinjuku Ni-chome*, a novel referred to in the gay boom discussion of chapter 2. The stories in these magazines are different from those in women's fiction about gay men in that the latter are more careful to build up a strong sense of character which aids reader identification before getting down to sex scenes. In women's comics, the men do not tend to drop their pants upon first contact, but only after a prior relationship has been established. Also, less emphasis is placed in women's comics upon huge genitalia. I have never seen a gay love scene in a women's comic where penis size was a site of particular erotic fascination, whereas the men's magazines, particularly the hard-sex ones, tend to obsess about penis size, ball size and amount of ejaculate as well as frequency of ejaculation.

Bamboo comics, which publishes comic serials from the now defunct gay magazine *Adon*, contains many manga drawn in the style of girls' comics (the boys are *bishōnen*), although the content is more sexual. For example, Murano Inuhiko's (1996) *Gakuran tengoku*

(Tumultous heaven) volume 1, opens to a scene in a locker room where a *sempai* (senior) inserts a popsicle into a younger boy's anus. This is followed by pretty relentless hard sex including an SM interlude where a young boy is kept in a locker and brought out for regular sex sessions with his *sempai*. The manga describes itself on the cover as 'a popular series dedicated to showing the real-life sweat and tears of a high-school boys' sports club' and clearly develops the theme of the erotic/violent potential in the *sempai/kōhai* (senior/ junior) relationship. This is a pervasive theme which has wider application than the 'rookie' genre of western (particularly American) pornography where a new recruit to the police force, army or prison is subjected to various hazing and sexual abuse. For example, the November 1998 edition of *G-Men* is dedicated to *taiikukai* (sports clubs) and contains a number of erotic scenarios built around the *sempai/kōhai* relationship in the context of school and university sports clubs (*see* Plate 10). One article, entitled 'Whether you enjoy or get enjoyed depends upon your position' (*Tachiba no chigai ni yoru otoko no kui kata kuware kata*) states that 'sports clubs are built around the senior/junior relationships *(kajō kankei de naritatteimasu)* of *sempai* and *kōhai*' going on to say that these relationships give a particular way of enjoying (*kui kata*) sexual interactions between men. It then lists a number of incidents purportedly reported by readers themselves of sexual experience in sports clubs where individual *kōhai* were sexually used (at times raped, but nobody seems to mind) by groups of *sempai*. It seems likely that, from the very open circumstances in which these incidents took place, they are more the product of fantasy than fact. However, the popularity of such stories suggests that the fantasy of being sexually abused or sexually abusing others according to status differentiations is an important erotic scenario.

There are similarities between the power differentials in the *sempai/kōhai* relationship and those between men and women in heterosexual comics. *Kōhai* are used and abused, and shown to be both deserving of such treatment, and also, secretly enjoying it, in much the same way as women are supposed to enjoy the sexual abuse they receive at the hands of men. In 'I love [your] mouth' (*Okuchi daisuki*), a manga in *Barazoku* (1994, vol. 5) (*see* Plate 9), a schoolboy football team's assistant, Tome, is shown secretly stealing his team-mates underwear. When this is discovered, his team mates force Tome to perform fellatio on them instead. Although protesting, the artist makes clear that the boy is secretly delighted at this turn of events. His team mates are shown lining up outside the locker room while the boy performs inside, one satisfied customer stating 'From now on every time I want to come, I'll use your mouth.' Interestingly, this manga parodies the figure of the *bishōnen* in that Tome is shown as a rather podgy, unattractive figure who endears himself to his team mates by his superb oral technique. However, the team's mascot, a beautiful boy who, when he first appears is surrounded by suns and stars with the big flashing eyes and flowing hair of the *bishōnen*, is finally rejected by the team because of his inferior cock-sucking potential. In gay manga, technique is everything.

It must be pointed out that although many of the *sempai/kōhai* stories revolve around the use of force and are somehow 'abusive' in nature (although the 'victims' are often willing accomplices) another style of story which focuses on this relationship stresses the nurturing aspect where a *sempai* initiates a *kōhai* into sexual pleasure. Extreme examples of this are the stories mentioned earlier where an adult man sexually initiates a boy into sex. These stories which detail the erotic imaginings of children are generally not paralleled in western gay pornography where very tight censorship surrounds the representation of childhood sexuality and where one of the enduring stereotypes that gay men have to work against is the perception of them as paedophiles. One story (purportedly a letter form a reader) in the April 1998 issue of *Barazoku* is entitled 'My lover is twelve years old' and is a letter from a twenty-four-year-old teacher who describes his growing infatuation with a boy in his class. The man explains that as his 'special feelings' for the boy turned to lust (*niku yoku*) he emotionally withdrew and became increasingly distant and cold to the boy who, confused by his teacher's treatment, confronted him after school. It was then that the teacher confessed his love, and rather than being repelled, the boy initiated a sexual relationship which continued until he graduated and moved to another school. The editor comments that 'This is a nice story isn't it? Love between a teacher and a pupil is one beautiful example of the ways of love.' Such a response to a story like this would be difficult to imagine in a western context. As Lunsing comments:

> There is little to compare to the American hysteria concerning minors and sex in Japan. Unlike in America or England, sex is not widely seen as likely to be dangerous, vicious or dirty, which makes it plausible that it is not seen as necessarily bad for young people (1997: 275).

Stories in which the age difference between *sempai* and *kōhai* is only a few years are also common. For example, there is a story in the June 1994 issue of *Barazoku* entitled 'Anxiety at that indistinct age' (*Fuan to kasukana jitai*) where an older boy initiates a young friend into the secrets of masturbation. The theme of initiation is also common in pornographic movies, and will be discussed later in the chapter.

Functions of gay magazines

Gay magazines in Japan are multivalent and read by men for a number of different reasons. They are large and relatively expensive publications which contain a wide variety of features ranging from pornographic images and stories to fairly high-brow discussions of movies and current affairs of gay interest. They also contain a lot of information aimed at getting gay men into contact with other gay men for both sex and friendship. The ads put men into contact with bars and saunas all over Japan which cater to homosexual men, as well as giving the numbers of chat lines which even men in isolated areas can use. Reports on cruising spots all over the country help men get together with other men for sex, and the personals help men find both friends and lovers.

However, unlike foreign gay material such as America's *Advocate* or Britain's *Gay Times,* the Japanese magazines do not do much in the way of promoting a 'gay lifestyle' other than sex. Also, there is little in the Japanese magazines which would contribute to the notion of a 'gay identity.' Unlike some popular western magazines, no Japanese gay publication addresses itself to a wider 'queer' community of gay men, lesbians and transgendered individuals or discusses issues which apply to both men and women who express a non-normative sexuality. The contents of Japanese gay magazines are very much oriented towards sex: where and how to get it, describing what it was like when you got it, and providing stories and images for masturbation. As Lunsing comments 'gay magazines ... present an image that is not entirely positive, i.e., gay men as sex maniacs' (1995: 71). This is largely true, though as is discussed below, some of the editors working on the magazines are aware of a need to expand gay magazines' range to include issues which affect the gay community such as AIDS while at the same time preserving the magazines' primary focus as vehicles for fantasy and entertainment.

In August 1998, I was able to meet with H-san, an editor working for the gay publication *G-Men.* H-san had been working on the editorial board of another gay magazine, *Badi*, when he decided to get together with a group of friends and an investor to create another magazine which catered to a niche market of men interested in what he termed 'macho fantasy.' This magazine, *G-Men*, founded in 1994, now has a circulation of 20,000 copies but its actual readership may be as much as twice this number as many homosexual men purchase back numbers of these magazines in second-hand book stores, or circulate used copies among friends. When I asked H-san why he thought Japanese homosexuals needed another glossy pornographic magazine, he told me that he had discerned a market for men who shared his 'type,' that is 'bears' or older, well-built men, often with body and facial hair who worked in manual professions. He wanted to create a magazine which had a more well-defined fantasy image, including manga and stories which continued from month to month, and which featured the same models in different identities and settings (but all revolving around a macho theme). When I asked why the magazine didn't feature what might be described as lifestyle issues, he countered that its purpose was entertainment, by which I assume he meant providing material for sexual fantasy. However, he did point out that the magazine runs regular features on AIDS and safe-sex. H-san, being HIV+ himself, said that the safe-sex features were his innovation and that he did think that gay publications had a responsibility to ensure that readers were informed of the practical implications of living out the fantasies that were portrayed. H-san writes many of these AIDS-related pieces himself, including the regular 'This month's information.' The September 1998 issue's information is a two-page article entitled 'Let's rethink HIV+ men's sex lives.' This is followed by another article entitled 'I'd like you to just remember this' (*Kore dake shitte okitai*) which stresses the importance of HIV+ individuals choosing a lifestyle which fits in with their course of treatment. This is obviously an improvement on the gay press' reporting on AIDS a decade ago, where, according to Treat (1994: 633) *Barazoku*'s editor, Itō Bungaku, wrote (in 1985) that 'there are few in Japan who use drugs and no one here has hardcore sex like in America. So what happened there can't happen here.' However, the amount of information about AIDS provided in *G-Men* is still extremely slight when compared to some American magazines such as *Out* and *Genre* which regularly feature updates on the latest AIDS medication and its side-effects.

Another of H-san's innovations is the production of a quarterly *G-Men Video Magazine* which features 'live' the models who appear in the pornographic stills in the magazine. H-san stressed that although the video contains a number of pornographic interludes, usually involving the models masturbating (the ubiquitous 'masturbation show' [*onanii shō*]) it also has interviews with the models themselves, who the viewers are requested to correspond with through a fan club. Other features in the video I saw (Vol. 14, Summer 1998) included shorts of the pornographic video production process, and an interview with the photographer who discussed how he achieved certain special effects, and a short about a *G-Men* club party which featured bears in drag, as well as comedy and dance routines. The video also features advertisements for other pornographic videos and speciality magazines. H-san stressed that the purpose of the video was to help the magazine's readers to further identify with the fantasy model figures by watching them 'live' as well as encouraging readers to participate in the *G-Men* community by joining model fan clubs and voting for the year's Mr *G-Man*.

Fantasy figures in gay pornographic videos

Gay pornographic videos are not readily available in Japan's video rental stores and many of the gay men I spoke to reported that they sometimes rented heterosexual porn and tried to block out the image of the woman while concentrating on the actions of the man. However, gay porn is easily bought through mail order and there are many companies specialising in different kinds of pornography advertised in the gay press. These videos are, however, expensive, selling for around ¥10,000 ($83) which is perhaps why dubbed versions seem to be freely circulated among networks of gay friends and acquaintances. Indeed, the informal gay organisation International Friends which meets monthly in Tokyo encourages its members to bring pornographic books and videos 'to share and swap' at its meetings. I asked a Japanese gay friend to let me have a 'typical' sample of gay Japanese pornographic videos from his massive collection and a week later he presented me with five tapes containing fifteen different pornographic stories upon which the following analysis is based[26].

Japanese censorship laws strictly forbid the exposure of genital organs and pubic hair which means that most Japanese gay videos have 'dancing squares' around the site of genital interaction. However, it is possible to buy some Japanese pornography in its uncensored state under the counter in some gay-speciality stores, and there is a lot of uncensored material circulating around networks of friends. It is quite common at a gay party for uncensored pornography to be put on the video while people are chatting, dancing or eating. A number of uncensored videos I saw actually featured Thai boys and were clearly made in Thailand although what little dialogue there was had been dubbed into Japanese. Interestingly, several of the Thai videos featured the same boys involved in genital interactions with girls as well as with other boys. However, these videos were clearly gay in orientation as the girls were never featured as objects of erotic interest in their own right but only as objects whose purpose was to stimulate and thereby display arousal in the boys. I did not see any Japanese gay videos which included girls[27].

A very common feature in Japanese gay pornography is the 'masturbation show' (*onanii shō*) in which a single man massages himself to a climax. In many of these displays the Japaneseness of the model is emphasised as in 'Muscle syndrome' (*Kinniku shindorōmu*) where the Japanese atmosphere is created by the youth appearing in a *fundoshi* (loincloth) and masturbating to the gradually accelerating pace of *taiko* drums. The traditional Japanese fantasy is also emphasised in 'Story of the sea in the fifteenth month' (*Jūgo gatsu no umi monogatari*) which features a variety of scenes creating a nostalgic vision of the Japanese boy including a high-school boy in traditional black uniform and white cap who slowly undresses in a school changing room. Another scene features a youth in a *yukata* (summer kimono) who is slowly undressed by a masked man dressed in black who resembles a bunraku-puppet operator. The youth is undressed to reveal a full back tattoo (suggesting that he is a yakuza or member of a crime syndicate) and a white loincloth. He is then masturbated by the masked man rather as a bunraku puppet is controlled. The association with 'tradition' is also made clear in 'Festival rough' (*Matsuri yarō*) where the scene is set by festival music featuring *taiko* and flute. A rose petal falls into a red-lacquer cup filled with *shōchū* (wine made from sweet potatoes), as the camera pans up to a youth dressed in a blue *yukata* which opens to reveal a red *fundoshi* (loincloth). He begins to masturbate as the *taiko* drums become increasingly frenzied. A maple-leaf ikebana by the youth's head also adds to the feeling of Japanese nostalgia. At one point the camera withdraws behind a latticed screen both to emphasise the Japaneseness of the situation by calling attention to a 'traditional' architectural feature but also to create a sense of *nozoki* or 'peeping,' a common trope in both hetero- and homosexual pornography with precedent going back to Edo-period erotic prints *(shunga)*[28].

Another scene features a youth in traditional labourer's clothes: tight waistcoat, ballooned trousers and split *tabi* socks. He undresses to the sound of *taiko* drums while sipping *shōchū* from a lacquered cup. He reveals a white *fundoshi* only to undo it and change into a red *fundoshi* through which he proceeds to masturbate. The purpose of the *fundoshi* change is presumably to display the correct way of tying the loincloth which is actually quite complex and has a greater erotic valency than someone merely slipping into a pair of briefs.

So far, two common tropes have been discussed, the creation of the fantasy figure of the 'traditional Japanese youth' as well as the *nozoki* or 'peeping' look at a youth masturbating. Another common feature is the *ijime* or 'bullying' scene which is common in Japanese pornography which features a vertical senior/junior (*sempai/kōhai*) relationship (as seen in the comic *Tumultous Heaven*, discussed above). A good example of this genre is 'Sports instructor' (*Taiiku kyōshi*) where a new recruit to a university sports club is taken off to a sports camp where his *sempai* subject him to a variety of hazing. He is bound up, pissed on, all his pubic hair is shaved off and then he has a cucumber inserted into his anus using mayonnaise as a lubricant which he is then forced to eat. The language is interesting as the victim is forced to use hyper-polite language (*keigo*) to his victimisers, who, as his elders, have the privilege of speaking to him in vulgar form. For example, in response to the vulgar command to eat, *kue!*, he must respond with the polite *itadakimasu*. The sharp distinctions in language level present in Japanese add a further element of erotic interest to the dialogue. A variation on the status division theme occurs in 'Muscle warriors' (*Kinniku senshi*) where a young salary-man asks his boss for a loan. The boss agrees but with conditions attached. These conditions are that he must meet the boss in a hotel room and masturbate in front of him. As the naked salaryman masturbates on the bed, the boss (with face hidden by dancing squares) shaves his pubic hair and then inserts a variety of toys into the salaryman's anus. The shaving of pubic hair is a common theme in Japanese gay pornography, both manga and video, and as the shaving is always done by the older/assertive partner it can be read as a means of reinforcing the verticality of the relationship. In Japan, because of harsh censorship laws only recently relaxed, the showing of pubic hair is considered taboo; such hair is thus associated with illicit adult sexuality. Through forcibly removing a younger/subordinate man's pubic hair, the younger man is divested of adult (active) sexuality and reinscribed as a passive (junior) partner.

The erotic implications of status distinctions are also explored in the video 'Hug me' (*Daki shimete*). Here, a cute young boy is interviewed by an off-camera voice about his sexual experience which up until now has been limited. The voice tells the boy that today he will experience 'everything' (*subete*) to which he replies 'please do' (*onegaishimasu*). The scene shifts to the bath where the now naked boy is washed by a masked man who is clearly much older. The boy is entirely passive as the man proceeds from body licking to fellatio to anilingus to anal penetration. Afterwards, the boy is shown again seated on the couch while the off-camera voice says 'Well done, how was it?' (*otsukare deshita, dō deshita*) to which he replies 'it was the best' (*saikō desu*). Unlike the above incidents, this video is not interested in exploring the potential for violence and exploitation in the *sempai/kōhai* relationship but is instead concerned with the 'indulging' aspect, discussed below.

Sons, brothers, fathers and lovers: *amae* in Japanese gay personal ads

Outside of the bar culture of major cities, men who desire other men have few chances to develop an identity based on their sexual orientation. Men who live outside the major metropolises have extremely circumscribed opportunities for meeting and socialising with other men who share their sexual interests. Even in Tokyo's Shinjuku Ni-chome district where hundreds of gay bars are situated, most of these bars are tiny, seating fewer than fifteen guests. Even the largest can only accommodate up to 100 (at a very tight squeeze). These bars are very different from the huge gay centres which can be found in London, Sydney or New York where hundreds of men mill about looking for friends or hoping to make new acquaintances. In Japanese gay bars, men often sit or stand around singly or in pairs watching a music video (Diana Ross and Madonna are big favourites) and cast furtive glances at the door every time a new face appears. In bars where they are known as regulars, it is likely that the majority of other guests will also be known to them and the video is usually replaced by a karaoke machine.

For men in rural areas, there may be a chance to have brief sexual encounters in the cruising spots (*hattenba*) of the nearest city but despite the strongly homosocial nature of Japanese socialising, it is difficult for these men to meet with other men as *gay men*. This is perhaps why gay magazines such as *Barazoku* contain so many personal ads where men can look for partners. In the June 1994 issue which I analysed, there were 607 personal ads covering forty out of 500 pages. In keeping with the general lack of opportunity for developing or expressing a 'gay identity' many of the men placing ads describe themselves as ordinary (*futsū*) or manly (*otokorashiki*) and are looking for other men like themselves who are cheerful (*akarui*) and honest (*shōjiki*). Very few men, except those with a fetish for transgendered men, specifically request feminine or effeminate partners (referred to variously as 'woman-like' *onnappoi, okama*-like *okamappoi* or 'big sisters' *onēsan*). Many ads definitively reject them along with smokers, guys wearing glasses, fat men and foreigners. In fact, such men are rejected so often in the ads, that some ads make a specific mention of not minding such things as glasses or foreigners. Activities proposed are the mainstays of Japanese recreation: driving, karaoke, going eating/drinking, travel and sports. Many men want a partner they can discuss their problems with (*sōdan aite*) as well as have a good time (*tanoshiku suru*). Some, of course, advertise simply for sex partners (*sekkusu furendo*); some specifically state that their purpose in writing is not sex, but the vast majority ask that a photograph be included suggesting that sex may be on the agenda at some future time. Many ads also place conditions on the type of person wanted. Even when age (*nenrei*), figure (*taikei*) or looks (*yōshi*) are said not to matter, character (*seikaku*) is always mentioned as important. The most frequent adjectives applied to desired characters are honest (*shōjiki/seijitsu*), sincere (*majime*), gentle (*sunao/yasashii*) and cheerful (*akarui*). The anxiety that many writers feel about the possibility of exposure is reflected in assertions of trust (*shinrai*) and confidentiality (*himitsu wa genshu*) as well as rejecting mischief-makers (*itazura*). The majority of writers are thus men who see themselves as being honest and ordinary, seeking other ordinary men to consult about problems as well as relax in very ordinary Japanese ways.

A sizable proportion of ads (about 25 per cent), however, request a specific type of vertical/horizontal relationship which is a common experience of Japanese socialisation. This is the senior/junior (*sempai/kōhai*) binary expressed in relationships throughout Japanese society. Among these ads, the most common requests are for older/younger brother (*aniki/otōto*) and father/son (*otōsan/musuko*) relationships. The verb most fequently used to describe the kind of relationship desired is 'to spoil/indulge' (*amaesaseru*), made famous by the psychologist Doi Takeo in his *Amae no kōzō* (Anatomy of dependence, 1985 [1971])[29]. Younger men want a father/brother figure to indulge them (*amaesasete kureru hito*) whereas older men want to indulge a younger brother/son (*amaetekureru hito*).

Doi (1985: 134–45) argues that 'homosexual feelings' (*dōseiai kanjō*) are particularly prevalent in Japan. I think what he means is that *homoerotic* sentiments are widespread because of the extremely *homosocial* environments in which young Japanese people are brought up and which they never successfully leave, even after marriage. He says that he doesn't mean homosexuality in the 'narrow sense' but in the case where 'emotional links between members of the same sex take priority over those with the opposite sex' (1985: 134–45). These strong emotional bonds are not so much prevalent among friends (which suggests an equality of relationship) but superiors/inferiors. He mentions teacher and pupil, senior and junior members of organisations, and even parents and children of the same sex. Doi stresses that these desires are quite normal and may continue to be the most important emotional attachments in a person's life even after marriage. He noticed that the situation in America was quite different where much greater value was placed upon the integration of the sexes and sharing activities with one's spouse was considered very important. He argues that Americans are anxious about showing too much familiarity with members of the same sex for fear of being 'suspected of homosexuality' (*dōseiai wo utagawareru*). Japan, however, has an extreme tolerance for the expression of homoerotic feelings. This is why, suggests Doi, foreign homosexuals seem to find Japan particularly attractive[30].

As Doi points out, a great deal of socialising in Japan is done in same-sex groups. Even when groups are mixed, men and women do not pair off into mixed couples but tend to sit together and interact as groups. Anne Allison in *Nightwork* (1994), an ethnography of a hostess bar, shows how the presence of female hostesses in a nightclub helps the men who visit the clubs in groups bond with the other men in their group. The hostess is there to facilitate this bonding by becoming the common object of the men's ridicule (or more seldom, appreciation). Sexual banter takes place but not on a one-to-one basis. 'The men' may joke about each other's sexual prowess or potency using the presence of a woman as a catalyst and thus defuse any overt homoeroticism. This kind of homosocial bonding is an integral aspect of Japanese business practice.

In the personal ads in *Barazoku* the status differentials familiar from family, school and work situations are carried over into visions of an ideal partner. Many men want, not a sexual or social equal, but a lover who stands either above or below them in the social hierarchy, most commonly expressed in terms of father/son (*otōsan/musuko*) or older/younger brother (*aniki/otōto*). In these ads, the homo*social* is rendered homo*erotic* or even homo*sexual*, as in this ad:

> Looking for a chubby father. I am a 31–year-old worker 162 × 50 × 15 [the last figure probably refers to penis size]. I want to suck my fat daddy's penis and I want him to put his erect penis into my Anus. Please send a sexy letter and a photo of your naked body. I'll give you a photo with my penis in it. I'd like your phone number. Distance isn't a problem. Anyhow, send me a letter.

But it is more common for these ads to focus upon personal relations involving 'indulgence' *(amasaseru)* rather than on sex, as in this example:

> Looking for an older brother. I'm 171 × 64, 26 years old. I'm looking for a fit older brother from late 20s to early 30s. It'd be nice if we could develop a natural (*shizen na*) relationship and do stuff like training, sports and trips. I'd like a person who can be nice (*amaesasetekureru*) to his baby-faced younger brother.

Offers of indulgence can be quite explicit, promising gifts and services, as in this ad: 'To my gentle son ... I'm looking for someone I can take to different places, take shopping and buy dinner for.' Or they can be phrased more in terms of offering emotional support: 'I want to be the person who is allowed to indulge you' [or 'whom you can come to rely upon'] (*kimi ga amaetekoreru ningen*).

These ads seek to replicate the verticality present in various same-sex relationships throughout Japanese society within a so-called gay relationship. This can cause some problems such as when a younger man who prefers to be anally penetrative (or at least have the upper hand sexually) seeks an older man on whom he can be emotionally reliant:

> Looking for an older brother. I'm a 22–year-old (166 × 57) who wants a kind older brother who I can feel relaxed with. I'd like an ordinary-looking salaryman, about 27 – 33 years old, who looks good in a suit. Although being like an older brother I can rely on, when it comes to sex, I'd like him to become my younger brother (*H no toki wa otōto ni natte kureru*).

In another ad, a twenty-six-year-old man wants to 'become a kind older brother,' offering to drive his younger brother to the ocean and to look at the night scenery, and at night he wants his younger brother to seek his indulgence (*yoru wa ore ni amaetehoshii*). These ads suggest that these vertical relationships are not simply about sexual stylisations but also psychological and emotional ones.

David Greenberg, in *The Construction of Homosexuality* (1988) identifies three patterns of homosexual behaviour which occur throughout the world's societies over time. He mentions *transgenerational* homosexuality where the partners' roles are divided by age, the younger always taking a passive or receptive role in sex acts. *Transgender* homosexuality involves a couple where one partner takes on the gender identity and role of a woman or an intermediate third gender, thus modelling the prevalent heterosexual pattern. And there are *egalitarian* homosexual relationships where differences in age, and status have no bearing upon sexual acts or roles. He identifies modern gay relationships as egalitarian. Outside of adolescent or peer group experimentation, however, egalitarian homosexual relationships seem to be limited to the modern world. Japan had a long tradition of both transgenerational homosexuality in Buddhist monasteries and among the samurai where youths were loved by adult men (known as *wakashūdō* or 'The Way of Youths') as well as a transgendered style prevalent in the kabuki theatre and associated pleasure districts where transgendered youths and men (*onnagata/kagema*) were courted by adult men. It is only recently that egalitarian options have developed where men can both give and take equally in the relationship, as one contributor puts it 'When we're alone we can have hard sex where we spoil each other,' (*futari kiri no toki wa amaetari amaeraretari hageshii H wo [suru]*).

Although transgendered homosexual partners are a minority interest in these advertisements, many writers stating explicitly that they do not want feminine partners, a very large number of men are looking for partners from a different age group. I have looked at those ads which express this desire explicitly in terms of looking for a father-, or older/younger-brother figure which comprise about 25 per cent. However, if we add to these the number of ads which specify a specific age (either younger or older than the writer), then the number rises to more than 50 per cent. This suggests that egalitarian homosexuality is still not the dominant paradigm for men seeking same-sex partners but that role play based on age is an important consideration when looking for a lover. We cannot however read this

Plate 1 'New Half from Shinjuku:' this magazine advert for a Tokyo theme park features a transvestite man. The caption at the bottom reads 'I came from Shinjuku' (the site of Tokyo's pre-eminent gay town).

Plate 2 This car sticker reads *okama ni chūi*, which can be read as 'watch your behind' or 'watch out for *okama*'.

Plate 3 The original *okama*: a pot for cooking rice.

Plate 4 School boys in love, from the women's manga *B-Boy*. The caption reads 'The last day we will walk in the same uniform.' (Courtesy of Biburosu publications.)

Plate 5 School girls in love, from the women's manga *EG*.

Plate 6 The character 'Mel', from the women's manga *New York New York*. (Courtesy of Hakusensha publications.)

Plate 7 In this scene from the women's manga *A Cruel God Reigns*, Jeremy is being tied up and raped by his step-father. (Courtesy of Shōgakkan.)

Plate 8 School boys make love in the women's manga *XY*. The top caption reads 'Does it feel good . . .?'.

Plate 9 In this comic from the gay magazine *Barazoku*, the 'beautiful boy' image of women's manga is rejected. The 'ugly boy' (on the left) is preferred by his team mates because of his superb skill at fellatio.

Plate 10 This feature article from the gay magazine *G-Men* describes how enjoying gay sex in a university sports club depends upon seniority. The chart places 'god' at the apex followed by the third years, second years and freshmen. The title of 'CASE 1' literally reads 'seniors eat juniors.'

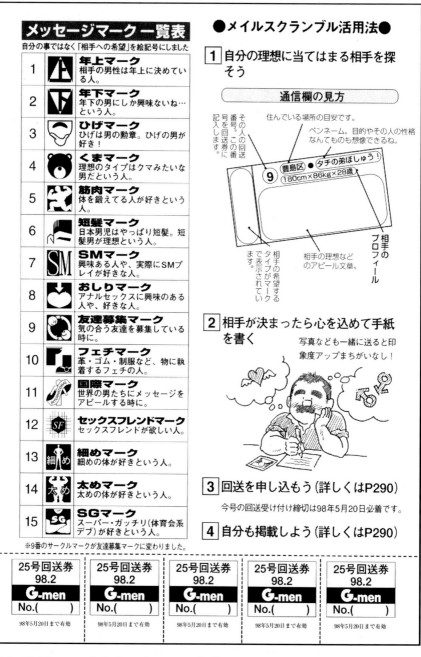

Plate 11 These symbols from the personal ads in *G-Men* help the reader to identify his 'type'. Included are symbols for age, facial hair, SM, and fetishes.

Dadism 12
by Pontaro

ついに念願の「お父さん」ができたと云うのに「どうしよう……また嘘ついてしまった」。

そもそも ポン太郎って男を化かすタヌキという意味で昔の男が付けた あだ名である。

最初から騙すつもりは無いんだけど 期待混じりで「もしかして君、○○な人ですか？」って聞かれるとサービス精神から つい相手の望む男を演じちゃう。

大抵は職業的なもので桜田門関係や 丁隊員。体育教師なんかが多いかな？ 年齢や性格的な場合もある。

先日知り合ったお父さんはこっちの世界を覚えてまだ2年の若葉者。見た目といい性格といいホント滝点。ただ、人と見る目がどうも無い相で「20代のウブな好青年」これが我輩の第一印象だそうです。

聞いた途端、気が遠くなった。『いくらなんでも 今回は止めとけよ！！』そんな心の忠告を無視して気が付けばすでにモジモジとはにかむ演技が始まっていた。（恐らく条件反射）現実の足とのギャップがあり過ぎて寒〜い口調に笑いをこらえるのが精一杯。

ポン太郎のパパ（略してPon-Papa）
プロフィール

●年 齢	55才
●身 長	175cm
●体 重	97kg
●血液型	O型
●ホモ歴	2年
●好きな物	ビール
●嫌いな物	白子
●好きな芸能人	南野陽子

なんで 南野陽子？ 今だも無いし、年齢的にも……

さあ、思い切り甘えてごらん！！

Pon-Papa の魅力は この屈託のない 笑顔と ノンケ転向組らしいマン汁焼け（キャッ おげれつ！！）で 黒ずんでしまった 大人のチンポなのである。

Plate 12 In this feature from the gay magazine *Samson*, which caters to men who like older men, the father figure says, 'Put yourself in my care (*amaete goran*) without hesitation.' Note the use of *amae*, a frequent term in transgenerational relationships.

Plate 13 In this scene from *Iron Man*, the hero meets his new boss for the first time. The boss is marked as homosexual both by his name, Kamasu, which incorporates the *kama* of *okama*, and by the rear view of his buttocks. He is ostensibly practising golf.

Plate 14 This advertisement for a host agency called 'Shibuya Dicks' describes the agency as a specialist in 'huge cocks'. The prices for its 'delivery' service are clearly marked ¥20,000 for two hours and ¥30,000 for the night. It also advertises part-time positions for men aged between 18 and 30 who possess 'big roots'.

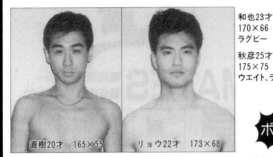

Plate 15 Some ads which use English are obviously inviting a foreign clientele but others use English (often incorrectly) because it is considered sexy as in Boys Culb (sic) which describes itself in Japanized English as a 'sexy boys' oasis'. The bottom ad offers part-time positions to 'short-haired university students who are active in sports clubs' as both hosts and video models.

Plate 16 'Boys love' is not limited to women's manga. This ad from a gay magazine is for a phone line specialising in sexy stories about school boys. The young boy says 'I'm ... coooommmming.'

Plate 17 IZAM, the beautiful cross-dressed lead singer of the boy-band *SHAZNA*, is also popular elsewhere in Asia. This article was featured in a Hong Kong magazine.

as implying necessary divisions in sexual acts, for the governing paradigm for these relationships seems to be *amae*: that is the older partner, or partner playing the senior role, indulges or 'spoils' the younger or junior partner. Thus, this indulgence may lead to the older partner subordinating his sexual needs to the younger even to the extent of giving up his role as the superior/power possessing (read 'penetrative') partner when in comes to activities in bed.

In this respect, Japanese gay relationships seem to mirror wider homosocial relationships where the concept of *amae* is paramount. In practically all situations, from kindergarten through to retirement, Japanese men (and women) are locked into a network of vertical relationships (*sempai/kōhai*) where those junior are required to respect and obey those senior who respond by putting up with their subordinates' mistakes, helping them with their problems and otherwise indulging (*amaesaseru*) them. It seems likely then, that the men who are seeking vertical relationships in these advertisements are simply extending to erotic dimensions power relations which are operative throughout Japanese society. Younger men want an older brother/father whom they can consult about problems (*sōdan aite*) just as they would their seniors at school or work, and who will also indulge (*amaesaseru*) them both in and out of bed. Older men who are looking for sons/younger brothers are also looking to extend to erotic dimensions relationships they probably already have with their subordinate co-workers: taking them out drinking and singing karaoke, organising company trips to a hot-spring resort, and giving career and family advice.

It is, of course, important not to read too much into what 607 men say they want out of a relationship in a few short sentences. However, the evidence provided by these advertisements (largely supported by another two issues of the same magazine that I have looked at as well as advertisements on the Internet) does problematize the largely taken-for-granted assumption that modern gay relationships are somehow 'egalitarian' unlike the unequal balance of power in heterosexual relationships between men and women. For many Japanese men at least, the ideal sexual relationship seems to be a companionship in which the status differences ubiquitous in Japanese society are extended to include otherwise segregated or private aspects of a person's life.

Gay Internet resources

Although the amount of printed material in Japanese dealing with male same-sex eroticism can be said to be large, the amount of information on the Internet is, for all practical purposes, limitless. There is so much material available, each website being connected to other websites by a network of links which are constantly being added to and updated, it is now impossible for one person to successfully monitor all the information available. For example, one webpage alone, *SindBad Bookmarks*, contains links to over 500 Japanese gay webpages and over 8000 world-wide. One Japanese website in particular gives an impression of the amount of material available. *Top 100 gay sites* (*Toppu* 100 *gei saito*), as its name suggests, lists in order of number of visitors, the 100 most popular Japanese gay-related websites. The average number of daily hits for the top three sites were as follows (in July 1998): *SindBad Bookmarks*, a links page: 2,654; *Twinkle Angel Video Factory*, a gay pornographic video production and sales company: 2,460; *Nude Boys Japan*, a site full of erotic pictures of Japanese boys: 1,713. Of course, these figures do not necessarily represent the number of different individuals who accessed these sites, as the same person could have entered each one on more than one occasion, however, it does show that a sizeable number of people are utilizing Internet technology to gain access to gay-themed entertainment and information on a daily basis.

Gay websites on the Internet fulfill all the functions of gay magazines only, in many ways, they do it better. For example, many sites feature personal ads where men can advertise for partners, usually under the headings of 'friends' (*tomodachi*), 'lovers' (*koibito*) and 'sex friends' (*sekkusu furendo*). However, unlike magazines which take over a month to publish, process and send back replies to personal ads, Internet ads can be posted and receive replies very quickly, or, in the case of a chat room, instantaneously. It is also possible with a sufficiently powerful computer to send digital pictures or even video clips to a prospective partner in order to check out before a meeting whether he is your type. For example, one notice board where men can advertise for partners, called *Boys Culb* (sic) states 'If (we) want lots of lovers and friends, let's appeal (to others) by posting our photos.' The same kind of 'typing' that characterises gay magazines is also apparent in the different Internet sites which cater to men with a certain fetish (*fechi*). These include sportsmen, body builders, blue-collar workers, students, 'Johnnies' and all the other popular types.

The discourse of *amae* (indulgence) which was shown to characterise junior/senior (*kōhai/sempai*) relationships in the gay magazines is also present on some web pages[31]. For example, *Aniki no heya* (Big-brother's room) which is number 84 on the top 100 list describes itself as 'strongly supporting the development of brotherly relations.' It encourages junior- and high-school boys to register on its notice board and wait to be contacted by older brothers (*aniki*) who offer them a variety of assistance. *Toshi's Page* has a section for men seeking younger/older brothers (*otōto/aniki*). Men of all ages seem to be looking for this kind of relationship, for example, one sixteen-year-old boy was looking for a younger brother with whom he could 'enjoyably amuse' himself. Some men deny that their interests are sexual at all: one thirty-four-year-old man looking for a younger brother states 'my motive isn't sex,' instead stressing that he wants to 'establish a meeting of hearts' with a baby-faced young man who wants to be indulged (*amaetagari*). A twenty-eight-year-old man wants to be able to offer advice (*sōdan*) to a primary or junior-school student. When sex is mentioned at all, it is usually in the context of watching pornographic videos together, for example 'let's play (*asobō*) while watching porno videos.'

Thus, use of the Internet has, for many men, replaced the more traditional ways of meeting partners either in the cruising grounds (*hattenba*), the bars or through magazine ads. As several of my informants point out (*see* chapter 7), the Internet has been invaluable in allowing them to organise their sex lives more safely and more freely. On *GayNet Japan*, for example, of the 3,510 ads which appeared in the above three categories between July 1997 and November 1998, 58 per cent were for 'sex friends' which suggests that a majority of men who use this service do so to meet sexual partners. Although *GayNet Japan* has a number of other bulletin boards including sections for jobs, travel, housing, meetings, news and general information, it is, apparently, infamous among some Japanese men as a *nampa netto* (*nampa* usually refers to men chasing women but here is used to refer to men chasing other men). Men who like sex with men are thus able to 'cruise' electronically without having to leave their homes. For example, one man, describing himself as a 'hung' GBM (gay black man) posted an ad on November 3 1998, inviting young Japanese men who lived locally to come round to his apartment and perform a certain sexual service. He stated that he would be checking his e-mail hourly for replies. Other men advertise their own statistics, preferred sexual activities, desired qualities in a partner, and available time slots when seeking contacts. Yet others advertise sexual acts that they are willing to perform on respondents who fulfill specific requirements (large penis size is most common, but others include such things as body hair or being well built), who are then invited to drop in at their apartments or meet at a convenient cruising ground. Men also use these notice boards to advertise the venues for orgies (*inran*) which usually involve apartments rented on a weekly basis. The advertisements refer men to a homepage which is password protected in order to find out the time and location. The browser must send an e-mail to the homepage administrator to get the password. Charges for these parties are minimal (usually about ¥2,000 [$16]) and seem to be organised by groups of friends on a non-profit basis. In this respect they differ from similar services offered for men who want to have sex with women in apartments hired for the purpose (known as 'adult parties' *[otona no pātei]*, men pay up to ¥20,000 [$160] and are guaranteed to get the 'real thing' *[honban]*, *see* Altbooks 1998: 183).

The Internet can also be used not only to inform men about already existing cruising grounds but to create new ones. For example, the site *Shinji no hatten jōhō* (Shinji's cruising ground information) which is number 90 on the top 100 site list has a board where men can give a time, date and place where they will be waiting in the hope of meeting a partner. Venues include public baths (*sento*) and sports clubs as well as the more traditional parks, toilets and shopping malls. The established cruising spots on this site have maps detailing their location as well as a description of the best times to go and the type of men that most often frequent them. Browsers can also add information to the site, describing their own good or bad experiences. One homepage, *Hatten densha/toire* (Cruise trains and toilets), details information about which train lines, including train times and coach numbers, are particularly good for men who want to feel up or be felt up by other men. Popular train station toilets and times they are most visited by gay men are also listed. On this site, men travelling on the bullet train also list the time and number of their seat and invite other men to make contact with them and have a sexual interaction in the train toilet. Making public assignations in this manner obviously involves some risk and some sites, such as *Shinji's* have a kind of protection designed to deny access to non-gay men by requiring would-be browsers to complete a questionnaire about gay life. Questions include the meaning of gay lingo such as *nonke* (straight) and *neko* (passive partner in anal sex) as well as naming brands of underwear popular with gay men. Only when all questions have been successfully answered is access granted, preceded by the message 'Congratulations, you are a fine gay' (*omedetō anata wa rippana gay desu*). Other sites require a password which can be obtained by contacting the site's administrator who may or may not test the applicant's gay knowledge before issue. This adds a small measure of security for men who make arrangements to meet with other men in semi-public places.

The term gay/*gei* is used on the Internet far more frequently than in the gay magazines and it is possible to speak of the Japanese gay Internet community. The community aspect of the Internet is evident in the interactive nature of many of the sites. For example, *Gei furenzu nettowāku* (Gay friends network; number ten on the top 100 list) has a number of interactive notice boards dealing with friends, lovers, cruise spots, love, and safe sex where men can post messages and receive answers; it describes itself as 'a communication space for gay men' (*gei no tame no komyunikēshon supēsu*). An interesting exchange on the *hatten* (cruise spot) board involved men who orgasm quickly who wanted to meet other men who did likewise, as one man put it 'it's terrible to have to make the effort to do it with ordinary guys.' Several men participated in this exchange, discussing places and times to meet to 'mutually enhance each other's pleasure.' The site also allows men to discuss problems with sexual technique, particularly to do with the difficulty of becoming the passive partner in anal sex.

Men also use Internet message services to offer sex for money or request money for sex. Not all the ads are placed by the men themselves, for example, an ad on the webpage *Takachin* (under the heading *keijiban*, or 'notice board') was from a man recommending the services of a particular call-boy outfit. This agency specialises in providing oral sex (either active or passive) in 30 minute slots which cost ¥10,000 ($83). The man placing the ad said that he had used the agency eight times and had always been satisfied by the boys provided (he thinks the majority were university students in their early twenties). He especially recommends the service for busy professionals who can leave their office for a quick session with a boy in a nearby toilet. Other ads are placed by boys themselves, often under the heading *enjo kibō* ('wanting assistance' but clearly parallelling the practice of school girls who sell sexual services for money to buy consumer goods, known as *enjo kōsai*). One boy, on the *Takachin* page, describes himself as a high-school boy with 'OK looks' who will do 'sexy things' in two-hour slots for ¥10,000. He suggests that what he is prepared to do depends on the money, stating that 'If I get more (money) I'd like to become more randy'. Older men who want to 'save' high-school and university students also advertise on these pages such as a man describing himself as in his thirties, who wants to save (*tasuketai*) a boy from late teens to early twenties. The nature of the help is not made clear but he promises not to do anything 'unpleasant.' Not all the boys offer sex. For example, on the *Boys Rush* webpage, there is a notice board for men selling various things and services which includes two notices from middle-school boys, one offering pictures of himself masturbating and the other offering to sell his swimming trunks and underwear. Such adverts are extremely common and occur on many websites, suggesting that some young men are as active as some young women in selling sexual services to older men. However, despite sensationalistic treatment of this phenomenon in Kiyohara's (1994) book *Homotaimu* and Hashiguchi's (1993) movie about a call-boy, *Hatachi no binetsu*, the press seems to have largely ignored it. This is symptomatic of Japan's double standard regarding male and female sexuality. The 'problem' of school girls selling sex is given widespread media attention, whereas parallel activities by boys are ignored.

Another way in which one function of gay magazines can be expanded on the Internet is the use of erotica in masturbation. Not only are websites full of pictures of naked men and boys having sex or masturbating, it is also possible, on one's own webpage, to provide pictures which are (purportedly) one's own. Thus a number of homepages show pictures of the owners and their partners engaging in sex which the viewer is (voyeuristically) requested to enjoy. A variant of this practice is the 'Penis notice board' *(penisu/chinchin keijiban)* where the ad placers can advertise and trade pictures of their own penis. Other men are invited to download these pictures and use them for masturbatory purposes which gives the owner a vicarious thrill. A variant of this practice is the very common 'masturbation inspection' (*onanii kenbutsu*) where the ad-placer puts pictures of himself masturbating onto a webpage and then invites men to drop by his apartment for a live demonstration. Other men request to be invited round to watch this kind of 'masturbation show' (*onanii shō*) and this is clearly a modern transformation of the long-attested erotic desire to 'peek' (*nozoku*) mentioned earlier. With the development of computer video links it seems likely that this kind of sexual interaction will escalate and many men will really be able to carry on a 'private gay life' in the privacy of their bedrooms even while living at home.

The Internet also offers the possibility for gay men to 'come out' on their own home page. For example, *Haeng-hong House* is the home page of a Japanese-Korean gay man which contains pictures (supposedly of himself) as well as a 'gay diary' of his doings. It is possible to post messages to him which he promises to reply to. Some men put up erotic pictures of themselves on their pages, and invite other men to engage with them voyeuristically. Of course, the anonymity of the Net gives great potential for performativity in that pictures of some other man can be passed off as one's own. Also, one can easily create a new personality and make up fantasized stories which are then passed off as real. It is therefore possible for homosexually inclined men, even in remote areas, to interact daily with other men and even carry out erotic relationships via text and photo exchange. The fact that many sites state that they are for gay men only and require a password or membership to access them confers a sense of community. One's normal, conformist self can give way on the Internet to a plurality of selves. It is possible to adopt a false name, age, personality or even body when interacting with others on the Net. It is also possible to make true statements about one's self and one's desires which cannot normally be acknowledged in everyday life, thus releasing pressure. Most sites register the total number of hits since opening and it is probably a cause of satisfaction and reassurance for many gay men to see the number of visitors to their sites climb. Many sites display the date (and time taken) to reach 50,000 and 100,000 hits, suggesting that attracting visitors is a source of great motivation and pride.

As with the gay magazines, gay Japanese resources on the Internet are predominantly geared to providing erotic titillation or for getting men into contact with other men (for sexual purposes). All of the top 100 sites on the webpage mentioned above were, to greater or lesser extent, oriented around sexual information, entertainment and titillation. Yet, although not as numerous, there are still a large number of sites concerned with 'sexuality' as opposed to 'sex' which contain discussions and essays about issues of sexual and gender identity. One such page, *Lulu's Homepage*, is written by an 'intersexual' (*intāsekushuaru*) person, describing him/herself neither as a man (*dansei*) nor woman (*josei*) but a 'middle sex' (*chūsei*). Lulu presents a number of essays s/he has written espousing *okama no feminizumu* (*okama* feminism). S/he writes, 'As far as I'm concerned, I think I'd like to discard this notion inside me of 'man' (*otoko*) and, if possible, think about feminism from the standpoint of neither a

woman nor a man (*onna demo naku, otoko demo nai*).' There are also
a large number of sites for lesbian and bisexual women, some of
which invite a gay male readership and others which stress they are
only for women. One site with a particularly large amount of
information and links, primarily for 'women who love women' (*onna
wo aishite iru onna*) is *Ruby in the Sky with Citrine* which describes
itself as a 'sexuality forum' (*sekushuariti fōramu*). The use of English
words is very common in Japanese gay websites, partly because
English is considered to be erotically charged and to have a certain
sophistication, but also because the discourse of sexuality is very
much a modern western one. Key terms which appear frequently on
the above mentioned pages are all *katakana* versions of English
originals and include: *sekushuariti* (sexuality), *toransujendā* (transgender), *intāsekushuaru* (intersexual), *rezubian* (lesbian), *baisekushuaru* (bisexual), *feminizumu* (feminism) and *menzuribu* (men's
lib[eration]). These fairly theoretical Internet discussions debating
the relationship between sex and gender are similar to those carried
out in serious journals such as *Gendai no esupuri* and *imago*
mentioned in chapter 2, but they do not seem to have filtered through
into popular culture. Certainly, none of my interviewees utilised these
foreign loan words for discussing issues of 'sexuality,' and those who
did use the Internet did so primarily as a means to make friends and
meet sexual partners as will be discussed in chapter 7.

An important information page for discussing widespread issues to
do with sexuality is run by Itō Satoru and his partner Yanase Ryūta
who have been exposed to media attention due to the books they have
published about their relationship and the difficulties they have
experienced in living together as a 'gay couple' (*gei kappuru*) (*see* Itō
and Yanase 1994, Itō 1996). Their page, *Sukotan kikaku* (Sukotan
plan) is very popular and in August 1998 had received 118,868 hits
since its inception in April 1997. There is a huge amount of
information on the site including resources for the study of sexuality
such as references to journals, books, magazine articles, films and
television documentaries, a media-watch section which comments on
the way homosexuality is treated by the popular media, a weekly
guest slot where prominent gay men, lesbians and feminists as well as
academics and social commentators answer questions about sexuality
or offer comments on contemporary debates, and a problem page
where both Itō and Yanase respond to people's questions and personal
difficulties. The site also advertises and promotes gay and lesbian
events and organisations and offers information about AIDS and safe

sex. This site is probably the most useful and informative source of information for gay men in Japanese and its interactive nature makes it invaluable to many men who can seek advice in a confidential and non-threatening manner. There are many testimonials from gay men who express their appreciation of the site and the efforts that both Itō and Yanase are making to make accurate information about homosexuality more widely available, one middle-school boy wrote that 'when I read that Mr Itō and Mr Yanase were visiting schools to give lectures, I couldn't stop crying.'

A look at the breakdown of visitors to the *Sukotan* page shows that more than half (56 per cent) of visitors are in their twenties. This is followed by 24 per cent in their thirties or forties, 9 per cent in their teens and only 5 per cent in their fifties and 2 per cent in their sixties and seventies respectively (statistics supplied by Sukotan based on an on-line questionnaire). Of these people, 58 per cent identify as 'gay' (*gei*), 24 per cent as 'bisexual' (*baisekushuaru*) 14 per cent as 'heterosexual' (*heterosekushuaru*) and 4 per cent as 'lesbian' (*rezubian*); although these figures must be treated with caution as respondents were asked to select the most appropriate term from a given list rather than proffer their own preferred self-determination. Most (64 per cent) came across the page while surfing the Net. In terms of most interesting feature, 43 per cent mentioned the problem page and 31 per cent opted for the basic information about homosexuality section, which suggests that there is widespread interest in gay information of a non-erotic nature. Some of the typical problems discussed and Itō and Yanase's responses to them will be outlined in chapter 9.

Other less serious information-related sites include *How to Be a Nice Gay* which has information on skin care, body building, dieting and dietary supplements and perfume. This page suggests that 'being gay' resides in taking better care of one's personal appearance. There are also a number of interactive pages such as *Chinpo jiman kōnā* (Penis pride corner) where viewers respond to a questionnaire on penis size and *Yūmeijin no asoko no saizu* (Famous people's cock size) where people who claim to have seen famous men's penises write in with a description (descriptions which are often contested by other claimants). Such pages provide a great deal of gay-related entertainment which cannot be found elsewhere in popular culture. More importantly, there are also a number of websites discussing issues relating to AIDS and safe-sex practices. Absent though, are webpages placed by fundamentalist Christian and other organisations offering assistance in overcoming same-sex desire or warning browsers of a supposed gay threat which one commonly comes across when doing a Net search in English for topics connected with homosexuality. This reinforces the position described by the *World Press Review* in September 1993 that 'homosexuality is not the hot social and moral issue in Japan that it is in the US and Western Europe' (vol. 40, issue 9, p. 24).

Although a great deal more could be said about homosexuality on the Japanese Internet, much of the material is similar to that outlined in the discussion of gay magazines and only the speed and convenience with which it is delivered differs. It is to be expected that growing Internet use and also better, faster technology such as the introduction of video links between users will assist a number of same-sex desiring men in their search for partners. Increased interaction between homosexual men may also affect the extent to which these men identify with each other as a 'minority' or 'community.' Likewise, men and women who would be uneasy about joining a social group or movement aimed at debating gender and identity issues may feel happier about participating in such discussions through the Internet. The internationalisation of sexual discourse through the Internet is also a factor which will surely add to the already extensive representatations of (homo)sexuality already present in Japanese society.

Conclusion

I have argued in this chapter that although Japan currently has a number of gay magazines, the emphasis of all of them is upon providing sexual stimulation through pornographic pictures and stories. Although there are occasional articles dealing with wider gay issues such as AIDS, these tend to be incidental to the main thrust of the publications which is to provide (erotic) entertainment. When providing information is a focus, it is usually information about how and where to get sex, as in the space dedicated to cruise-spots or bars and areas in foreign countries where it is possible to meet other male partners (again, primarily for sex). I suggest that these magazines represent images of homosexuality primarily in terms of sexual acts. Homosexuality is defined through genital acts and not through any kind of interior identity or exterior lifestyle.

It is clear that perhaps the most pervasive erotic fantasy is that which includes a senior/junior (*sempai/kōhai*) relationship. This takes two forms: the senior partner(s) either abuse or indulge the junior partner(s) in relationships which actually mirror the relationships that many Japanese men experience in real life. Throughout their lifetimes, Japanese men will be networked into extremely hierarchical homo-social environments where their seniors have considerable power to either help or hinder them. The psychologist Doi Takeo has illustrated how Japanese people tend to seek out indulgence from their seniors in a variety of circumstances. I have argued that Doi's analysis also holds true for many of the pornographic scenarios discussed above. I also argue that his analysis is useful when accounting for the very large number of personal ads which fantasize an ideal partner in hierarchical terms: the most common being father/son and older/younger brother. This brings into question the applicability to Japan of Greenberg's characterisation of modern homosexuality as 'egali-tarian.' Rather, in terms of *idealized* partners sought through personal ads, many Japanese homosexual men still seem to desire a relationship which corresponds with the transgenerational pattern of same-sex interactions which were an obvious aspect of the Tokugawa-period *nanshoku* code. And when Japanese men fantasize their *idealized* sexual interactions, stories which involve a *sempai/kōhai* dynamic are the most popular.

Hence, the power differentials which disadvantage women in representations of heterosexual pornography are also apparent in gay pornography, except it is the junior partner who is forced to submit to the senior. Like the women in heterosexual pornography, junior partners are shown to be both deserving of the treatment they receive and also grateful for it. The representations of sex between men in gay magazines, then, have little in common with the aesthetically crafted and tender relationships between the beautiful youths *(bishōnen)* in women's comics. What relationships exist in gay pornography are there only to frame the action, to establish who is in control. Potentially horrific scenarios, such as schoolboys being kept in lockers to be used as sex slaves, become not only permissible but even desirable in that the subordinate partners are shown to secretly desire their abusers. Their protestations are all part of a sexual game in which 'no' really means 'yes' and the pleasure of resistance lies in its inevitable defeat. In gay pornography, struggle as the *kōhai* may, *sempai* always wins.

Conspicuously absent in Japanese gay media are images of the 'feminine' man so recurrent in media directed at women. In gay media, the gay male body is, if anything, hyper-masculine, and the gay man is presented primarily in sexual, not emotional terms. Just as men are presented as using women for their own sexual gratification in men's comics, in gay media too, senior men use their subordinates for their own erotic ends. Men are shown using and being used in a variety of violent and sadistic situations in which the penis and the orifices it penetrates are the main focus of the action. When gay men address themselves, then, they do not depart from the mainstream tropes associating sexuality with violence and penetration prevalent in men's magazines and comics generally. In gay media, too, sex is still something that one partner 'does' to another. There is here little to support some women's hope that an alliance with gay men will bring about a radical reinterpretation of Japan's sex and gender system[32].

Chapter 7

Interviews with
Japanese Gay Men

Introduction

In the preceding chapters, I have been primarily involved in looking at media representations of homosexual men, both those representations prevalent in popular media such as magazines, women's comics, television and film and in specifically gay media including gay magazines, videos and the Internet. Among these different media, three broad categories of representation can be discerned: in the news media (both print and television), a characterisation of the homosexual as a deviant personality, often conflated with *gender nonconformism* and *cross-dressing*; in popular culture directed at women, a representation of gay men as *best friends* and *ideal lovers;* and in the gay media, an emphasis upon homosexuality as a series of sex acts engaged in by *hyper-masculine bodies*. In this chapter, I will show that none of these representations reflects, in any very clear way, the lived realities of men who experience same-sex desire in modern Japanese society. I shall be arguing that although discussion of homosexuality is fairly widespread in a variety of Japanese media, none of these representations seek to document actual lived experience but rather they construct a fantasy of the gay body which is largely divorced from the concerns of men who experience same-sex desire.

My information about Japanese gay men was gathered in a number of ways. Firstly, I lived in Japan from 1988 to 1994 when I regularly participated in Tokyo's gay scene, meeting with a large number of gay men in a variety of contexts. Since 1997, I have been visiting Japan with the purpose of interviewing Japanese homosexual men about their experience and understanding of same-sex desire. I have also participated in meetings of gay organisations and visited gay businesses. In addition to this I have been in regular e-mail contact with a large number of Japanese homosexual men resident outside Japan who have been helping me by answering questions and

volunteering information about their experience as Japanese homosexuals living abroad. As mentioned in the introduction, my method
of initially contacting Japanese gay men through the Internet has
resulted in an over representation of *gaisen* or Japanese who like
foreign men. I found that most, but not all, of the men who responded
to my advertisements in both Japanese and English were primarily
interested in meeting with me because I was a white man. I cannot
therefore claim that my interview sample is representative of Japanese
gay men in general among which *gaisen* are a minority. In fact, I am
not sure who would qualify as a 'representative' Japanese gay man or
whether I would recognise such an individual were I fortunate enough
to meet one. However, my interview material has also been
supplemented by a great deal of information from novels, coming
out stories, biographies and other writings by Japanese gay men as
well as studies about gay men by other researchers, particularly
Yajima's (1997) book of interviews with gay men, the gay men
interviewed by Summerhawk et al. (1998) and the tapescripts made
available to me by Ōhama George (1994). The information I present
here therefore represents many but by no means all of the concerns
expressed by the very wide variety of same-sex desiring men in Japan.
    With regard to interview methodology, Heaphy et al. (1998: 460)
have pointed out that 'Perhaps the only point that is widely agreed on
by qualitative researchers with regard to interviews is that there exists
no one qualitative method or technique that can guarantee the
production of valuable, useful *and* unproblematic data' (emphasis in
the original). My own interview method was very informal. Rather
than a list of questions I would ask the interviewees directly, because of
the highly personal nature of the discussion, I had a number of themes I
tried to bring into the conversation when it seemed natural to do so. I
tended to avoid taking notes while talking and, instead, would write up
what I remembered of the conversation later the same day. Although
this approach meant that my data was filtered through my selective
memory, I found it to be most conducive to creating the kind of friendly
and relaxed atmosphere necessary in order to help my informants open
up and discuss intimate matters. However, I found that with informants
who I interviewed exclusively through e-mail, I had to be more specific
when requesting information. Even so, I rarely asked questions as blunt
as 'Tell me about your coming out experiences' but preferred to
approach such topics in a more round-about manner. Of the interviews
described below, the majority were conducted through face-to-face
meetings preceeded by and some times followed up with further e-mail

or postal communications. Only those with Sato, Hiroaki and Satoru were conducted exclusively through e-mail.

Profile of interviewees

I have tried to provide a useful outline of my informants' lives which has involved carefully selecting and editing the information they made available to me. Occasionally, elsewhere in the book, I have used information from informants which is not recorded in their biographies here, particularly from those conversations which were recorded. I have also referred to informants whose biographies are not included in this section. Although I spoke to or corresponded with sixteen men in detail about their lives, I also met many other men who provided me with incidental information which I have occasionally seen fit to use. All names and a few key details such as times and places have been changed to protect the anonymity of my informants.

'Tommy'

Tommy is forty-one years old and currently lives in Canada. He has an older brother who is married and an older sister who, because of recurring illness, has remained unmarried. His father has passed away but his mother continues to live in the family home with his unmarried sister.

When he was five or six years old, Tommy first became aware of an attraction to other men. He remembers being fascinated by the body of a male colleague of his sister's who was spending time with them at his family's rented beach house. He never acted upon same-sex desire until he was twelve years old when he remembers being in a gang of boys who were bullying a younger boy. At Tommy's instigation, the younger boy was forced to strip and he remembers feeling aroused by the power he had to control the younger boy. It was about this time that he discovered masturbation, during which images of older boys at the school would naturally occur to him. However, he doesn't remember ever discussing masturbation or sexual fantasies with his friends and he had no idea that these desires were unusual or uncommon.

After graduating from university, Tommy went on a six-month tour of Europe. In Wales, he met an Welsh girl who accompanied him on his travels and they began a sexual relationship. This was his first sexual experience. He does not remember having been troubled by the fact that his actual sexual experience involved a woman but his sexual fantasies involved men. He did not at this time consider himself to be 'bisexual' as the discourse of sexual preference was not something he was familiar with.

When Tommy was twenty-four, he was working in Tokyo when some colleagues suggested they go to drink in Shinjuku Ni-chome for a prank. This was the first time that Tommy had heard of Ni-chome and its association with the homosexual subculture. After this event, he went back to the bar alone and met an American man. This was his first sexual experience with another man. However, he still did not accept the label 'gay' as he was at this time casually involved with a Japanese woman; although he did continue to visit Ni-chome and have occasional sexual encounters with foreign (white) gay men.

At twenty-nine, Tommy was posted by his Japanese company to Canada. In Toronto, he first encountered openly 'gay' men and was impressed by the size and scope of Toronto's 'gay scene.' He began a relationship with a Canadian man and gradually came to think of himself as 'gay.' However, he only uses the term 'gay' when he speaks English. In Japanese, he avoids the use of nouns referring to sexual identity, instead describing himself as 'a guy who likes guys' (*otoko ga suki na otoko*). It wasn't until his early thirties that he experienced an identity shift and decided that he would not or could not marry a woman. Influenced by Canada's progressive legal reforms relating to same-sex partnerships, he is now looking for a permanent male partner with whom he can settle down and establish a household. So far, although his Canadian friends mostly know about his preference he is only out to a few Japanese gay friends he met in Canada who have subsequently returned to Japan. He does not socialise with the Japanese community in Toronto and has no intention of returning to Japan on a permanent basis. This is primarily because he is attracted to white men and would like to live with his lover in a registered partnership. He does not feel that this would be a possibility in Japan even in the future.

'Sato'

Sato is forty-six years old and has lived in Vancouver for the last fifteen years. He became sexually active as a teen in the late-1960s. He writes that 'gay' was not used in Japan at this time except in the term 'gay-boy' which meant prostitute. He did not identify with the term *okama*, he writes '*okama* implied prostitute or something inferior and I did not think I was *hentai* [perverted]). I think it [the term he used to describe himself] was *homo* or *dōseiaisha*.' Since leaving Japan, he has been surprised by the changes that have taken place over the last fifteen years. He writes that being homosexual in Japan in the 1970s was 'a totally hidden activity' so he was very surprised to hear about Japanese gays participating in 'Gay Games' abroad and campaigning for 'gay rights' in Japan.

There was a little pressure from his older brother and sister to get married but, after he told them that he was not interested in women, they stopped pushing him. He writes: 'My brother understands what "being gay" means, my sister probably does not. She just gave up pushing me. Overall the pressure was not so strong.' However, his sister insisted he went to see a doctor:

> So we went to see a university hospital [doctor]. I had an interview with the doctor at first. His question was very simple. 'You don't think that you can change your homosexuality do you?' I said 'No' [then the doctor said] 'Now I'll talk to your sister.' I went out of the room and she entered. It did not take five minutes for her to come out of the room. She did not say a thing after that. I sometimes wonder now if I should ask her what the doctor told her.

In reply to the question 'Are there any differences between gay men in Canada and in Japan?' Sato replied that:

> Here in Canada, they [gay people] are much more open. There is an area in Vancouver where many gay men and women live. It is called West-End of Downtown. In West-End, you can see many pink flags on the balconies of their apartments and condominiums which means the residents are gay. Also, there are some openly gay celebrities including some members of parliament ... I could not think of this kind of situation in Japan, at least while I was there. Westerners are very individualistic compared to Japanese. While I was in Japan, I was always feeling some pressure from the society. It was like 'I have to go to bars after work with my colleagues,' 'I have not to have too many pleasure trips because of neighbours eyes' or 'The prices of gifts to friends and relatives for their special occasions have to be almost the same as other peoples.' The society in Japan is like that. In other words, everybody has to be the same in Japan. I had to behave as if I was a straight man who wants women all the time. When I was socializing with my colleagues or friends, I had to say

something, which I actually did not think, like 'that woman is sexy . . .,' etc. I can say that was one of the hardest parts of my life in Japan. I just hated it. Anyway, many of my Canadian friends know that I am gay, although very few of my Japanese friends know that. Well, the Japanese community here is a kind of extension of the society in Japan. So I have to be careful.

'Hiroaki'

Hiroaki is thirty-one years old and has lived in the US for the last ten years where he works in the travel and tourism industry. Even as a child, he was familiar with American culture as his family regularly took trips together to the US because his parents thought that the trips would be educational for himself and his brother. He writes that

> Ever since I was little, by visiting America, I was unconsciously taught that it is OK for everyone to be different. Not everyone has to have straight black hair and [dark] eyes [with] one language and culture. Inside myself, I was always fighting . . . Japan's homogeneous culture, tied up with old tradition . . . I always tried to convince myself that I am different and that is good. But I found moving to the US was the key to be me.

While still a child, Hiroaki remembers feeling different from other boys. He was not interested in typical boys' play such as baseball but preferred to keep his own company, listening to music or playing the piano at home. He became aware of a strong attraction towards older boys at his school about the age of ten, but hesitates to call the attraction 'sexual.' Because of his retiring personality and lack of interest in boys' activities, he was called 'okama' and 'homo' behind his back by schoolmates. He recognised that he was different from other boys but did not know how to articulate the difference. He remembers having no idea about the difference between the terms okama, homo and dōseiaisha, although these words were all applied to him. He was also referred to as 'onnappoi' (girlish) and 'nayo-nayo shiteiru' (soft-acting). This was largely due to his preferring the company of girls over boys. He remembers being popular with girls at his junior school. However, he had no sexual interest in them.

Hiroaki remembers being very concerned about his future in Japan and actually asked his parents to send him to a foreign high school when he was fifteen. He writes, 'In many ways, I did not feel like I fit in Japanese society and ... the only idea I had in mind [was] to get out of this country.' Hiroaki had the impression from the Japanese media that both San Francisco and New York were places where large numbers of gay men lived and where an open gay lifestyle was possible. He felt that there was no possibility of being open about his sexuality in Japan, writing 'In Japan, I was blinded as a gay person. I did not know who to turn to or talk to. I eventually decided to keep quiet about my sexuality. In the west it seemed less taboo to talk about gay people. It almost seemed healthy to be openly gay there.'

He writes that he is 'in the middle of the coming out process,' commenting that:

> I come out only with very close friends whose friendship is strong enough to last no matter what I am; my American gay friends, my best friends (straight), and a few Japanese gay friends. After all, I guess I only come out ... where people are happy to hear I'm gay. Now, by looking at the situation in the US I come to think that it is a lot easier to come out because there are people like me all over the States and it is very important for everyone to be out to change the society.

Hiroaki likes to travel and has found that the Internet is a very valuable tool for making contact with gay men all over the world. He uses it both to make contact with gay men in a given area before he visits as well as to get general information on the kind of gay life and facilities he can expect to find there. He writes that the Internet is more valuable than gay magazines or guidebooks because the information is constantly updated. Before he was online, he used his 'gay antenna' to find out gay-sympathetic people and places but this was often a hit-and-miss affair. Most of his information about gay life in Japan is found through the Internet. He writes: 'I sometimes check Japanese gay web sites to see how society changes. It is amazing how many gay people are active in Japan. I wish I knew some of the people while I was growing up so that at least I had information about where to go, what to do, find someone to share thoughts or get advice from.'

While living in Japan he was aware that Shinjuku Ni-chome was a gay area but only heard it mentioned when it was made fun of. He has never visited the area. He feels that young Japanese have an advantage in that they can learn so much about gay life from the Internet, however he feels that he himself has been lucky and that it would have been much worse had he been growing up homosexual in his father's generation.

'D.J.'

D.J. is a twenty-one-year-old university student studying International Relations at a prestigious university in Tokyo. His family live in Kobe. D.J. is a tall, very handsome boy who was very popular with girls. He was also very good at sports while at school but never really enjoyed playing them, preferring to get involved in dramatic productions. He still enjoys going to the theatre today. Although conscious of being attracted to other boys from age thirteen, his first sexual experience was with a female classmate at age seventeen. She suggested that their relationship become sexual and they had sex on several occasions. D.J. had no problems performing sexually with his girlfriend and remembers enjoying the interaction. However, he is not sure if he could still have sex with women now that he is more sexually experienced with men.

D.J. came to Tokyo at age eighteen to attend university. He rented a small one-room apartment so as to have more personal freedom than staying in a dorm would allow. He very quickly went to Shinjuku Ni-chome which he had heard about through various Japanese media and met a German man whose lover he became for nine months. The relationship eventually ended because D.J. was interested in making friends with other gay men and going out on the scene, whereas his lover, being much older, was more interested in staying at home. This was his most substantial relationship although he has had subsequent casual interactions with foreign men. He is only interested in older, taller, white men.

The university at which D.J. studies has no lesbian or gay organisation and none of his classmates know about his orientation. Other than his lovers, only two people know that he is gay, a flamboyant Japanese man who works with him at his part-time job and a female colleague also at the job. The three of them often socialise together, going to see gay-themed plays and movies. He feels no pressure to come out to his parents, siblings or classmates.

After university, he has decided to work for an American bank which has a policy of welcoming workers from a variety of backgrounds. He chose the company against the advice of his parents who wanted him to accept an offer from a prestigious Japanese bank because he felt that a foreign firm would exert less pressure upon him to conform to Japanese stereotypes. He hopes that working for a foreign company will lead to a posting abroad as he feels that America, in particular, would be a more sympathetic environment for him to be gay as well as providing him with more opportunity to meet men.

D.J. is 'not sure' if he is bisexual or gay. He feels emotionally unsatisfied with his relationships with men but finds sex with men more exciting. He is currently wondering whether he should try dating girls again as he is very popular among his female classmates. He feels emotionally close to women but is not sure whether he would still respond sexually to them having had sexually fulfilling relationships with men.

'Yūichi'

Yūichi left Japan at age seventeen to do an ESL course in America. Finding that he enjoyed life in the States, his parents agreed to let him attend an American university where he studied Sociology. After graduating, he remained in the US for a total period of seven years. He has recently returned to Japan where I met him in Tokyo while he was still living with his parents and looking for a job.

Yūichi remembers being criticised by his parents for being overly-interested in girls' things. He often used to play with his younger sister and her friends, playing with dolls or at making house. He remembers preferring the company of girls to that of boys because girls were friendlier, more relaxed and better at conversation. He remembers boys in his school as being rough, violent and vulgar. As a consequence, his way of speaking was a little girlish and he was referred to as okama-like (okamappoi). He was aware of being sexually interested in other boys from his early teens but didn't really think much about it. His desire to study in America wasn't really motivated by the idea that he could be openly gay there, as he had very little notion of a 'sexual identity' at that time.

While studying as a freshman in college, he had occasional sex with his roommate, a black guy. His roommate would occasionally get into Yūichi's bed, lie on top of him and have intercrural intercourse until he came. This was entirely without affection and was never spoken about. The roommate had no interest in sexually fulfilling Yūichi but would leave the room as soon as the act was accomplished. Yūichi assumed for a time that this is what gay sex was. While at university, Yūichi still did not consider himself 'gay' although he knew that he had no interest in women. His entry to the gay scene was only accomplished after graduating when he was picked up in a gay bar by an older white guy who was heavily into SM. He had a relationship with this man for over five years and was gradually assimilated into his lover's group of gay friends. However, his lover would frequently bring home casual acquaintances and expect Yūichi to join them in sexual play; again Yūichi assumed that this was typical for 'gay' relationships. Although he occasionally came back to Japan for holidays, Yūichi never socialised on the Japanese gay scene. His understanding of 'how to be gay' was entirely predicated on American models: how to act in bars, how to signal interest to a potential partner, how to cruise malls and parks. Thus, when he returned to Japan, he had no idea how to cruise other Japanese men or even how to interact with them in bars. He finds Japanese gay men very hard to read and was experiencing difficulty in establishing a relationship with a Japanese man.

Yūichi had already 'come out' to his mother by telephone when he was living in the States with his lover. He had told his mother that there was 'something else' (*hoka ni aru*) other than friendship to their relationship. He did not think that his mother would have the vocabulary to discuss 'sexual orientation' and indeed, she seems to think that it is just a matter of time before he meets the right girl with whom he will feel comfortable enough to get married. He has not come out to his father or sister as he has very little in common with either of them and does not feel that they have a sufficiently close relationship to make such a personal disclosure relevant.

Yūichi had assumed that there were no books in Japanese about gay life in Japan (other than pornographic magazines) because he had been looking in the wrong sections in the book stores. He had been looking in the 'Psychology' section (*shinri*) whereas most stores stock gay-themed books in the 'Women's' (*josei*), 'Family' (*katei*) or 'Gender' (*jendā*) sections. When I took him to a section in a large Tokyo book store which had over twenty publications in Japanese about gay life in Japan, he was very surprised. He bought a book on basic information about homosexuality, intending to give it to his mother but he later changed his mind about showing it to her as he felt that she would not make the effort to read it.

However, when I met Yūichi again a few months later, he informed me that his mother's attitude had shifted somewhat and that after an initial period of embarrassment, she had begun to inquire about his personal life, asking him about the break up of his previous relationship and suggesting that he introduce her to his current partner. He felt that the shared secret of his same-sex attraction had somehow brought them closer and that it had strengthened their bond against his father. Although Yūichi's mother was interested in meeting his partner, she wanted to do this in a neutral environment and did not envisage his (Japanese) partner being recognised by or integrated into the family as a whole. Consequently she rejected the idea that Yūichi and his lover should both come home to celebrate New Year with the family, leaving Yūichi and his partner to celebrate by themselves. Yūichi also confided that although he was very pleased to have finally established a relationship with another Japanese man, there were a number of factors both personal and social which were putting strain on the relationship. Firstly, his lover lived in one of Tokyo's satellite towns which meant that their homes were over two hours away, thus making meeting up on a week-day night difficult. Also, Yūichi, inspired by American models of courtship, wanted to spend what he termed 'quality time' with his lover which involved doing things together like going to the cinema, and making trips at the weekend. However, his boyfriend, who is a little older, is on a managerial promotion track in his company and is required to put in or at least *be seen to* put in a lot of overtime work, including some Saturdays. This means that in the little time they spend together, his boyfriend is so exhausted that they never managed to do anything. A further strain on the relationship was the rumour that Yūichi's boyfriend might be posted to a branch office in Osaka. Japanese companies notoriously move their managerial-track employees around their branch offices with little consideration for their personal circumstances. In the case of Yūichi's boyfriend, who is unmarried, he could scarcely cite the strain that a move would put on his gay relationship. Yūichi expressed regret at the fact that a long-term cohabiting relationship such as he had enjoyed with his American lover seemed impossible in Japan.

'Aki and Shinji'

Aki is a thirty-seven-year-old graphic artist who works as a freelancer on a variety of projects including a gay magazine. Shinji is thirty-eight and used to work as an accountant in a *juku* (cram school) but has recently resigned hoping to pick up part-time work which would give him more time to pursue other interests. They have been living together in Tokyo for eight years.

Aki is from Hokkaido and Shinji from Kyushu. Both stressed that it was impossible for them to live as they would have liked while living in these rural areas and both cited their move to Tokyo as being influenced by a desire to live a more open gay life. After meeting in

Tokyo, it was only six months before they decided they wanted to live together but they had difficulty first in finding an estate agent that would accept two single men who wanted to live together as clients and then in finding a landlord who would agree to let a single property to two men. Eventually they decided to 'pass' as cousins (on their mother's side so as to explain the difference in surnames) who wished to live together in order to save money. They were fortunate to find an estate agent who believed this story and they have had a very harmonious relationship with the landlady who lives opposite to them. The high rent in Tokyo has been a useful excuse to explain to their families why they are living together, and they have succeeded in convincing their rural parents that this is a common custom in Tokyo when in fact it is extremely unusual (perhaps less so for two women). They were both adamant that a similar living arrangement would be inconceivable in their home towns. As Aki said 'compared to the countryside, in Tokyo I feel I have been able to become more free.'

Aki considers himself fortunate that his job allows him to work with a variety of gay organisations as a gay man. He has a full and busy social life and is well integrated into Tokyo's gay scene. He was able to give me introductions to a gay magazine for which he had done some art work which enabled me to interview some of its employees and see a Japanese gay business at work. He also has many gay friends abroad and often makes trips to the US where several Japanese gay friends have moved to live with their American lovers. Working freelance as he does, Aki is often at home and therefore takes on more of the household tasks such as shopping and cooking. Shinji's demanding work schedule which meant he had little time or energy to put into their home as well as his rather homophobic work environment were factors which led him to retire from his job.

With regard to the development of a 'gay identity,' Aki feels that he has always been gay, saying that he was always attracted to older boys in his neighbourhood from his earliest memories. However, he learned not to disclose this attraction to straight people after an unpleasant experience at high school when he confessed his love to a straight classmate. He says that from that time he has learned how not to divulge the fact that he is gay (*gei de aru koto*) to others. However, of all my interviewees, Aki is perhaps the only one who can unequivocally be said to have a both 'gay identity' and a 'gay lifestyle' in that much of his time is spent as openly gay with other gays. For example he lives with his gay lover and works for a number of gay businesses as well as socialising almost entirely with other gays both while in Japan and when travelling abroad. However, he is not out to his parents or family and still maintains the story that he and Shinji are cousins in order to explain his living arrangements to the landlady and neighbours.

He is very happy with his life and says that 'It's good that I was born gay' (*gei ni umarete yokatta*). He cites that fact that his job is unproblematic and that he can live happily with his boyfriend (*bōifurendo*). Also, being gay has enabled him to make a lot of contacts with interesting people which if he had been straight, he would have been unable to do. While talking on the train on the way to his home he showed absolutely no reticence about using the adjective '*gei*' to describe himself, me and his friends even though the topic of our conversation and the fact that it was being carried on in Japanese between a Japanese and a foreign man in public was obviously being noticed by the people around us.

'Hara'

Hara is a forty-five-year-old finance professional who lives alone in a large apartment in Takadanobaba, Tokyo. He is not married but experienced intense pressure from workmates and family until he was thirty-five. After this point when he still remained unmarried, people began to suspect that there was 'something wrong' and stopped asking him about his marriage plans. He expects that there is some speculation about his sex life, but as he pointed out, there are plenty of other reasons why some Japanese men find it hard to find a partner (suspected mental illness in the family, *burakumin* [hereditary sub-caste facing discrimination due to ancestors' connection with 'polluting' professions] or Korean ancestry, etc.).

Hara is primarily interested in SM sexual interactions where he usually takes the dominant role. He likes to tie up his sexual partners and subject them to punishment which usually involves whipping and scourging with a variety of implements. He has been interested in this kind of sexual interaction since childhood where he was fascinated by comic books and animations in which the handsome young hero was captured by the villain and subjected to torture before escaping. He became aware of sexual urges in the late-1960s at a time when there were no specific gay magazines. At that time there were magazines which included a variety of perverse (*hentai*) sexual situations such as SM, scatology, paedophilia and homosexuality. He used to buy these magazines in second-hand stores since they were not readily available in mainstream book stores. These magazines often ran articles about the SM world in New York and Los Angeles which was much more developed than anything in Japan. He decided that after graduation, he would go to the States to check out some of the venues written about. When he made a two-month trip to California, he was cruised in Los Angeles by an older man in a car. The man drove him round to a variety of gay venues and then took him home. This was his first sexual experience.

In the early-1970s, the first gay magazines appeared and Hara was able to find out the addresses of gay SM bars in Japan but he found that he wasn't particularly attracted to Japanese body types and preferred foreign men so he has always made regular trips to California where he visits SM venues. He is not particularly interested in having a stable relationship with another man but instead prefers casual sex-play with a number of partners. Recently, the Internet has proved a valuable way to make new contacts as he is able to exchange photographs and also discuss sexual likes and dislikes before setting up a sexual interaction. He says that his sexual interactions now go more smoothly as both partners have negotiated in advance what they would like to do and what their limits are. He said that most of his partners were married white men living in Japan who were bored with their standard sex lives.

He isn't out in Japan except of course to his partners and to two close female friends. He feels no need to make this kind of declaration to the people around him, commenting that he does not expect his straight friends to discuss their sex lives and sees no reason to bring up his own. He accepts the label 'gay/*gei*' in both English and Japanese but stresses the recent nature of this terminology. He says that the word '*homo*' used to be much more common in the 1970s and that in the 1960s, the *hentai* (pervert) magazines he was reading were still using some of the vocabulary inherited from the indigenous tradition of *nanshoku* (male eroticism), although that has now been entirely replaced by American-derived vocabulary such as *homo* and *gei*.

'Hiroshi'

Hiroshi is a thirty-year-old man who has been HIV+ for three-and-a-half years. He has had a very international background, being educated at a university in the States and then working for a number of firms in America and Hong Kong. He recently returned to Japan in order to receive subsidised medical treatment. He lives next to his parents in a flat with separate entrance.

Hiroshi's family background is unusual in that his father is rich and owns an import/export business. As a consequence, he and his brother and sister spent much of their childhood living and studying outside Japan. Hiroshi is bilingual and bicultural. After discovering his HIV status, he returned to Japan where he felt obliged to come out to his brother and sister. As the oldest son, he felt a responsibility to inform his siblings that he would be unable to fulfil the role expected of him, that of looking after their parents in their old age, firstly because he was gay and did not want to marry, but more importantly because he was HIV+ and therefore could not guarantee that he would survive. He spoke of this as a 'double coming out' which was very difficult for him to do. However, his siblings were supportive, his sister helping him in small ways by going to the hospital to get his prescription when work makes it difficult for Hiroshi to attend. He has tried to tell his parents on numerous occasions but has always faltered at the last minute. He has made a New Year's resolution for three consecutive years that he will tell his parents about his condition but has been unable to do so for fear of causing them worry.

As the oldest son of a wealthy family, he is under constant pressure to marry. His mother has started to talk of marriage introductions *(omiai)*. Recently she suggested that he might like to meet the daughter of an acquaintance whose father had died leaving her a house and a piece of real estate in a central Tokyo location. His mother's interest in the real estate, as opposed to the personality of the girl, is an example of the business-like understanding of marriage which prevails in his family.

Hiroshi has gained a lot from working with two Tokyo gay groups, OCCUR and Second Coming Out (an AIDS organisation). When time allows, he works on their phone lines and participates in discussion groups. However, he has a full-time job which he must keep up because, although his medication is subsidised, he must still pay 30 per cent of the costs. Also, because one of the drugs in the cocktail he is currently taking has yet to be licensed in Japan, he must import it directly from New York at his own expense.

Although Hiroshi would like a committed relationship, he has found it difficult to meet a partner in Japan. He received only three replies to an Internet advertisement looking for a HIV+ partner or a partner for whom his status was not an issue. He occasionally meets men he likes but is afraid to come out to them as HIV+ for fear that the disclosure will either frighten them away or attract them to him for the wrong reason. He will not have a sexual encounter without disclosing his status so he often dissembles and pretends not to be interested in someone when he actually is. This situation has caused him a great deal of frustration and regret. He would like to return to the States where the possibility of meeting a similarly HIV+ partner is much higher and where both the Internet and magazine personals are full of such men advertising for partners, but is stuck in Japan for financial reasons. Also, he feels that the US discriminates against HIV+ people and that he would not be granted a visa if he declared his positive status.

'Tomo'

Tomo is a twenty-eight-year-old telecommunications engineer. He has never been abroad except for a short trip to Hawaii. He has a younger sister who is already married with a baby. He lives with his parents in order to save money and also because it is more convenient. Since he needs to be on call whenever problems arise with his company's clients, he does not have the time to run his own apartment or look after himself and needs his mother to look after him.

Tomo had his first sexual experience with a girl he met in university. They had a sexual relationship for a year which broke up when he decided he wanted to start having sex with men. He is only attracted to white men and uses the Internet to meet with partners interested in becoming 'sex friends.' He is not interested in romantic attachments with these men, nor does he imagine ever having a committed relationship with another man or living together with a man. Tomo considers that he is still attracted to women, although he has not had any sexual contact with women since he first started to see other men two years ago. He expects that he will get married in his early thirties but does not consider giving up his sexual contacts with men. He will continue to meet men casually as he does now, only instead of hiding these affairs from his parents, he will hide them from his wife. He uses the Internet (aided by a mobile phone) to contact his partners.

Tomo was unused to discussing his 'sexuality' and seemed uncomfortable with the labels 'gay' and 'bi' although he understood them. He has never discussed his sexual preference with anybody and has no intention of 'coming out.' He is unsure why he only responds sexually to white men and Japanese women. He feels that white men are 'more masculine' because of their greater body size, stronger facial features and body hair. He thinks that western women are 'too masculine.' He is interested in expanding his experience of sexual acts. He has enjoyed anally penetrating other men but has so far been unable to accept being anally penetrated himself. This is not because of inhibition but because of the pain involved.

He has only been to Shinjuku Ni-chome once. He was not impressed with the scene and does not consider himself to have anything in common with gay Japanese men. He is only interested in having casual sexual encounters with white men and has found the Internet the most useful means to meet partners. This is largely to do with his extremely busy work schedule which means that he has little time to waste going through the motions of courtship.

'Shin'

Shin is thirty years old. He has an older brother who is already married and a younger brother who lives away from home to be closer to his office. Shin still lives at home with his father (his mother has passed away). He is responsible for looking after his father who has not yet retired. He does all of the cooking, shopping and cleaning and has recently given up his full-time job to work freelance so as to be able to spend more time at home.

Shin is only interested in foreign men and has had several short-term relationships with foreigners passing through Tokyo. He has met these men in Ni-chome bars but has constantly been disappointed with the quality of relationships he established, his partners either leaving the country or carrying on with other men. He has not had a relationship for four years. He would like a long term relationship but despairs of finding the right person on the 'scene.' He has never used the Internet or personal magazines to meet partners; nor does he have any interest in participating in gay social groups. Although he considers being gay to be 'the most important' aspect of his life, he says there are other aspects of his life which must be sorted out first. He needs to ensure that his father is well looked after (which means that he can never live with another man while his father is still alive). Also, he has to put a lot of energy into finding enough freelance work to survive. He is also studying English translation so as to increase his career prospects.

He has never come out except to his previous boyfriends. No-one in Japan knows that he is gay and he has no intention of declaring this to his family. He has no close friends and describes his relationship with his brothers and father as 'cool.' He does not feel that disclosing his sexuality would be well received by his family. Recently, he is being pressured by relatives to think about marriage. He fears that some members of his family may suspect his orientation as he is very quiet and gentle, qualities usually prized in Japanese women. Ironically, in giving up his job to look after his father, he is fulfilling the role that would usually be performed by a daughter (or eldest son's wife). His real-life experience is closely parallelled by the self-sacrifice of Goh in *Okoge* (Murata Takehiro 1992), discussed in chapter 5, who similarly steps in to care for his ailing mother.

'Kōji'

Kōji is a twenty-four-year-old university student studying Broad-casting at a large private university in Tokyo. He lives with his parents. He has an elder sister who is already married.

As a child, Kōji spent a lot of time playing with his elder sister and her friends, as a result he spoke rather effeminately and was referred to as '*okama*-like' (*okamappoi*) by other boys. He didn't particularly like doing girlish things but his small body frame (he was always among the smallest in the class), high voice and feminine speech pattern marked him out as different. He had no idea what *okama* signified other than 'a boy who was too much like a girl.' He remembers feeling attracted to much older men from age nine. He would stare at attractive men on the train and imagine what their bodies looked like, particularly their body hair and smell. Although he discovered masturbation at age twelve, he does not recall any fantasy element, he was just interested in the physical sensation and used to enjoy looking at himself as he did it. At this time he had no concept of how to have sex with men. By the age of fifteen he knew that he was sexually attracted to men not women but had no label for the experience. There had never been any mention of homosexuality at school, either in sex education classes or among the students. He had heard the term *homo* but wasn't sure what it connoted. Although he had seen the American movie *Torch Song Trilogy* (which features several gay partnerships), he regarded this as something foreign (*mukō ni aru koto*) and could not relate it to his future life in Japan. It never occurred to him that he might have a relationship with a man or live with him. His primary feeling at this time was one of regret, that he would be unable to get married and produce grandchildren for his parents.

While at university, he spent one year as an exchange student at a college in the US where he became aware of a gay and lesbian group on campus. However, the leader of the group was a very visible and aggressive lesbian whose presentation Kōji disapproved of. He did not feel he had anything in common with the rather confrontational members of this organisation and never spoke to them. However, he had heard of San Francisco's reputation as a gay Mecca and so made a trip there one vacation. He was picked up in a coffee bar in the Castro on his first day by a white American with whom he spent the remainder of the vacation. However, upon returning to campus, he was upset to find out that his boyfriend was seeing other guys and so broke off the relationship. On his next vacation, this time to Los Angeles, he was picked up in a coffee bar by another white guy. This man was much older and a more steady figure who made effort to keep in contact with Kōji when back at campus. Although Kōji has now returned to Japan, he still considers this man to be his boyfriend and hopes to visit him again.

Kōji has never been to Ni-chome and has no interest in going; nor is he interested in participating in any kind of gay group. He sees no scope for developing a gay identity in Japan as he would be too anxious about his parents or colleagues finding out. So far he has only come out to a Japanese girl who was hoping to have a relationship with him. She responded rather coolly and has subsequently moved away from Tokyo. Were he able to move to America (to be with his boyfriend), then he would consider telling his parents because he would want them to know that the reason he was leaving Japan was to live with his lover. He feels that he could live as a gay man in America, but that this would be impossible in Japan. He has used the Internet to meet foreign gay men living in Japan, but just as friends, because he does not feel he could have a sexual relationship with a man while residing in Japan.

With regard to the future, Kōji hopes to be able to find a job in the international division of a Japanese film or television production company that would enable him to make trips abroad. When I asked if he intended to move away from home once he had found a job, Kōji seemed surprised that I should think this a desirable thing to do. 'Renting an apartment is so expensive in Tokyo' he said 'and anyway, while I live at home my mother does everything for me, so it's more convenient.' When I pointed out that living at home made it difficult to have a private life, he seemed unconvinced, commenting that 'I can always visit my friends in their apartments.'

'Jirō'

Jirō is a thirty-eight-year-old university administrator who lived with his parents until he was thirty-seven. He has now purchased a small apartment near his parents house. He has a younger sister who married fifteen years ago. He is being pressured to marry by his parents but has told them that he is in love with an American woman living in Los Angeles who he pretends to visit often (actually he is visiting his boyfriend and the woman in the pictures in his apartment is a lesbian friend). He would like to have a fake marriage with an American woman in order to get a green card and be able to live with his boyfriend.

Jirō describes his childhood as 'regular.' He was originally interested in girls and when he discovered masturbation at age twelve, he used pictures of girls from men's manga. While at university he had a girlfriend who was already sexually experienced. She suggested that they have sex and they checked into a love hotel. Although he managed to have sex, he felt under a lot of pressure to perform and was surprised he did not enjoy it, and, as he didn't want to repeat the act, after a while they broke up. Although he was aware of being interested in men's (especially white men's) bodies, he didn't cognise this as sexual and certainly never suspected that he might be gay. He says he never thought about his 'sexuality' at this time. However, at age twenty-five he came across a gay pornographic magazine in the rubbish outside his apartment. He took it home and read it. It had a strong and immediate effect upon him and he used the pictures as masturbation images. This was the first time that he had ever thought there was a 'gay world' (*gei no sekai*) and he realized instantly that he was gay. Although the magazine had advertisements for bars and personal ads, he was far too nervous at this stage to check them out.

At age thirty, he had still had no sexual contact with a man. However, on a trip to Hawaii, he found himself in a gay bar and was picked up by a white man who told him about a gay beach. He spent the rest of the week on the gay beach and had five different partners in a week. Subsequently, he went back to Hawaii every year for sex. Five years ago in Hawaii, he met the man who became his boyfriend. This man is much older than Jirō and more interested in romance and affection than sex. This suits Jirō as he likes to have regular sex with his sex friends whilst feeling secure in the emotional relationship he shares with his boyfriend. He visits his boyfriend twice a year, and his boyfriend has also visited Jirō in Japan.

Jirō is sexually very active. He has two 'sex friends' in Japan, both of them white men married to Japanese women. He has a boyfriend in Los Angeles and he also visits Hawaii yearly where he estimates he has had sex with over fifty men. Because of his full sex life, he has regular twice-yearly HIV blood tests at a local hospital. Although he has been to Ni-chome, he finds the Internet a more useful tool for meeting partners and used it recently to make contact with men before a trip to Korea. He subsequently had sex with one of these men although he turned down another who was not his type. He has no interest in having a long term relationship in Japan but would like to live with his boyfriend in Los Angeles. He would consider telling his family about himself only if he moved permanently to America where he sees it as possible to live a gay lifestyle. He does not think such a lifestyle is possible in Japan. He is not a member of any gay organisation and has no interest in meeting Japanese gays as he says he has nothing to talk about with them.

'Ichirō'

Ichirō is a twenty-one-year-old unemployed man living with his parents. He has an older sister who is married although she recently returned home as her marriage has been under stress. She is considering divorce. Ichirō's parents, although still living together at the time I spoke to him, are also considering divorce. Ichirō, because of personal problems at school, was unable to pass the entrance exam to go to university and has had a variety of part-time jobs since leaving school. At the moment he is not working but rather half-heartedly studying in an attempt to gain entrance to a university as a mature student.

Ichirō is a very gentle and retiring person who, as a child, spent a lot of time with his elder sister and her friends. As a result he developed rather feminine mannerisms and a female way of speaking. At school, he was ostracised by other boys and forced to spend time with girls. By the time he reached middle school (age thirteen) this ostracism turned violent and he was repeatedly bullied by gangs of boys. This led to him refusing to go to school for long periods, and, eventually, at age fifteen, to a period of hospitalisation for unspecified 'emotional problems' (I think he may have been hinting at a suicide attempt). His emotional problems continued at high school and as a result he was absent from school more often than he attended.

At this time he became aware of his attraction to other men which he understood as being part of his general 'emotional problems.'

Although he never disclosed this attraction to anyone, he worried about it constantly and felt utterly hopeless about his future. His parents, who both work, were very impatient with him about his unwillingness to go to school and his failure to *gaman suru* (put up with problems). His relationship with them is still strained but he is financially dependent upon them and has no educational qualifications with which to get a job and make himself independent. Consequently, he feels trapped and hopeless in his life at home.

At age seventeen, he was approached in a movie theatre by an American man who took him out for coffee. They began to meet as friends and the American eventually told Ichirō that he was gay, and that he suspected that Ichirō was too. Ichirō felt a tremendous relief that he could finally acknowledge this part of himself to someone, and he started a relationship with the American man. However, six months into the relationship, his lover became sick and discovered that he was suffering from full-blown AIDS. Within a year, he had died. During the time of his lover's hospitalisation, Ichirō was the only person to visit him. This was a tremendous strain on him as he was only eighteen at the time. He had nobody to discuss this situation with. After his lover's death, Ichirō became increasingly depressed.

Ichirō's next relationship started in the same way: he was approached by a foreign man in a movie theatre. This relationship lasted a year before his lover returned to America. They still keep in contact but have not met since his lover's departure. Ichirō despairs of meeting another man. He is only attracted to foreign men but as he cannot speak English, his choice of partner is limited. Also he does not have the financial resources to hang out on the Shinjuku Ni-chome scene and as he does not have a computer, he is unable to access the gay websites.

Recently, he saw an advert for an international gay group that meets every month in Tokyo and went along to one of their meetings. Although there were foreigners there, he could not speak to them because they did not speak Japanese. However, he made friends with a Japanese university student who introduced him to some other young gay Japanese. At a subsequent meeting he made friends with a foreign student. He now has a small circle of gay friends with whom he socialises. Ichirō hopes very much to find an older foreign man who will look after him. He has very high expectations of a relationship: it should be monogamous, long-term, and he would like to live with his lover. He sees the ideal gay relationship as patterned on a heterosexual marriage. He has been very disappointed that the foreign men he has met so far have been only interested in casual relationships.

When I met Ichirō a few months later, he told me that he had a new American boyfriend (*koibito*) whom he spoke of in very positive terms as 'kind' (*yasashii*) and 'pure' (*pyua*). However, as the conversation progressed, it became clear that he had only met this man one week previously and had high expectations of what was still a very recent acquaintance. Furthermore, he also told me that he had decided to study in order to pass the entrance examinations into medical school which, given the difficulty of the examinations, his poor academic record, and the Japanese education system's inflexibility towards older students who have 'missed the boat,' seemed a very unlikely prospect. I was left with the impression that the dreary realities of Ichirō's past experience had encouraged him to fantasize about the kind of future he would ideally like to have, as opposed to taking positive steps towards achieving a less glamorous but possible future. For example, despite his professed exclusive attraction to foreign men, he still had not taken steps to learn English, thus seriously limiting the number of foreign men he could interact with.

'Satoru'

At the time of interview, Satoru was a thirty-one-year-old post-graduate student coming to the end of his studies and looking for a job. He lives in the small city of Okayama in southern Honshu in a one-room flat near his parents house. He is the eldest son and has two younger sisters. He also has a boyfriend who is much older than himself whom he rarely sees because they are both very busy; however, they maintain regular contact through e-mail.

Satoru writes that he was a little 'girlish' during his youth because of the amount of time he spent playing with his younger sisters and their friends and as a result he was name-called by his classmates, usually *okama*, *onnappoi* (womanish) and *onna-otoko* (girl-boy). However, he had a cheerful disposition and as a result was fairly popular at school and was never physically bullied. He remembers being interested in older boys' and male teachers' bodies from about age eleven. He was particularly fascinated by the change in his peers penises during puberty and their growth of pubic hair. On one occasion, he bribed an older boy to show him his pubic hair in the school toilet. He also used to check out men's groins to see if he could see the outline of their penises and used to examine his father's underwear for semen stains. He used to conjure up images of older boys' penises while masturbating.

Early on Satoru realised that these desires were not to be spoken of and he conceptualised them as a kind of sickness which he hoped to outgrow in time. He never acknowledged these desires to anyone for fear of their response. He assumed that he was the only person to feel these transgressive desires and assumed that he would never meet a male partner. He felt very lonely and isolated as a result, even wishing that he could die rather than grow up loving other men. Satoru continued to feel lonely and confused into his undergraduate days until he met and fell in love with a female student at the same university. They started a sexual relationship and he was relieved to find out that he could respond emotionally and sexually to women. However, he was troubled at the time because his masturbatory fantasies were still exclusively about other men. After this relationship came to an end he continued to have intermittent sexual relationships with women, but none as substantial as the first.

Satoru had picked up from the mass media that there were gay venues and meeting places but he found it difficult to visualise what gay men were actually like and did not consider himself to be 'gay' at this time. It was not until he was twenty-nine that he made contact with the wider gay community, which he did through the Internet. He replied to an ad on a gay bulletin board and communicated with a man for a few months via e-mail before he felt confident enough to meet him. Although this meeting did not lead to a sexual relationship, the man was very supportive and removed Satoru's fears about gay men (that they were somehow strange, or 'obviously gay') and he felt more confident after this about meeting other gay men. As he says, after this first meeting 'I thought gay men were normal.' Although he subsequently had sexual relations with several men, he was dismayed by their lack of emotional investment, stating 'As a rule, since I attach great importance to feelings more than sex, I was very disappointed in gay men.' After a number of one-night stands, he 'felt a repulsion towards gay men for a while' but his desire for sex kept him active on the gay scene. When I questioned him about the different motivations he had for pursuing sex with women and with men, he suggested that what he wanted from a man was 'to presume upon his love. When we have sex, he would lead me ... ' which suggested that he was looking for the kind of *amae* (indulgence) commonly described in gay personal ads (*see* chapter 6). However, when thinking about women, he thinks more in terms of 'a companion for life,' defining this in emotional rather than sexual terms.

Satoru is the eldest son from a provincial town and expects to get married in the near future. He has no expectation of living with a male partner and does not see this as a desirable alternative to marriage as 'In Japan people would regard me as a gay man if I lived with a male partner.' He feels that privacy is important and feels that living with one's (male) lover would be claustrophobic. Interestingly, he does not feel that this would be an issue with a wife. Although he hopes to meet a marriage partner 'naturally,' he does not discount the possibility of an *omiai*. After marriage he will 'try to stop my habit towards men and love my family' although he says that his gay friends ridicule this idea, saying 'soon your wife will be a mother and will be busy taking care of the children, then you will come back to look for another kind of love,' an attitude which again illustrates the extent to which motherhood is considered to remove a woman from the realm of desirability.

'Yukio'

Yukio is a twenty-year-old part-time student from a small town in Hokkaido currently living alone in Tokyo. Yukio's first sexual encounter took place during the first grade of middle-school (age thirteen) when a male classmate showed him how to masturbate in the school toilet. From this time on he regularly met with this friend and they engaged in mutual masturbation sessions. From the age of about fifteen they also began to have oral sex with each other, having picked up the idea from a heterosexual pornographic magazine. Yukio enjoyed the sex he had with his friend and did not analyse it in terms of hetero or homo, assuming that he would in time also begin to have sex with women. However, as he got older, he began to realise that he was interested in having sex with other male friends but never with female friends. It was not until he saw the movie *Philadelphia*, starring Tom Hanks, about a gay lawyer who loses his job because he contracts AIDS, that Yukio realised that he too was probably 'gay' (*gei*). He became a great fan of Tom Hanks whom he fantasized as his ideal partner and began to collect all his movies. From this time he became increasingly interested in foreign (white) men and his sexual fantasies began to revolve around foreigners, replacing the figures of his schoolmates.

Yukio realised that he had to leave his hometown because of the restrictive nature of the small-town environment. He said that people (*seken*) exerted a lot of pressure upon their neighbours to conform. For example, he mentioned a school friend who had been bullied at school because it became known that his father had had an affair with another boy's mother. He realised that he had no chance to get into an elite or even a good university because his hometown lacked the extracurricular support given by *juku* cram schools which is necessary to pass the exams. Instead, he decided to go to Tokyo at age eighteen, work part time and study English in order to get into a foreign university. His parents fully supported him in making this move.

In Tokyo he got a job as a salesman in a branch of a large shoe chain and was able to earn over ¥160,000 ($1,330) per month, enough to rent a one-room apartment and pay for English classes three times a week. It was soon after arriving in Tokyo that he bought his first gay magazine and found out about the *gaisen* bars (places for Japanese who like foreign men) in Shinjuku. On his first visit to one of these bars, he met an American man who became his boyfriend. However, they split up after six months because his partner was playing around. After this experience he decided not to commit to a relationship but to meet foreign men casually for sex. He began to meet men using the 'sex friend' section of *GayNet Japan*. He generally received a large number of replies to his ads and found it easy to meet foreign men for casual encounters.

Although Yukio has a number of foreign sex friends, all his regular friends are straight Japanese men and women of the same age. He said that he was out to all his friends in Tokyo and that he considered it 'taken-for-granted' (*atarimae no koto*) that his sexual preference should come up in conversation. He is networked into a large floating population of young part-time workers who had gravitated to Tokyo from rural parts of the country in order to escape interference in their lives from parents and neighbours. These young people seemed to move easily from job to job, saving up money in order to pay for courses to improve their employment skills or for specific projects such as foreign travel. However, Yukio did say that the kind of openness he experienced with his friends in Tokyo would be inconceivable in his hometown in Hokkaido and that he would never come out about his same-sex preference to anyone from his hometown lest rumours spread and cause trouble for his parents.

Shortly after I met him, Yukio was offered a place at a university in the southern United States. He was planning on leaving Tokyo in the near future in order to spend some time with his family in Hokkaido before leaving for the States. He intended to use the Internet to make contact with gay men living near the campus in order to find possible partners before arriving. I asked him why he was uninterested in having a more long-term relationship and he commented that as far as sex was concerned 'This week I might want to do it [have sex] but next week I won't feel like it.' He didn't seem to feel the need to have a partner who was interested in more than just sex. When I mentioned that the university probably had a lesbian and gay student organisation, he said he was uninterested in meeting people solely because they were gay and expressed surprise when I suggested he might want to check out whether it was even *safe* to become known as gay on campus given the conservative nature of the southern American states. He had assumed that the relaxed attitude his Japanese peers had towards homosexuality would be the same among young people in America.

'Kazuo'

Since my informant Kazuo is deaf, most of our communication has been through writing: letters, e-mail and, on the occasions we have met, written notes. Kazuo has also written a long memoir about his experience which has been translated into English and appears in Summerhawk et al. (1998).

Kazuo is currently thirty-four years old and lives in a large city in the Kinki district of Japan with his parents. His father, although now in his seventies, is still a director of a small production company and his mother is a home maker. Kazuo himself is a computer programmer in a software company.

After a serious illness while still an infant, Kazuo became deaf and has remained so. Although he went through the regular school system, his disability isolated him somewhat both from his peers and from mass culture in general. As a result, he says that even when he entered high school at the age of sixteen, 'I didn't even know the word "gay"' ('gay' *to iu kotoba sae mo shiranakatta*). His high school shared the same campus with an affiliated university and one day he was approached by a university freshman while looking for a book in the library. When the freshman learned that Kazuo was deaf, he was very kind and attentive and became his friend. As Kazuo says, 'For a year we carried on a relationship as senior and junior (*sempai to kōhai*).' He says that he felt the same love towards this student, whose name was Hide, as one would to an older brother. Hide made a great effort to learn sign language so that he could communicate better with Kazuo and they began to meet daily.

On Kazuo's seventeenth birthday, Hide invited him to come to his room for a birthday party where they ate and played games until

late. Given the lateness of the hour, Hide invited Kazuo to stay over.
While Hide was out of the room taking a bath, Kazuo looked
through his magazine collection and came across a copy of the gay
magazine *Barazoku*. He was astonished to see pictures of naked men
and to read the comics and short stories detailing sex between men.
Previously, he had no idea that such things happened. When Hide
came back and found Kazuo reading the magazine, he was furious
and reduced him to tears. Kazuo kept apologising until Hide
eventually forgave him, finally taking him in his arms and then
kissing him. Kazuo says 'I had no idea what was happening' as Hide
began to make love to him. Although Kazuo asked him to stop, Hide
continued to undress him, Kazuo saying that 'It was neither pleasant
nor unpleasant, I felt as though something inside of me had been
shaken and a different me had woken up.' Suddenly, he found
himself reciprocating and 'It was as though another me had taken
over inside.' After this night, they became lovers, Kazuo commenting
that 'This is how my gay path (gay *no michi*) started, with Hide and
me.'

   After Hide had graduated from the university they spent a year
apart until Kazuo could join him in Chiba where they rented an
apartment together. Kazuo says that they took great pains to disguise
their relationship so as not to arouse the suspicions of their
neighbours and friends. It was now eight years since they had first
met, and apart from one year of separation, had spent time together
every day. However, one day Hide left on a business trip and never
returned: he died in a plane crash. Kazuo says that after the crash, he
sank into a deep, dark depression and though of killing himself. It was
one year before he became himself again and tried to get his life back
on track.

   Kazuo feels immensely grateful to Hide for befriending him and
also for helping him to realise that he was gay. He says that without
Hide's influence he may never have 'woken up' (*mezameru*) and
would have lived an 'uneventful life' (*heibonna jinsei*). Although
Kazuo once thought about getting married to a woman, he has not,
until recently considered looking for another male lover. He feels that
finding a male lover would show lack of deference to his dead partner,
but that taking a wife would not. However, although he talked about
marriage with a number of women, his total lack of sexual desire for
them led him to realise that a marriage would be impossible.

   Kazuo's life has expanded greatly since his partner's death. He is
now networked, not only into a community of deaf people, but also

deaf-gay people with whom he can share his special experiences and frustrations. This has led to increasing contact with foreign gay men, both hearing and deaf with whom he keeps up a hefty correspondence. He also travels, when his work allows, to visit his friends and meet with deaf-gay men in Australia, the US, Germany, and Holland and interview them for a book he plans to write about international deaf-gay life. Given his rudimentary English and the fact that deaf sign languages are not universal, he faces considerable problems in interfacing with foreign men but is extremely resourceful in overcoming these difficulties. Having observed the better living conditions for foreign deaf-gay men, in terms of job opportunities and lack of discrimination, he feels that he would like to leave Japan and live in either Australia or Holland but, given his age, his lack of English and his disability, he is not optimistic about being granted a work visa.

Furthermore, Kazuo is becoming something of an activist on behalf of the deaf-gay community in Japan and is in the process of setting up an Internet *minikomi* (a contracted loan word based on 'mini communication' the opposite of 'mass communication') which will contain articles in Japanese and English about international deaf-gay issues based on his personal experience as well as that submitted by his friends. He also has a massive archive of gay-related books, comics and newspaper and magazine articles in his bedroom dating back ten years which was an invaluable resource for me when I was researching the current book. He hopes to raise money to open a small office which will house the literature collection and provide office space for the *minikomi*. Although he is becoming increasingly active as a spokesperson for the deaf-gay community, he has not disclosed his sexual preference to any member of his family or to his work colleagues and has no intention of doing so. In this respect, he is virulently opposed to the Japanese gay rights organisation OCCUR's emphasis on 'coming out' which is based very much on American models of sexual-identity. He identifies himself as part of the 'anti-OCCUR faction' (*han akā ha*) which disapproves of OCCUR's political stance on homosexual issues.

When I stayed with his family, Kazuo was most insistent that I should never refer to homosexuality in conversation with his parents, which seemed odd in that almost every book in his room had the word 'homosexual' (*dōseiai*) or 'gay' (*gei*) on the cover. When we were watching television and Kazuo grimaced at a famous female teen idol who was acting in a particularly irritating manner, his mother commented to me that 'That child (i.e. Kazuo) doesn't like girls' (*ano ko wa onna no ko wo kirai nan da wa*) which seemed to me an implicit recognition of his orientation. Rather than speak of Kazuo as 'closeted' then, it seems more likely that he and his family have an unspoken agreement that sexuality is not to be discussed.

Chapter 8

Japanese Gay Men's
Self-Understanding

Introduction

The following discussion is based primarily on common themes
deriving from the interviews I conducted with the men outlined in the
previous chapter. However, in order to show that the issues raised are
not particular to my group of informants, I have supplemented this
with references to the interview data collected by Ōhama (1994),
Yajima (1997) and Summerhawk et al. (1998) as well as references to
other gay men I have spoken to or corresponded with, whose
biographies I have not given. I have also occasionally referred to
biographical information taken from Japanese gay websites and
published in books and magazine articles.

When I came to write this chapter, the information about their lives
provided by my informants as well as other biographical details
available in published media presented me with an extremely large
and varied resource and it was difficult at first to see how these very
different views, experiences and perspectives could by synthesised into
a coherent account typical of 'Japanese gay men' in general. However,
after looking over my interview data and reading again Yajima's
(1997) book of interviews with Japanese homosexual men, I realised
that although there were multiple views on any one issue, the same
issues did occur with some regularity. These were largely 'affective'
issues to do with personal relationships with friends, family and
colleagues and concerned whether to tell or not to tell: in English (and
Japanese parlance) whether to 'come out' (*kamu auto*) or not. Other
affective issues included how to negotiate sexual relationships, how to
keep such relationships secret and how to deal with inquiries about
marriage. I deal with these concerns in sections on coming out, sex
and relationships, marriage and family and living situation.

Other issues, particularly those to do with 'gay identity' and 'gay
community' were not necessarily emphasised by my informants.

191

However, I chose to deal with these topics here partly because the idea of 'gay identity/community' is so central to much western debate about what homosexuality is that it is important to interrogate what these terms might mean in a Japanese context. This theme is continued in Chapter 9 when I address the question 'Is there a Japanese "gay identity"?'

In this chapter, I also take up some issues particular to my group of interviewees. As many of my informants were contacted via the Internet, it became clear that the Internet (and other new technologies like the mobile phone) were of particular use in organising sexual relationships and carrying on a 'private gay life'. As Internet use is rapidly expanding in Japan I chose to discuss the implications of this in a section on new technologies. Similarly, life in Japan vs 'the west' is not necessarily a concern in Japanese gay media generally, but given the *gaisen* bias of many of my informants, and my role as a 'western' researcher, I felt this was an important topic which it was necessary to discuss.

Gay identity

It is clear from the brief biographies of the sixteen homosexual men outlined in chapter 7 that they do not necessarily share a discrete, separate 'gay identity' that separates them from a supposed heterosexual majority. It is worth, at this point, considering again Kinsey's problematisation of the homo/hetero binary division of human sexual behaviour. The data presented above lends support to Kinsey's (1948: 639) findings that men cannot be neatly divided into opposing homo- or hetero categories.

I do not want to enter into arguments here about whether some of my informants are 'really' bisexual. However, it is clear from the stories of Tommy, D.J., Jirō, Satoru and Tomo that their first sexual and emotional relationships were with women although none of these men is currently involved with a woman. Both Tommy and Jirō were quite clear that heterosexual involvement was a closed chapter in their lives and that they were looking for long-term and significant sexual and emotional relationships with other men. However, D.J. suggested that he might be interested in pursuing some of the women who have expressed interest in him, as he has been unsatisfied with the level of emotional commitment in his relationships with men, whereas Tomo and Satoru are fully confident that they will at some point in the future get married, although they doubt that they will give up their casual sexual interactions with men.

Although all my informants, with the possible exception of Tomo, acknowledge and sometimes use the term gay/*gei* when talking about themselves and their sexual preference, it is by no means clear at what stage in their lives this understanding or experience of 'gayness' developed. In Jirō's case, his realization that he was gay, at age twenty-five, was extremely abrupt. He instantaneously understood that he was gay when he happened across his first gay magazine and this new understanding of himself as gay replaced a previous understanding of himself as 'normal.' Even so, it was another five years before he was able to act on his newly cognized identity when he found himself in a gay bar in Hawaii. Kazuo, also, was precipitated into a new self-understanding extremely rapidly when he was seduced, at age seventeen, by his best friend. As he comments, 'It was as though I had been woken up.' Kazuo speculated that had he not had this homosexual experience, the very possibility of which had never occured to him, he might well have gone on to live 'an uneventful life.' Tommy, however, came to understand himself as gay more gradually. Like Jirō, his first sexual experience was with a woman and he continued to be sexually involved with women even after discovering Shinjuku Ni-chome and having casual sex with men. It was not until his early thirties that he finally decided that he was 'gay' (a label he only uses in English) and that happiness for him lay in establishing a long-term cohabiting relationship with another man.

Other informants such as Hiroaki, Yūichi, Kōji and Ichirō all report feeling different from other boys as children and mention that they were ostracised to varying degrees for appearing too feminine. This latter point is interesting for it was not these men's same-sex attraction which was being stigmatized (for at this time it was barely cognized even by my informants themselves) but their failure to perform masculine gender. This supports Lunsing's finding that 'a minority of gay men ... felt discriminated against at school because of their homosexuality ... femininity in men, regardless of sexual preference, was more likely to cause problems' (1997: 284). As discussed in chapter 3, the *okama* or the feminine man is often treated as a figure of ridicule and contempt in Japanese popular culture. The gay activist and writer Yanase Ryūta points out in an autobiographical piece that 'The basis of Japanese people's hatred of homosexuals (*dōseiaisha*) starts with hatred of unmanly men (*otokorashikunai otoko*) and effeminate men (*onnappoi otoko*)' (Itō & Yanase 1994: 167). However, not all my informants necessarily felt themselves to be differently gendered because of their attraction to men and in terms of gender performance most were indistinguishable from their peers.

Hence, Epstein's insistence that 'There is no "homosexuality" but rather "homosexualities"' (1998: 146) is largely borne out by the interview data outlined above. It is as impossible to give a coherent description of *the homosexual* as it is of *the heterosexual* in Japan: neither can be reduced to ideal types of sexual being. As Halperin suggests '"The homosexual" is an identity without an essence' (1995: 61). It is therefore no surprise that my informants do not display a uniform progression towards the development of a 'gay identity;' nor do they necessarily feel a sense of commonality with other gay men solely on the basis of a shared same-sex attraction.

None of my informants seemed particularly interested in the 'cause' of their same-sex attraction; the search for causes generally being the concern of people who perceive such attraction as unusual or pathological. And none of them expressed regret about their feelings or showed a desire to change their orientation. However, several men did report being subjected to other people's construction of homosexuality as a physical condition which both could and should be 'cured.' As Sato's experience shows, when he came out to his siblings, his sister insisted they went to see the doctor who presumably told her that homosexuality was not a disease in that she never referred to her brother's 'problem' again.

A similar response was reported by a Japanese friend whose mother overheard his Australian high-school basket-ball coach pleading with him to come back to Australia to live with him:

> My mother asked me, 'Why did *sensei* say that he loved you?' I told her that we had been lovers for two years and that I was leaving school to go to Australia and live with him. She ran out of the room calling to my father 'Get the doctor, call the doctor.'

Other friends have also confided that the response of many of the people they came out to was to suggest a trip to the doctor. However, in all these cases, it was medical doctors and not psychiatrists who were referred to, suggesting that the 'cause' of homosexuality is considered to be more physiological than mental. This medical model is pastiched in one of the 'gay boom' movies, *Okoge* (Murata Takehiro 1992) where Goh's mother blames herself for his condition, believing that some 'gay bacteria' (*homo no baikin*) infected her during pregnancy. The idea that homosexuality is a medical problem probably derives from the pop-psychology described by Jolivet (1997:

79) who analysed pre-natal care literature directed at Japanese mothers. Some of the (medical) authors of these texts suggest that homosexuality results from a hormonal imbalance and is caused by stress during pregnancy.

However, despite the social discourse constructing homosexuality as a physiological condition along medical lines, none of my informants recognised themselves in this kind of model. Although their same-sex attraction resulted in a wide range of social difficulties, my informants were generally free of any kind of psychological distress or anxiety regarding their homosexual feelings. These feelings *per se* were not considered sinful, bad or a cause for worry, although the implications of these desires (such as disappointing one's parents by not getting married, fear of being discovered etc.) were. To this extent, the situation of homosexual men in Japan is not dissimilar to that of Thai gay men described by Jackson (1995: 270) who writes:

Thai gay and heterosexual males have considerably fewer points of difference than Western gay and heterosexual men. Historically, the Western homosexual male has been distinguished from the heterosexual male by having his sexuality defined as illegal by the state and as sinful by the dominant religion. And he has been subjected to homophobic violence and discrimination in everyday life.

Although several of my interviewees do report facing discrimination and bullying at school, in all cases this was a result of a perceived gender deviance (being too girl-like). In these instances, the conflation of terms such as *okama* and *homo* with *onnappoi* (woman-like) and *nayo nayo shite iru* (soft acting) suggests that the target of animosity was not primarily same-sex attraction but transgenderism. In these cases my informants' same-sex desires were incidental to the fact that they were bullied; they were bullied for failing to satisfactorily embody male gender, for being too girl-like. So, those of my informants who did successfully 'perform' masculine gender seem to have less sense of difference or isolation from their peers. Despite experiencing same-sex desires that they recognised as transgressive (in that they knew they were not to be verbalised) several of my interviewees, such as Tommy and Jirō, regarded themselves as 'normal.' Kazuo went so far as to suggest that had he not been seduced by his best friend he would have gone on to live a 'normal life,' apparently unaware that same-sex eroticism existed. Hence, although not socially sanctioned in the same way as extramarital sex is for men, homosexual sex is not attacked by the media in Japan in the same way that it is in Britain or America. What is criticised is not so much homosexuality *per se*, but images of the 'feminine' man. Gay men who are gender normative do not, then, necessarily see themselves in these images or feel themselves to be necessarily different from their straight counterparts solely on the basis of their same-sex attraction.

With the exception of Aki who lives and works in a gay milieu, and Ichirō who is unemployed, all my informants were networked as gender-normative 'men' into mainstream institutions, either studying at university or working for a variety of companies. None of them saw their same-sex attraction as definitive of themselves as individuals, preferring to situate themselves in relation to workplace and family. Sexual interaction with other men was something they tried to fit into their busy schedules after office hours, at weekends or during trips abroad. Where family or work demands were such that carrying on a same-sex relationship became difficult, men such as Shin and Tomo were happy to prioritise their social obligations over their personal desires. Although many would have liked to live together with a same-sex lover, this was understood to be something only possible 'abroad.'

Coming out

It is clear that most of the men I spoke to were extremely hesitant about coming out to both family and friends. To a large extent, this is because, as Goode has claimed, 'to most heterosexuals, the category "homosexual" is a dominant prepossession. It obliterates all other features or characteristics of a person; homosexuality is a *master trait*' (1997: 269). Hence, through coming out, a person's sexual preference, which is just part of who they are, assumes an exaggerated role in how that person is understood and evaluated by others. Given that most of the information about homosexuality in Japanese society consists of negative stereotypes, many gay men feel that they have little to gain in becoming publicly associated with those images. Furthermore, many men feel that sexuality, whether homo or hetero in orientation is a private matter, not something to be divulged in public. Hara, Tomo and Jirō, for instance, feel that they have nothing to come out about as none of their friends or family ever discuss their sex lives and they see no reason to talk about their own. As one of Ōhama's informants says (Ōhama 1994), disclosures about one's sexuality are inappropriate except to very close friends. He comments

'You don't go to buy lunch and tell [your colleagues] "Hello, I'm gay".'

Another of Ōhama's informants, a thirty-two-year-old salaryman, interestingly comments that to come out is *amae* (which Ōhama glosses as 'taking unfair advantage of another's kindness'). He comments that '[homosexuality] is something very important to me but [you should] think about whether it is also important to the person you work with; I don't think my whole existence as an individual means that much to them.' The reticence which many of my informants felt towards coming out to friends and family was closely connected with anxiety about other people's responses and the desire not to cause them trouble. This seems to be a widespread concern, one of the men interviewed by Summerhawk et al. commenting that 'coming out should not be pursued purely out of self complacency, but in consideration of the hardship it may force on others. I just cannot come to terms with the idea of doing something that would add to the many hardships already faced by my mother' (1998: 68). Men who write in to Internet problem pages on the issue of coming out frequently mention not wanting to upset or disappoint their parents. One man, writing on Itō Satoru's homepage *Sukotan*, says that he owes a debt (*giri*) to his parents for having brought him up and that he thinks it 'unforgivable' (*mōshi wake nai*) that he cannot provide them with descendants (literally, cannot show them the faces of their grandchildren). He says that he cannot get it out of his head that by telling his parents that he is gay, he will somehow be harming them.

Many of the men I spoke to do not regard their same-sex desires as particularly significant or interesting but they fear that if they were to make their homosexuality known to the people around them, they would encounter an unnecessarily extreme response. Hence, my interviewees tended not to adopt a confrontationalist stance towards friends and families and were conciliatory when faced with negative responses. As one gay man in his late twenties wrote to me:

> For some people, small things can become a huge wave and carry them away because the values that people place on different things are different ... It's to be expected (*atarimae*) that you can't always understand what it is that upsets other people, especially with regard to being gay. Although I've been rejected by my parents and beaten, I don't feel bad and live a happy life.

In many ways the above response is typical of other stories I heard from Japanese gay men. My informants tended not to 'other' heterosexual society in a confrontationist discourse which posited society and its institutions as somehow against them. Instead, many of the men I spoke to tried to understand why it might be difficult for others to accept their homosexual inclination. Partly, as Hiroshi mentioned to me, through coming out to one's family, one puts them in the awkward position of having to decide whether or not to come out to the wider society about having a gay son. As outlined in the discussion of marriage practices in Japan in chapter 5, friends and family actively interest themselves in a young person's future, particularly with regard to marriage. Thus, although coming out to one's immediate family may ease the pressure felt from parents to get married, one's parents themselves will still be bothered by inquiries about their son's single status. Hence, when a gay man comes out to his parents, he puts them in a difficult position regarding their social network: should or should they not disclose the reason why their son is not getting married? As one of Summerhawk et al.'s female interviewees points out, pressure to get married in Japan is felt not only by children of marriageable age but also by their parents. She says that at the time she was being pressured into marriage 'parents felt that their task of raising their children was not over until their children had married ... on the other hand, if a child didn't marry, parents felt publicly humiliated because it meant that they had failed' (1998: 98).

So, just as some members of an individual's social circle may see themselves as 'stakeholders' in the future life of that individual, a gay man may also see his own life as inextricably linked with that of his family and colleagues. He may not want to disrupt these important relationships by making a declaration about his private sexual life which is unlikely to be understood or accepted by the people around him. As another of Summerhawk et al.'s gay interviewees says 'All of us in our heart of hearts have a secret that we dare not reveal to anyone ... my secret just happens to be my sexual orientation' (1998: 68). Another man interviewed by Summerhawk et al. stresses that what he found difficult about coming out was not the 'gay bashing' that gay men abroad might suffer but rather, 'coming out for me was essentially about the shame that had to be faced' (1998: 149). In Japan, coming out as 'gay' inevitably means letting one's friends and family down by failing to conform to society's expectations.

When Japanese gay men come out, they tend to do so selectively. Both Tommy and Sato, for example, are out to their Canadian friends but have not disclosed their preference to Japanese friends living in Canada or back in Japan. Aki and Shinji, although a cohabiting gay couple with a high profile in Tokyo's gay scene, still put up an elaborate pretence about their relationship to family and neighbours. Some informants, such as Shin, are in the position of being out only to those men (foreigners) they have slept with and have no intention of ever disclosing their preference. Shin, like Hara, thinks that people around him suspect some problem and may even suppose he has a homosexual inclination, but in Japan there is great cultural pressure against vocalising these suspicions. This is nicely illustrated in the coming out scene in *Okoge* where Goh has to declare his homosexuality twice (the first declaration is ignored), the second declaration is greeted by his family rising from the table and carrying on a loud conversation about the weather while his elder brother practises golf swings. This kind of pretend nonchalance is evident in real life too.

Even when some men make a disclosure about their sexuality to Japanese friends and family, it is often received rather coolly and seldom referred to subsequently which leads many men to wonder what the point of telling one's family is if it fails to bring them closer or resolve misunderstandings. The reticence of many Japanese people to acknowledge diversity in human sexuality was definitely the deciding factor in the lives of Tommy, Sato and Hiroaki to leave and live outside Japan, where they have remained. As Hiroaki says 'I found moving to the US was the key to be me.' The disorientation that many Japanese gay men who have lived openly as gay while abroad feel when they return to Japan is eloquently expressed in this excerpt from an Internet chat page: 'I don't know if it's possible to be actively gay in Japan ... I'm Japanese and don't know if it's possible to be WHO I AM in Japan' (emphasis in original). This man, a recent returnee from America, later adds that 'I am forced not to discuss any matters that relate to gay people at work because it makes people uncomfortable.' This feeling of discomfort is common in Japan when aspects of life which are normally understood to be part of the private sphere are brought out and discussed in public. It is this reticence which leads men such as Tomo to argue that his same-sex attraction is as irrelevant to his family and colleagues as is their opposite-sex attraction to him, as one's sex life is not something that needs to be shared with others. In this respect, Kazuo is an interesting case in that he has never discussed his sexuality with his family and forbade me to even mention the topic in front of his parents. However, unlike my

other informants who went to great length to hide anything that
might be construed as remotely gay from their parents, his room is
packed full of gay-related publications which he makes no attempt to
hide. I took his mother's comment that 'That child [Kazuo] doesn't
like girls' as an implicit acknowledgement of her son's sexuality. She
was extremely circumspect in asking about both my 'research' and
about my connection with Kazuo, including how we had met, which I
took as a further indication that she knew more than she let on.
However, to have verbalised all this would have been a considerable
faux pas.

The author Fushimi Noriaki, in *Gay Style* (1998a) presents a short
essay on 'coming out' (*kamingu auto*) where he talks about the
unhappiness he felt as a teenager constantly having to change
pronouns from 'he' to 'she' when discussing his love life. He states
that first one must come out to oneself by considering that 'I will
probably always like men and if that's called being gay (*sore wo gei to
iu no nara*) then I'm probably gay (*boku wa gei na no darō*)' (1998a:
35). He then lists the advantages which follow on from this
acceptance: you can think about a man you like without feeling
bad; other people will come to think of two men having sex as
nothing unusual; you won't have to lie about your life at work; your
parents won't be kept waiting for you to get married; it will come
about that you will be able to walk down the street arm in arm with
the one you love; people will come to no longer regard two people of
the same sex living together coldly; and you won't be made fun of just
for not being masculine (1998a: 39). He argues that these advantages
will 'come about' through gay men acknowledging their same-sex
desires and openly expressing them through 'coming out.'

However, Fushimi, having previously worked as a musician and
recently become a gay rights activist and media talent on the basis of
the success of his first book *Private Gay Life* (1991) seems rather
optimistic about the consequences of coming out to friends, family
and workmates. It is clear that many of the men I interviewed do not
feel that by coming out, they will necessarily be able to live less
encumbered lives in the manner envisaged by Fushimi. First of all,
'being gay' is neither a simple ascription nor a unified experience and
it is clear that not all of my informants necessarily feel comfortable
with this label. Furthermore, Fushimi seems to assume that once a
man has 'come out' about his sexuality, his family, friends and
colleagues will simply accept the announcement, and their world view
will be suitably expanded, thus producing a more comfortable

environment for other men to come out. Unfortunately, declarations about their sexual preference seem to be met with silence rather than acceptance in the case of many of the men I spoke to. Sato's declaration resulted in a trip to the doctor, and was never subsequently referred to. Ichirō, partnerless, jobless, and uneducated feels he cannot take the risk of making a declaration about his homosexuality for fear of the adverse effect this may have upon the already strained relations which exist both between his parents and between his parents and himself. Driven to depression and a (possible) attempted suicide while at junior school because of his same-sex desires and failure to embody masculine gender, he had to suffer alone through the death of his first lover from AIDS while only eighteen. However, he feels unable to discuss this with *anyone* from inside his own world. His whole story came pouring out to me, a foreign researcher, on only our second meeting, while the people he has lived with all his life know nothing.

Other men, although financially independent, fear for their jobs or promotion prospects and maintain elaborate ruses to hide their homosexuality from friends and colleagues. Yet, some of my informants such as Hara, Tomo, Jirō and Satoru cannot really be said to be 'hiding' anything as they do not view their 'sexuality' as an appropriate topic of conversation. They do not feel that discussing their same-sex sexual adventures is necessary in much the same way that straight men who play around while married would not feel any inner compulsion to 'come out' about their inner identity as 'adulterers.' Indeed, what would Hara, for example, come out as? A gay man, a sado-masochist, or as a 'master' in SM interactions with male slaves? In a culture where sexual peccadilloes are understood to be 'hobbies' (*shumi*) or 'play' (*asobi/purei*), men such as Hara, Jirō and Tomo, for whom their same-sex sexual interactions are spare-time activities undertaken much as other men might plan a golf trip, feel no inner compulsion to acknowledge these activities in public, much less base their 'identity' upon them.

A further consequence of 'coming out' is that it sets up a false dichotomy between being 'gay' (*gei*) and being 'normal' (*futsū/nōmaru*). Men such as D.J., Tomo, and Satoru, who have all had sexual interactions with women and have not ruled out future heterosexual contact do not necessarily see their same-sex attraction as equalling 'gay.' It is by no means clear that simply producing another category, another label, that of 'bi' in order to file away their experience is helpful. These men all acknowledge a strong sexual desire towards other men, but strong emotional desire towards women; they are looking for different things from the different sexes, a differentiation which the label 'bi' does not acknowledge. They would consider themselves to be gender normative, and in all respects other than choice of bed partner to be ordinary men. The big danger in coming out is, as Halperin argues, gay people 'make [themselves] into a convenient screen onto which straight people can project all the fantasies they routinely entertain about gay people, and to suffer [their] every gesture, statement, expression, and opinion to be totally and irrevocably marked by the overwhelming social significance of their openly acknowledged homosexual identity' (1995: 30). This is perhaps why, as Lunsing (*in press*) suggests 'working without labels seems to be more effective because most labels have negative connotations attached to them.' All this suggests that Fushimi's neat evolution from self-acceptance to self-labelling to coming out to social acceptance is problematic.

Gay community

The extent to which the men interviewed feel a sense of community with other men who experience same-sex desire differs widely. Satoru, for instance, despite his same-sex attraction still speaks of gay men as 'other,' commenting that he feels 'disappointed in gay men.' It took him several months of correspondence with a gay man before he had the courage to meet him, feeling relieved to find out that gay men could be 'normal.' This is partly due to the media's distorted representation of homosexuality and its focus upon the gay scene's more exotic aspects. As one of Summerhawk et al.'s interviewees states, 'I only knew [Shinjuku] Ni-chome as a place full of weirdos and sex perverts, not only was I filled with a sense of embarrassment for wanting to visit there, but it required a lot of courage to venture forth' (1998: 47).

For many, being homosexual is simply about having sex with men. Yukio, Hara, Tomo and Jirō are primarily interested in meeting with other homosexual men in order to find sex partners. None of these men participates in the gay scene, preferring to use the Internet to make contact with prospective partners and set up sexual encounters. For example, Jirō came along with me one time to an international gay meeting but refused to come along the next week because he had not met anyone there who was his 'type.' Tomo was extremely explicit about why he had no interest in socialising on the gay scene. He told me that he was only interested in having further sexual experiences with foreign men and was not interested in making friends with foreign or Japanese gay men as he simply did not have the time for social activities. Hara, interested as he is in SM interactions, told me that it was a waste of time chatting up a man in a bar only to discover that his partner wanted to have 'ordinary sex.'

For many gay men, their first encounter with other gay men on the gay scene can be disorientating. For instance, there are many letters on Itō Satoru's Internet problem page complaining about the atmosphere in gay bars and clubs. One twenty-seven-year-old man writes that 'although I am now trying to find gay friends and lovers, no matter how I try, I just can't get used to the atmosphere in gay bars.' He finds the way in which many men on the gay scene communicate using camp speech (onē kotoba) alienating. Another man states that he hates the way in which conversation ceases when a new face comes in the door and that sometimes when he enters a bar, the way in which some men look at him makes him feel that he is being 'licked all over.' A twenty-year-old man who says that he has just 'debued' on the scene expresses confusion about the incessant questioning he receives as to his preferred 'type' and whether he is a penetrator (tachi) or a recipient (neko) in anal sex. He asks 'if I want to be a proper gay (ichinin mae no gei), must I decide these things?' Just because a man experiences same-sex desire, this does not necessarily mean that he will feel welcomed or at home in a gay bar. Indeed, several of my informants avoided Tokyo's gay scene because of its emphasis upon sex. Even though Tokyo provides extensive recreational space when gay men can relax as *gay men*, not all men who experience same-sex desire in Japan necessarily see this space as supportive.

For other men such as Hiroshi and Ichirō, however, socialising with others in gay organisations is an important part of their lives. In Hiroshi's case, being HIV+, he receives a lot of help and support from his gay friends and tries to contribute to the community by giving up his free time to work on telephone help lines and participate in discussion and support groups. For Ichirō, discovering a gay organisation and participating in its meetings has been a way for him to make friends and finally vocalise the pain and depression he has been experiencing connected with his own homosexuality, his experience of being bullied at school, and the death of his first lover from AIDS, none of which he can share with straight society, or even with his own parents who have become increasingly hostile towards him over his lack of direction and motivation in life.

Kazuo has found that the sense of connection and purpose in life that he once found in his relationship with his partner now comes from his international connections with deaf-gay men all over the world. He maintains regular contact with all his friends through e-mail and visits them at every opportunity, making at least three foreign trips a year at Christmas, Golden Week (beginning of May) and Obon (mid August).

Not surprisingly, given the number of *gaisen* in my sample, a number of my interviewees seemed to split their lives into 'gay' and 'straight' components along ethnic lines. Among those men living abroad, Tommy, Sato and Hiroaki all lived 'out' gay lives with their foreign friends (both straight and gay) but were very cautious about which, if any, Japanese friends they were open to. Sato, in particular, seems to feel that 'Japanese society' is incapable of accepting his sexual orientation, stressing that 'the Japanese community [in Vancouver] is a kind of extension of the society in Japan. So I have to be careful.' Other men who live in Japan showed a similar split in that they only had sexual relations with foreigners. For instance, the only people who know that Shin is gay are the foreign men (and their friends) he has slept with. Jirō and Tomo, too, only sleep with foreign men and say there is 'no point' in socialising with Japanese gay men (to whom they are not attracted). Thus, many of my interviewees feel a sense of connectedness only with men they are sexually attracted to. The more abstract notion of a 'gay community' based on a mutual subjective experience (same-sex attraction) or a shared experience of oppression was not a meaningful concept for the majority of the men I spoke to. Indeed, why would busy men like Jirō, Tomo or Hara, whose energies were almost entirely taken up by work be interested in talking to men who were not their 'type?'

A nice illustration of the differences between American and Japanese expectations of 'gay community' is given by the lesbian activist Sarah Schulman who was taken to several gay bars in Shinjuku Ni-chome during a brief visit to Tokyo in 1992. She was very surprised by the large number but small size of the bars where the same small groups of Japanese gay men would visit the same bars night after night. She wonders:

> Why would hundreds of gay people choose to come to the same building night after night and then divide up into privatized units of friends thereby ignoring the possibility of community contained within those walls? (Schulman 1994: 246).

She admits to returning home the next day 'bewildered' by her experiences of gay life in Japan which were in many ways so different from her experiences in America. The reason why Japanese gay men would prefer to break up into small groups to visit specific bars is, as is described in chapter 6, largely to do with wanting to meet specific sexual 'types' who have their favourite bars.

Sex and relationships

There is an obvious lack of uniformity among my informants regarding their attitudes towards sex, promiscuity and monogamy. Hiroshi, for example, describes himself as a very monogamous person who has no interest in casual sex. It is the cause of great pain in his life that because of his HIV status he cannot find a long-term partner. Ichirō and Shin, too, feel depressed because they cannot find a partner in Japan who is willing to commit to a long-term relationship. Aki and Shinji are in a long-term monogamous relationship much like a conventional marriage.

Other men, though, such as Hara and Tomo are honest about the fact that their interest in other men is primarily sexual. Hara is only willing to put time into a relationship with a man who is willing to play a 'slave' role in SM interactions, whereas Tomo is interested in having foreign sex friends with whom he can expand his sexual experience. He says he has no time for a relationship. Jirō, in a long term relationship with a much older man where the sex is subordinate to the affection, is on the lookout for 'sex friends' with whom he can have occasional non-committal sexual interactions. These three men had extremely active and varied sex lives. As Jirō said, he has had sex with over fifty men during his trips to Hawaii alone.

Yukio, having been disappointed by his first lover, decided to give up on relationships and instead cultivate a number of 'sex friends' met through the Internet. He finds this a more convenient way to meet people as he can contact his sex friends as and when he feels the desire for sex. As he said 'This week I might feel like doing it [having sex], but next week I won't.' Being a very young and attractive man, he has a large number of sex partners with whom he enjoys different styles of sexual interaction and is always able to find a partner when he feels the desire for sex. The way in which Yukio experiences himself sexually is very much structured by gay pornography. Sometimes, he and his partners will watch a pornographic video and simultaneously act out the sexual scenarios. Occasionally, he will get a new idea from watching a gay video and then contact a potential partner through the

Internet and suggest that they act it out. Yukio told me that although he has never had sex with more than one man at a time, he has had up to three partners in the same day. Other men I spoke to, including Jirō, also said that they often had sex binges, especially at the weekend or during holidays, during which they would have sexual interactions with multiple partners. Yet, other men I spoke to expressed their dislike of this kind of sexual interaction, Satoru going so far as to say he 'felt a repulsion' towards gay men after a number of one-night stands. It would be mistaken to say that the kind of sexual scenarios imagined in the gay media are entirely fictional. Many gay men do meet together regularly for extensive sex sessions with multiple partners in which pornography is used as a focus or a model for the interaction. Yet, by no means all gay men find this kind of interaction an attractive proposition and some men even go so far as to express a revulsion towards it. Attitudes towards sex, then, are as multiple among gay men in Japan as they are among straight.

Aki and Shinji are still in a monogamous, committed relationship, after eight-and-a-half years together which is considered to be an exceptionally long time by the people who know them. Kazuo, who was involved with his first lover for eight years, even ten years after his lover's death, still feels a resistance to searching for a new man to replace his lost partner. Kōji and Jirō, who have boyfriends living in Los Angeles, are not interested in having a relationship in Japan because they fear exposure to parents and colleagues. However, both would like to move to America to live with their partners.

Other men, such as Hara, Tomo and Yukio, are disinterested in relationships altogether, albeit for different reasons. Hara, since he is not interested in 'ordinary sex,' only wants a relationship which involves SM role play. Tomo, who describes himself as 'too busy' for a relationship, wants to seek out male partners to expand his sexual repertoire; and Yukio, disappointed by his first lover, has found that he prefers to seek out casual encounters as and when the mood strikes him. Informants such as Shin, Ichirō and Hiroaki, however, expressed a desire to have a monogamous relationship much like a conventional marriage. Unfortunately, they have not found it easy to meet such a partner on Japan's gay scene which is a cause of considerable dissatisfaction in their lives. None of them is interested in casual sexual interactions, stressing that they are looking for a primarily emotional relationship.

Significantly, several men draw distinctions between the erotic attraction they feel towards other men and the more emotional feelings they have for women. D.J. and Satoru have both been disappointed with the lack of emotional commitment they have experienced with their same-sex partners and contrast this with the more affectionate relationships they have had with women. Satoru goes so far as to say he 'felt a repulsion towards gay men for a while' after a series of one-night stands with men. Satoru, although clearly more interested in men sexually, intends to get married, partly because he is the eldest son of a provincial family but also due to the fact that he wants a 'companion for life' who, he feels can only be a woman. Both these men feel a lack in their relationships with men and express an intention to look for more emotional relationships with women, relationships which do not exclude but are not reducible to sex.

In fact, D.J.'s apparent openness to starting a relationship with a woman can be seen to parallel the desire some women have to seek a relationship with a gay man. Although enjoying his sexual interactions with men, D.J. feels that something is missing, a kind of emotional empathy that he used to experience with his female partners. He says that he may look for a companion among his female peers, with whom he is very popular. Although he is 'not sure' if he will still be able to perform sexually with women now that he is more sexually experienced with men, he is at least considering starting a relationship with a woman. D.J.'s apparent willingness to prioritise affective considerations over sexual satisfaction can also be discerned in the attitudes of some women who would prefer a gay man as their 'best partner.' Hence, it is not possible to say that the media discourse which presents gay men as women's ideal partners is *entirely* the product of fantasy as, at least in the case of D.J. and Satoru, there are some gay men who explicitly reject the gay media's (and mainstream men's media's) obsession with sex, and say they want a more emotionally fulfilling relationship, a relationship that they believe women are more capable of offering.

Marriage and family

Attitudes towards marriage are similarly very diverse. Kōji seems to have understood very early in life that his same-sex attraction meant that he would not marry and have children and this was a cause of regret, mainly because it meant disappointing his parents. Other men, such as Tommy, did not come to a decision that they would not or could not marry until much later in life. Kazuo, after the death of his lover, wondered for a time whether it might not be in his best interests to get married and even went so far as to discuss the possibility of marriage with several women. However, he eventually realised that his lack of sexual desire for women made marriage unfeasible. Tomo fully intends to get married in a few years when he reaches thirty. Satoru too, as the oldest son feels obliged to get married and was relieved when, as a university student, he found that he could be both sexually and emotionally responsive to women. D.J. has left the question of dating girls in the future (and maybe getting married) open.

None of my interviewees was married and they employed various strategies for explaining to friends and families why this was so. Some of the men (Sato and Hiroshi) came out to their siblings, whereas Yūichi came out to his mother. However, none of my informants was out to all members of their family and so occasionally had to fend off intrusive questions or offers of *omiai*. Jirō has made up a story about a romance with an American woman who he pretends to visit on his twice yearly trips to Los Angeles. He has pictures of himself and his 'girlfriend' (actually a lesbian friend of his boyfriend) in his apartment, but has no pictures of his boyfriend on display. Other men, such as Shin and Hara, resolutely ignore the questions about marriage. Hara, now in his mid forties, is so far past the normal marriage age that all enquiries have ceased (people assuming that there must be something wrong). Shin, however, is still bothered by such enquiries although he now thinks that his relatives suspect his orientation.

Unlike Satoru, whose desire to get married was expressed in terms of seeking a 'companion for life,' Tomo expressed his desire to marry not in terms of settling down with a lifetime companion but in terms of both social obligation and practical necessity. As the only son, his parents expect him to marry and, as he said, his busy workload requires that someone look after him (at present his mother). It is perhaps permissible to speculate that marriage to Satoru and marriage to Tomo would be quite different. Satoru is more like the image of the gay man created by women: a man who values love and affection over sex and role play. However, Tomo seems to have a more traditional attitude towards women: for him, a wife is necessary as a helpmate, not as an emotional or sexual partner. Satoru expresses his hope that he can give up his need for sex with men, whereas Tomo fully intends to carry on seeking out same-sex partners. These two men thus show very different attitudes towards their own homosexual feelings and their expectations of a relationship with a woman. Tomo clearly has much in common in his attitude towards women and the way he expects to treat his wife with many straight men.

Living situation

In Japan it is considered quite normal even for adult children to continue living with their parents until well into their twenties. Often, a child will not leave the family home until marriage and even then it is not unusual, especially in the countryside, for a married couple to continue to live with the parents (particularly in the case of an eldest son). Again, Japan should not be viewed as deviant in this respect, nor necessarily unusual. Kirby and Hay (1997), for instance, found that eight out of their twenty-one gay interviewees in Adelaide, Australia, lived with their parents and that younger, less educated working-class men were more likely to remain in their parents' home than their more mobile middle-class peers. However, although poorer young people in Europe or America may remain with their parents longer than they would wish because of financial constraints, in Japan many adult children still prefer to continue to live at home even when they have the economic resources necessary to set up their own apartment. As both Kōji and Tomo expressed to me, living in the parental home is simply 'more convenient.'

Cohabiting with parents obviously places restrictions upon an individual's private life. Of my interviewees, Yūichi, Tomo, Shin, Kōji, Kazuo and Ichirō all continue to live with their parents whereas Hiroshi lives next door to them in a self-contained unit. Jirō, who is thirty-eight, had only recently moved out of the parental home into a flat nearby. Of these men, Shin is committed to remaining in the parental home in order to look after his father which he sees as a duty which transcends any personal desire he might have for a cohabiting relationship with a male partner. Tomo's motives, however, are self-confessedly self-serving, he prefers to live at home because of the 'convenience.' As he pointed out to me, his work schedule is so busy and so unpredictable (as a telecommunications engineer, he must be on hand when problems arise) that he does not have time to care for himself and is totally reliant on his mother. Kōji, likewise continues to live at home because it saves on expenses, is convenient and also his parents expect it. When I jokingly suggested that his mother might eventually tire of looking after him, he seemed surprised and said 'oh but that's her job.' Even at the age of twenty-four, he will not stay out overnight and still calls his mother to tell her if he will not be returning for dinner. Kazuo had to move back in with his parents because, after his lover's death, he was emotionally incapable of getting by on his own. Unlike my other informants, however, Kazuo seems to feel no need to go to extreme lengths to hide his interest in homosexual issues, although he shares with them the reluctance to broach the topic in conversation. Yūichi, too, having only recently returned from the States moved back in with his parents but he is very keen to move out as soon as he finds a job and saves the money for a deposit.

The limitations of living a 'gay lifestyle' while living with one's parents are obvious. Several of my informants told me that they never read gay magazines or books or watch gay videos because they fear their mothers will discover them while cleaning. Some of the men who visited my apartment were very interested in my collection of gay books, videos, comics and magazines and obviously wanted to look at them; however they all declined my offers to lend them out. Apart from having to conceal one's reading matter, receiving and making phone calls to gay friends and partners is problematic. Tomo solves this by using a mobile phone which he can switch off (but which records messages) when it is not appropriate for him to hold a conversation. All of my informants living at home had to create elaborate excuses as to why a foreign man (myself) should be calling them in Japanese. I was thus explained away as an English teacher, a foreign exchange student, and a co-worker. The most elaborate excuse was that I was a friend of a friend's sister who had recently arrived from Australia and was looking for Japanese friends who spoke English! Only Yūichi explained me to his mother as a gay researcher who was interviewing Japanese gay men, an explanation which was met only with an *ā sō desu ka* (oh, really?). Given the difficulties of even holding a telephone conversation in one's own home, it is easy to appreciate the advantages that the Internet has brought to gay men who want to keep in regular contact with their friends as well as make contact with sexual partners. Of my informants living at home, all except Ichirō and Shin had Internet access in their bedrooms. Of course it is impossible to bring home sexual partners and it was this latter point which finally motivated Jirō, at age thirty-seven, to get his own apartment. His two regular 'sex friends' are both American men married to Japanese women and they had to meet for sex in love hotels. Even though Jirō now has his own apartment, he still has to be cautious as his mother, who lives nearby, has her own key and is likely to pop round in order to do some cleaning or stock his refrigerator.

For many men, not just leaving home, but leaving one's home town is the key to developing a more overt gay lifestyle. Aki and Shinji exemplify this in that they both left rural areas in Kyushu and Hokkaido in order to come to Tokyo. The mystique of the capital has been useful for them in explaining to their rural families their unusual living arrangements. Tommy, Hiroaki and Sato went one step further and left Japan altogether in order to live a more open gay life in North America. However, not all homosexual men feel the need to make such a decisive break with their family and Japan. There seems to be a connection between the extent that a man feels he has a 'gay identity' which he cannot express and his desire to break away from the family home and even Japan. Tomo, for example, who has no use for the term 'gay' and feels no connection with gay people or gay culture, is quite happy to continue living at home while having casual sexual encounters with foreign men in their apartments. For Shin, his filial obligations to his widowed father override any sense of a gay identity. Jirō, who only recently moved out, did so not because he felt he couldn't express his gay identity while living at home, but because living with his parents interrupted his busy sex life. Even Hiroshi, after spending most of his twenties in America and Hong Kong, has returned to Japan and moved in to his parents' converted annexe. Despite being gay and HIV+, he is still performing the role of eldest son and simply cannot bring himself to tell his parents about his situation.

The close connection between children and parents in Japan which continues well into adulthood is thus another factor working against developing what might be termed a 'gay identity.' Most of my informants were very cautious about possessing or displaying anything in their personal spaces, their bedrooms in the parental home, or even their own apartments, which might suggest a homosexual orientation. This means that, despite Nomura Sachiyo's statement to the contrary, most gay men in Japan are not free to express their sexuality through interior decoration and do not see their sexuality reflected back at them from books on their book-shelves, calenders and posters on the wall, or sex toys in their closets. Jirō is a good example in that he actually 'straightened' up his apartment with photos of an American lesbian friend who he passes off as his girlfriend. Although he owns his own place, it is only five minutes from his parents' house and his mother can turn up any time unannounced and let herself in with her own key when she comes to do his cleaning. He is therefore very careful to make sure that his gay magazines and videos are locked away in a box in his closet.

Ayres mentions that certain 'artifacts' of gay culture are necessary when manufacturing a gay identity or of representing what 'homosexuality is' (1999: 90). He mentions such things as pictures, magazines, porno videos, books, movies and television programmes. The close association which many of my informants maintain with their parents makes it impossible for them to display signifiers of their homosexual orientation in their living space. When they do possess gay artifacts, these are kept locked away and hidden which reinforces the understanding that sexuality is but one aspect of their lives to be compartmentalised and hidden away as opposed to an 'identity' which must be given voice to.

New technologies

Given that the majority of my informants were initially contacted through the Internet, the number of Internet users is necessarily over represented in my sample. However, Internet use is a growing trend globally and it is only to be expected that Japan, which is already a high technology society, will also see increased use of the Internet in the coming years. In chapter 6, I have already outlined the variety of information and services which can be found on the 'Gay Net' in Japan. Here I will discuss how the use of the Internet, e-mail and mobile phones has enabled several of my informants to better organise their love and sex lives.

Firstly, the Internet has enabled those men who are still living at home to have private access to information about the gay world in Japan and internationally. Both Kōji and Tomo live with their parents and are unable to keep any gay literature or videos in their bedrooms for fear of it being discovered by their mothers while cleaning. However, through the Internet, they are not only able to access gay websites which feature erotic pictures and stories but also contact friends and sex partners. Tomo is further aided by the use of a mobile phone which he keeps switched off (it records messages) so that he is able to choose when and where to respond to a phone call or not to respond at all. This use of mobile phones is similar to that noted among gay men in Hong Kong by Chou (1997).

Another convenient aspect of the Internet, apart from its privacy, is that it enables prospective partners to introduce themselves and discuss their hopes, likes, and dislikes before actually meeting. It is also possible to send digital pictures which enables men to decide whether or not their correspondent is their type. This obviously saves a lot of time and is more convenient (and less risky) than cruising a public place or chatting in a bar, only to discover that one's partner has different expectations or sexual interests. Hara, who is not interested in 'ordinary sex' uses the Internet as his primary means of meeting new partners. Another of my informants (whose biography is not given here) who shares Hara's interest in a specific type of sex, advertises his sexual services on an Internet information board. He provides this service free to men who meet his anatomical requirements. Tomo and Jirō, too, neither of whom is interested in a relationship use the Internet to contact and make arrangements to meet with their sex friends.

The anonymity of the Internet also enables men such as Satoru to communicate with other men in a safe environment without any strings or attachments. As he told me, after he first made contact with a man through a chat room, he was able to carry on a correspondence via e-mail for a few months before finally getting the courage to meet him. Once he had met his first 'gay man' he realised that gays were much like ordinary people and from then on continued to use the Internet to meet partners. The use of e-mail has also proved invaluable for men such as Kōji and Jirō who are carrying on long-distance relationships with their American lovers. They are able to communicate with their partners on a daily basis without arousing the suspicion that receiving frequent foreign mail would cause. E-mail is also important in establishing and maintaining friendship networks among gay men, particularly among Japanese who like to make friends with and date foreigners. Once these foreign men have moved on, it is easy to keep in contact with them. Kazuo, in particular, is networked into an international group of both hearing and deaf-gay men with whom he corresponds primarily through e-mail. Also the Internet is a convenient means of finding new friends and contacts before visiting a new town or country. Jirō was able to contact via the Internet several gay men in Korea before his visit to Seoul, one of whom became a sexual partner with whom he still corresponds.

Finally, although the majority of my informants used the Internet to meet new people, this technology has great potential for the dissemination of information. Kazuo, who is a professional computer programmer, uses his specialised knowledge to create and edit an Internet *minikomi* aimed at the deaf-gay community in Japan. As Internet use increases and younger people become more computer literate, it is to be expected that this kind of information sharing and community building through electronic means will develop rapidly.

Japan vs 'the west'

Virtually all of my informants drew sharp distinctions between gay life in Japan and in the west. The greatest distinction is apparent in how these men come out. In most cases they are out to a greater number of foreign friends than to Japanese friends. Sato expresses this distinction clearly when he writes 'Many of my Canadian friends know that I am gay, although few of my Japanese friends know that. Well, the Japanese community here [in Vancouver] is a kind of extension of the society in Japan. So I have to be careful.' Many gay men do not feel they can discuss their sexuality with other Japanese people. Hiroaki comments that 'In Japan, I was blinded as a gay person. I did not know who to turn to or talk to. I eventually decided to keep quiet about my sexuality,' adding that 'In the west it seemed less taboo to talk about gay people.' Anxiety about how the disclosure of their homosexuality will affect their relationships keeps many of the men I talked to silent.

One thing that became apparent as I discussed the issue of a 'gay lifestyle' with my informants was the extent to which they regarded this as possible only outside Japan. This was clearly expressed to me by Kōji who described to me the impact the film *Torch Song Trilogy* (Paul Bogart 1988) had upon him when he saw it, by chance, at age fourteen. This movie features a number of gay relationships in San Francisco, including a gay family where an adopted (gay) son lives with his adopted parents (a gay couple) (*see* the negative response of gay film-critic Osugi to this movie, discussed in chapter 5). This film did not encourage Kōji to imagine such a possible future relationship for himself; instead he had the very strong impression that such gay relationships were only conceivable abroad (*mukō ni aru koto*) and he felt the film had no relevance for his life in Japan. Indeed, ten years later, Kōji still considers a 'gay lifestyle' to be something that (although desirable) is only possible in America or Europe and is consequently extremely cautious about socialising on the Shinjuku Ni-chome gay scene or having sexual relationships with other men while in Japan, fearing exposure to his family and colleagues. Jirō, too, although maintaining several clandestine sexual relationships with other men while living in Japan, sees a 'gay lifestyle' (such as that lived by his American boyfriend in Los Angeles) as possible only in America. When he visits his boyfriend he moves primarily in a social world where everyone is gay and where he is introduced to his boyfriend's friends and family as his lover. However, when in Japan, he maintains the story that his reason to visit America twice yearly is to visit his *girlfriend*, whose picture he has around his apartment.

Kazuo also perceives western nations, particularly Australia and Holland, as better environments for living as a gay man. However, he has had a lot of contact not only with foreign gay men but foreign deaf and deaf-gay men, which means that he does not regard 'abroad' as some kind of paradise, he is well aware that other societies' tolerance of homosexual people or people with a disability is both fragile and provisional. Yet, he feels that the situation in Japan is so much worse, and the likelihood of change so remote, that it would be in his interest to leave Japan so he could be more open about his sexuality and interests.

Many of the men I spoke to who do not live abroad would like to. For instance, Jirō would prefer to live with his older lover in Los Angeles but has to content himself with twice-yearly trips. Kōji, too, would like to work in the US while living with his lover, but realises this is impossible and instead lives a celibate life in Tokyo, afraid that if he started a relationship in Japan it would be found out by his family. D.J. turned down an offer of employment by one of Japan's top banks despite his parents' opposition and instead took a job at an American bank in the hope that it would have a more flexible attitude towards its workers' lifestyles, and also hoping that he would be posted abroad. Yukio, too, rather optimistically, is looking forward to going to university in the southern US where he expects to find similarly relaxed attitudes towards homosexuality as exist among his young friends in Tokyo.

Needless to say, as is discussed in the next chapter, the acceptance of a homosexual lifestyle in Europe or America is tenuous, provisional and very geographically specific. However, the fact that many of my interviewees perceive 'abroad' (*mukō*) as a more open environment in which they can express their sexuality is interesting. As Hiroaki said 'It seemed almost healthy to be openly gay [in America]' but he goes on to stress that 'In Japan I was blinded as a gay person.' The extent to which 'Japan' is experienced as a constraining environment and 'America' understood as a liberating one is largely tied up with the expectations that an individual has about living a 'gay lifestyle.' If living with one's same-sex lover is understood as a central and definitive aspect of 'being gay' then, quite clearly, the Japanese social structure disadvantages men who wish to live together, just as it disadvantages unmarried men and women who want to do the same. However, if being gay is primarily understood in terms of preferring a certain kind of sex, then Japan is actually quite an easy society in which to live. Unlike many places in Europe and America, Japan's legislation has a hands-off approach to male-male sexuality and men can meet and form a variety of sexual interactions without worrying about arrest and exposure. Even when caught up in legal proceedings for some other reason (as in the case of the finance official described in chapter 3), same-sex sexuality is often described as a 'play' (*purei*) or a 'hobby' (*shumi*) and does not have the same moral valency as is attributed to it in the west. Homosexuality is not considered sufficiently serious to spark off moral panics, as happened recently in America, when a children's television character with purple fur and a handbag was denounced by Christian fundamentalists as setting up a gay role model (*see* the Reuters report of 22 February 1999, on Jerry Falwell's 'outing' of the Teletubbies character Tinky Winky). In fact, as outlined in chapter 4, explicit homosexual scenes are prominent in comics directed at young girls in Japan and a transvestite man can even be used in advertisements for a family theme park (*see* Plate 1).

Conclusion

Although my sixteen informants cannot be taken as representative of Japanese gay men in general, I think it is clear that none of the men I interviewed embody, in any very clear way, *any* of the stereotypes about gay men that are produced by both mainstream and gay media. The confidence with which Nomura Sachiyo claims that 'Gays are, as you'd expect, somehow woman-like' seems misplaced. None of my informants displayed any particularly feminine mannerisms and in many respects embodied characteristically masculine attitudes to-wards sex and relationships. Also conspicuously absent in the apartments of the men I visited were other 'artifacts' of their homosexuality, namely chandeliers, lace curtains and rococo-style furniture. The 'splendour' and 'refinement' that women are supposed to appreciate in gay men according to the *CREA* article discussed in chapter 5, were also absent in the lives of the gay men I interviewed. The gay man as he appears in women's media discourse is, therefore, largely a mythical figure.

Although several informants did report that they were often stigmatised for being too 'woman-like' while they were growing up, this was no longer a concern for them. With the exception of Ichirō and Shin, who were exceptionally mild-mannered and reserved, even by Japanese standards, all the men I spoke to seemed gender normative in that there was nothing in their speech, dress, demeanour or lifestyle that marked them as any different from their straight peers. As for the image of gay men as women's best friends and ideal partners, although both D.J. and Satoru expressed an interest in starting a relationship with a woman in the hope of gaining the emotional satisfaction that had so far eluded them in their relationships with men, my other informants either expressed total disinterest in emotive factors, or hoped to establish sexual and emotional relationships with *other men*. Only Satoru saw himself as establishing a companionate marriage with a female partner; Tomo, who also expressed a desire to get married, was quite cynical about his motives for doing so and had no intention of giving up his sexual interactions with men. Satoru himself admitted that he was required to marry as the only son of a provincial family, and so his desire for a companionate marriage must be placed in this context. Certainly, none of my informants expressed any antagonism towards women, but female friends hardly figured as important in their lives. Indeed, several of my informants barely had time in their busy careers to schedule sex sessions with their male partners, and none, other than D.J. and Satoru seemed to feel the need to look to women for emotional support not forthcoming from other men.

The image of gay men as sex maniacs prevalent in gay media has slightly more basis in reality in that many of the men I spoke to were open about their preference for a large number of sex partners (or 'sex friends') over and above one long-term companion. Although even this picture is complicated by the fact that men like Jirō had both a steady lover with whom they felt a substantial emotional connection while simultaneously using the Internet and foreign trips to maximise the number of sexual partners. Yet it must be remembered that some men explicitly condemn this kind of behaviour, finding it repellent. Hiroshi and Shin avoid the Shinjuku Ni-chome scene precisely because of its perceived emphasis upon one-night stands. However, Hara and Jirō avoid it for entirely different reasons, Hara commenting that there is no point chatting up a man in a bar only to find out that he is interested in 'ordinary sex' and Jirō preferring to negotiate sexual interactions from the comfort of his home by using Internet chat rooms. Hence, although some of the men I spoke to do frequently engage in sexual interactions that seem to be pornographically scripted (in that lengthy and at times explicit negotiations on what is to happen take place via e-mail), by no means all of them found this kind of rapid partner turn over attractive. It is therefore not possible to characterise gay men as a whole as overly interested in sex. Men such as Hiroshi and Shin endure long periods of celibacy, not because they experience less sexual desire, but because for them it is important that this desire be expressed in the context of a committed relationship; as Shin expressed to me 'sex means commitment.' Thus the cultural myths that structure the ways in which many people perceive homosexuality in Japan seem to have little relevance to the lives of those men who experience same-sex desire.

There are, however, a number of social realities that repeatedly occur throughout these narratives suggesting that gay men do face similar problems in relation to life in Japan, but how they deal with these very much depends upon the person. I shall discuss these briefly below.

(1) Most prominent among these is the issue of 'coming out' which my informants were, on the whole, reluctant to do. There were a number of reasons for this, the most important being a lack of a sense of necessity requiring public statements about private realities. Many of my informants saw no necessary reason to discuss their sex lives with family or colleagues as they regarded their sex lives as purely private matters.

(2) Tied to the difficulty of coming out was the issue of marriage. Because my informants did not feel that making a disclosure about their sexual orientation would make sense to their friends and families, they had to dissemble about their reluctance to get married. Although two of my informants had decided to pursue marriage to women as a viable option, most were reluctant to even discuss the topic. As outlined in chapter 5, marriage is not considered to be solely the concern of the individual but various other 'stakeholders' interest themselves in the marriage process, helping an individual to make sure it happens 'on schedule.' Thus, a number of my informants report difficulties to do with the marriage issue.

Various strategies are employed to defuse the situation. For instance, Jirō says he is in love with an American woman living in LA whom he pretends to visit twice a year. Hara resolutely ignored pressure from family and colleagues to get married until he was thirty five when, being so far past the 'scheduled' age, people began to fall silent on the issue, suspecting that something must be wrong. Shin, now thirty, has the convenient excuse for delaying marriage of having given up his job to look after his father. Kazuo can cite his disability as sufficient reason for avoiding marriage. My other informants Ichirō,

Kōji, Yukio and D.J., all being under twenty five, are too young so far to have to worry about fending off intrusive enquiries about their marriage plans.

(3) Not all my informants said they were interested in establishing long-term relationships with other men. However, among those who did uphold this as an ideal, a number of difficulties were mentioned. First and foremost was the difficulty in finding and establishing a relationship. Several men commented that most men on the Shinjuku Ni-chome bar scene had a 'one-night-stand' mentality which made them reluctant to go out and seek partners. As many of my informants were *gaisen*, there was an added difficulty in that foreigners in Japan tend not to settle there for life but move on to other places after a few years. Thus both Shin and Ichirō were in the unfortunate position of having been left behind when their foreign lovers returned home. However, this does not exclusively apply to Japanese men who date foreigners as can be seen in the case of Yūichi and his boyfriend. As the corporate structure of Japan's larger companies requires that employees be available to move around Japan without regard to their personal feelings, even relationships between two Japanese men can be disrupted by geographical relocation.

(4) Another factor limiting the kinds of relationships that gay men in Japan can create is time. Japanese men are generally extremely busy as I found when trying to schedule interviews. I often had to hang around in the evening for several hours in coffee shops near my informants' offices waiting for them to contact me to tell me when they could get off work. Few were able to tell me in advance when they would be available as it was rarely possible to know when they would be able to leave the office. Men like Tomo, for example, are so busy that they say they have no time for relationships, having to schedule quick sex sessions in their limited free time. Thus the amount of time men have to spend with their lovers is seriously circumscribed by work-related pressure.

(5) Many of my informants reported experiencing difficulty connected with their living situations. As pointed out earlier, it is considered quite normal for a son to continue to live with his parents until he marries and establishes a separate household. When living with one's parents is a possibility it is considered unnecessary or even unusual to want to move out on one's own. On top of this social expectation that a son will remain in his parents' home is the often prohibitively

expensive procedure of finding one's own place. The rents in Japan's major cities are among the most expensive in the world and, in addition, it is not uncommon for a new tenant to have to part with up to four months rent in advance in order to move in. Hence, many of my informants continued to live with their parents. Even among my informants who lived alone, the small size of the apartments and the social prejudice against unrelated men living together, made cohabitation an unlikely prospect.

The story of Aki and Shinji, who must pass as cousins in order to explain their unusual cohabiting relationship, shows that it is difficult to live with one's same-sex lover in Japan. Satoru explicitly rejects this possibility when he says that 'In Japan people would regard me as a gay man if I lived with a male partner.' According to gay activist Itō Satoru, the cohabiting relationship between himself, his elderly mother and his lover, has not been sympathetically received by the neighbours. He cites an incident when a neighbourhood gossip grabbed his mother's hand in the car park and pleaded pathetically 'You must not give in till Satoru is married' (Summerhawk et al. 1998: 80). He adds that the neighbours' hostile looks were so intimidating to his partner Yanase, that for a while he refused to leave the house.

Even if a gay couple did not mind the social suspicion that they would face if their cohabitation became known, it is no easy task in Japan to rent an apartment as a male couple. Thus, given the constraints on free time and the difficulty of living together in Japanese society, it is not surprising that some men express disinterest in establishing and working at relationships, preferring instead to schedule in sex sessions as and when possible.

(6) Several of my informants came from very provincial areas. Aki and Yukio were from Hokkaido and Shinji was from Kyushu. They all spoke of living a gay lifestyle in Tokyo which would be unthinkable in their home towns. Aki explicitly states that 'compared to the countryside, in Tokyo I have been able to become more free.' In fact, his provincial relatives' lack of understanding of how things work in the big city has enabled him to pass off his cohabiting relationship with another man as usual in Tokyo, when it is in fact unusual. Yukio, too, deliberately left Hokkaido and came to Tokyo in search of more freedom, a freedom which he found among Tokyo's large, young population of migrant workers.

Other men went one step further and left Japan altogether. Hiroaki says that 'I found moving to the US was the key to be me.' My informants locate the freedom that they experience with regard to their sexuality abroad in terms of North America's greater tolerance or support of gay rights. Living in gay-friendly environments in international cities such as Vancouver or San Francisco, they look at their more closeted peers in Japan, and feel that they cannot return without 'killing' a part of themselves. When some of these emigrants do return, they experience a difficulty assimilating into the Japanese gay scene. As Yūichi described, when he returned to Japan after having been socialised on the American gay scene, he had no idea how to relate to other Japanese gay men.

It is clear that there are social factors which structure and limit but also facilitate sexual interaction among men in Japan. Yet the extent to which an individual experiences constraint or freedom in relation to these factors largely depends upon individual expectations. If a man expects to live a gay lifestyle predicated on urban-American models of interaction, he will clearly find this difficult in Japan, just as he would find it difficult in small-town America. However, Japanese society, with its clearly delineated double-standard relating to male and female sexuality, provides plenty of opportunity for men to interact with each other sexually.

Chapter 9

Is there a Japanese Gay Identity?

Introduction

In chapters 3 to 6, I was concerned with outlining and analysing the various representations of homosexual men and the gay male body as they are constructed in popular as well as specifically gay media. The common representations of gay men as 'feminine,' as 'ideal lovers' or as macho sex machines are the cultural myths I refer to in the title of the book. In chapter 7 where I presented my interview data, I was attempting to show how the social realities faced by real men in actual daily interactions with family and workmates challenge these popular stereotypes. Although some gay men may consume these fantasy figures, they do not identify with them. These popular representations tend to homogenise gay men and present them *all* as feminine or *all* as obsessed with sex; therefore, I do not want to contribute to this process by suggesting that there is a singular reality or even a narrow band of social realities which would similarly homogenise gay men and their experience. In this chapter, I want to expand this theme of diversity by challenging the notion that there is an homogenous 'gay identity' which is conditioned and circumscribed by the same social forces. Human sexuality and people's responses to it are invariably multiple. There can be no 'ideal types' either homo- or heterosexual.

The sexual identity model

Problems with a model of identity based on sexual object choice are not limited to Japan alone. As outlined in the introduction, the very possibility of predicating a personal identity upon sexual orientation is a recently evolved notion limited to large urban areas of modern postindustrial societies. Thus, contrasting a supposed monolithic western 'gay identity' with weak or non-existent sexual identities in Japan is a flawed approach. Recent work by Dowsett (1996) and others has shown that even in supposed 'gay Meccas' such as Sydney or San Francisco, it is difficult to give empirical content to the notion of a uniform 'gay identity.' Dowsett speaks of the 'impossibility of identity' (1996: 274) in relation to Sydney's gay community in that the variety of sexualities subsumed under the trope of 'homosexuality' is so diverse, and the ways in which same-sex desiring men interact with the wider 'gay community' (if they do interact at all) are all so different. He argues that academic research conducted by lesbian and gay scholars as well as medical research into HIV/AIDS infection 'both box (homo)sexuality into a marginalized compartment within and from which little movement [is] possible' (1996: 274). The problem with perspectives that take 'homosexuality' as an empirical category is that 'They leave out what is difficult to fit into the picture. They delete the ambiguities we experience in relation to object choice and in the emotional-sexual relationships we make. They omit the ambivalence we experience toward our own and others' bodies' (1996: 274).

Other Australian theorists such as Offord and Cantrell (1999) also question the validity of gay or lesbian 'identities' arguing that they are rendered possible only at the price of conformity to 'fixed images' or what they call 'supra' identities (1999: 210). They point to the way in which gay media are complicit in producing, regulating and maintaining sexual identities where 'there is no space for ambiguity' (1999: 210). The existence of gay media, then, do not necessarily enable the expression of pre-existent and previously repressed sexual identities but themselves are necessary for their production. So, again, it is simplistic to argue that Japan 'lacks' sophisticated gay media in which gay men are given a voice as the existence of western-style gay media is very much predicated on western-style understandings of sexuality, selfhood and identity.

Issues of identity aside, Kirby and Hay (1997), also with regard to Australia, point out that living a 'gay lifestyle' outside of the safe areas provided by developed gay residential communities in major cities, is extremely circumscribed by the necessity to appear 'normal' in order to protect oneself from homophobic reactions. They also point out that only those men who can control who gains access to their living space are free to display items that might suggest a same-sex orientation and that many gay men regularly 'straighten' up their home before an outsider's visit. Many of the concerns discussed by their Australian interviewees closely parallel those brought up by my Japanese informants.

It is clear from my interview data that my informants all have very different understandings of sex, emotion, and their relationships with men and women. They experience the very 'ambiguities' which western notions of 'gay identity' tend to elide. Thus, D.J. for example is still considering whether to try to establish sexual relations with women with whom he feels a closer emotional bond than with men. Jirō, after an initial 'straight' period, now maintains a close (but relatively sexless) relationship with his older male lover while simultaneously meeting with two sex friends as well as regularly visiting Hawaii in order to make casual sexual contacts. Tomo is uninterested in 'relationships,' which he claims not to have time for, and is seeking out same-sex partners with whom he can expand his sexual experience; he still plans to get married. Aki and Shinji live in an enduring, cohabiting monogamous relationship and socialise as a couple on the gay scene. Hiroshi, Tommy and Ichirō are searching for their 'life partners' with whom they can settle down and build a home. Shin has put off his own emotional and sexual fulfilment in order to look after his father and Kōji would only consider having a cohabiting relationship with a male lover if he lived abroad. Hara is not interested in relationships or 'ordinary sex' but instead uses the Internet to contact prospective partners and negotiate a variety of SM practices. It is clear even from this limited sample of men that each has a very different way of expressing his same-sex attraction.

Mainstream Japanese media are also full of contradictory representations of homosexuality. I have argued above that in some Japanese media there is a conflation of same-sex desire, gender nonconformism and cross-dressing. Thus, young Japanese people who experience same-sex desire but who are 'ordinary' in all other respects, do not tend to identify with these cross-dressed figures. The relative absence in the media of discussion of homosexuality as an identity and lifestyle choice, whether positive or negative, means that Japanese people who experience same-sex attraction are unlikely to conceptualise themselves in terms of a politicised gay or lesbian 'identity.' Also Japanese society is more tolerant of same-sex intimacy (what Doi [1985] terms 'homosexual feelings,' or *dōseiai kanjō*) than Anglo-American societies which means that intimate relationships between age groups or between seniors and juniors are unlikely to be under suspicion. However, being perceived as too woman-like (*onnappoi*) can lead to bullying. In these cases, the boys' perceived gender non-conformity (dislike of sports, rough play and bad language etc.) caused them to be ostracised and abused with terms such as *okama*, *boigāru* (boy-girl) and *homo*. It is not homosexual attraction *per se* but its association in most people's minds with transgenderism which is the problem.

According to my interviews with homosexual Japanese men as well as coming out stories contained in the gay press and the Japanese gay men's life stories collected by Yajima (1997), an awareness that a 'gay community' exists usually starts with stumbling across a gay magazine which lists gay bars and cruising spots. Given that until the early-1990s, information about Japan's gay life was almost entirely absent in the Japanese media, many men who grew up experiencing same-sex attraction felt themselves to be completely isolated and even had difficulty envisaging how two men might have sex together. Thus, many men mention the extreme shock they felt when coming across gay magazines with their graphic representations of sex between men and promise of a whole world of homosexual possibilities. The gay activist Yanase Ryūta, for instance, says 'I shall never forget until the day I die the shock I felt when I came across pictures of nude men [in the magazine *Barazoku* he found in a second-hand book store]' (Itō and Yanase 1994: 169). He continues 'I was both delighted and surprised that I had found the thing I was looking for.' However, homosexual men coming across these magazines for the first time do not necessarily recognise themselves in the images portrayed. As Yanase says 'I noticed the word *homo* occurred many times [in the magazine] and I wondered what this could mean. I wondered if I could be called *homo*' (1994: 170). After checking the meaning in the dictionary and learning that it referred to an 'abnormal love' (*ijō seiai*), he felt 'I must on no account become this.'

More recently the role of the Internet in disseminating information about gay identity and lifestyles has also grown. However, the realisation that a community of same-sex desiring men exists and that organs of communication such as gay magazines, videos, and Internet *minikomi* and notice boards are plentiful, does not necessarily reassure all men who experience same-sex desire. For example, although Satoru first made contact with other gay men through an Internet chat line, it was months before he got the courage together to actually meet one of the men because of his image that gay men were somehow strange, their gayness being marked on their bodies. Participation in the gay community also requires a certain amount of spending power. Ichirō, for example, does not have the money to buy a computer and cannot access the Internet. He lives at home and cannot buy and keep gay magazines in his bedroom and, being unemployed and having a two-hour commute into central Tokyo, he is unable to even afford to drink in the gay bars of Shinjuku. Other men, such as Shin, although they have the financial resources to participate more in the gay community, often become disillusioned with its emphasis upon sex and one-night-stands, and participate in it only intermittently. Some Japanese men engage with this world only peripherally, using it to find sexual partners or services, for some it becomes their primary recreational space and others use it to find a partner and then drop out of the scene for as long as the relationship lasts.

However, those Japanese who do become networked in the gay community in Japan, and through the presence of foreign gay men, into the international gay community, are exposed to a new range of discourses. In the context of the gay world, there is the tension between some foreign gay men's 'political' construction of sexual identity and indigenous Japanese understandings of sex as purely recreational (expressed in Japanese as *asobi* or 'play' and *shumi* or 'hobby'). In other words, western, particularly American identity politics makes the personal political and in the case of same-sex desiring individuals accepts the mainstream projection that what is most important, unique and individual about this group is their sexuality, thus making sex speak for the entire person and inadvertently reinforcing the hetero/homo binary. Yet, participation in Japan's gay scene does not automatically result in the adoption of a 'gay' identity because of the very plurality of sexual types and terms which exist there. For instance, my informant Sato, who was active in Japan's gay scene in the early-1970s, pointed out that he failed to identify with terms then current such as *okama* because 'that implied something like prostitute' or with *gei* 'which was not used in Japan except in the term *gei bōi* which meant prostitute.' He adds, 'I did not think I was *hentai* (perverted)' and instead, seems to remember using the terms '*homo* or *dōseiaisha*.' Another informant, Tommy, who lives in Canada and socialises on the gay scene in Toronto, uses the word 'gay' to describe himself only when speaking in English but avoids using nouns at all when speaking Japanese, preferring to say 'I like men' (*boku wa otoko ga suki*). Most of the men interviewed by Yajima (1997) use the phrases 'my sexuality is gay' (*watashi no sekushuariti wa gei*) or 'my sexual orientation is gay' (*jibun no seishikō wa gei desu*), suggesting that for them 'gay' is a description of sexual acts rather than personal identity.

The less politicised stance of same-sex desiring individuals in Japan is made clear by the difficulty of finding a single term in the Japanese language that all same-sex desiring individuals, both men and women, identify with. Other than *dōseiaisha*, the Chinese-character translation of 'homosexual' which exists primarily as a sexological term, there are no terms to describe both homosexual men and women. Hanawa, who has done work on constructions of nationality and sexuality among Japanese communities living in the US, problematises terms used to describe sexual orientation in Japanese. She says:

> While the word *resubian* has had some currency in Japan since the 1920s, it exists in the Japanese language only as a transliteration and for the most part in terms of a discursive locus of social problems, not a site of identity... it is crucial that we understand the construction of sexual identity in a social-cultural context such as Japan, where the very idea of identity raises so many vexing problems (1996: 479–80).

Japanese has no single lexical item like the word 'gay' in Anglo-American culture which serves as a site of identity for both same-sex desiring men and women. Clearly, the term *okama*, which applies only to men, is inadequate because of its transgender connotations. *Onabe* (pan) was popularised during the gay boom as a parallel term for same-sex desiring women, but it never caught on. *Gei* (gay) is most often understood to mean gay men (as in the magazine *Za Gei* [The Gay]), and similarly, *rezu* is a term applicable only to women. Buckley notes that 'Japanese lesbians frequently speak of the difficulties in creating any shared agenda with the male homosexual community' (1994: 174) and this lack of a feeling of a 'shared agenda' is partly reflected in the lack of a term, inclusive of both gay men and lesbians, which acknowledges that the two groups might be connected. As outlined earlier, there are also no media which address gay men and lesbians as a common constituency. Hence, the fact that no unitary term has developed in Japanese popular culture which serves as a rallying point for all people who experience same-sex attraction, and there is no organ of communication aimed at both gay men and lesbians, means that such people are less likely to rally behind a label and, highlighting their sexuality, use it as a weapon in a confrontationalist-style social movement aimed at gaining greater sexual rights. They are more likely to negotiate their way around existing social structures rather than challenge those structures head on.

As I pointed out in Chapter 4, Japanese women's comics which contain many images of male homosexuality, often avoid any political discussion and tend not to label the boys as 'gay,' as their actions take place in a fantasy world where same-sex eroticism has been naturalised. Even recent works such as Ragawa's *New York New York* which depict gay men's problems in a homophobic society are hardly politicised; these gay men gain sympathy through the heart-wrenchingly sentimental situations in which they are placed, rather than on the streets shouting slogans. Likewise, the 'gay boom' movies are not univocal on nomenclature, *Okoge* (Murata Takehiro 1992) predominantly uses *homo*. However, when Goh comes out to his family, he says of himself that 'I like men' *(otoko ga suki nan dakara)*, only when this fails to generate a response does he add 'I'm gay' *(homo nan da yo, boku)*. Likewise, *Kira kira hikaru* (Matsuoka George 1992) avoids nominalisation, the 'gay' lead saying of himself that 'I'm a guy who dates guys' *(boku wa otoko to tsukiau otoko)*. It is his father-in-law who supplies a label, 'I heard you were a homosexual' *(kimi wa dōseiaisha da to kiitan)*.

The gay press too, as argued in chapter 6, is mainly oriented towards (sexual) entertainment and tends to avoid discussion of politicised issues. There are no glossy magazines like the American *Advocate* or Britain's *Gay Times* which focus on gay lifestyle and contain information about human rights issues. There is little support then, in either mainstream or gay media, for the idea of a specific 'gay identity.'

The sexual rights model

As I have outlined above, 'homosexuality' is openly represented in Japanese society, even in comics directed at young girls (a signifier of its harmlessness), but it is viewed as a form of fantasy or entertainment and rarely taken seriously. Yokoyama, interviewed by Yajima (1997: 82), reports that in the seven years that he attended classes in social work, homosexuality was discussed only once and 'at that time the topic was Sweden's family law.' When homosexuality is discussed in terms of 'human rights' *(jinken)* at all, it is often by Japanese men who live or have lived abroad. They view America in particular as being advanced in this respect with Japan lagging behind. The Japanese man interviewed by Kurigi (1996: 109) says that 'In America awareness of human rights is progressing, privacy is stressed,' whereas in Japan, he feels his private life is always under surveillance, people being overly-interested in why he isn't married. He concludes that 'If I returned to Japan I'd have to kill my selfhood' *(Nihon ni kaeru to jibun wo korosanakerebanaranai)*. When I asked my informant Hiroaki, who moved to the US while a university student, why he thought the situation was better for gays outside Japan, he commented:

> In Japan I was blinded as a gay person. I did not know where to turn ... or who to talk to. I eventually decided to keep quiet about my sexuality. In the west, it seemed less taboo to talk about gay people. It almost looked healthy to be openly gay there. In Japan, the situation is too far behind even for asking for gay rights.

Another informant, Sato, who lives in Vancouver, gave this reply to the same question:

> Here in Canada they [gay people] are much more open. There is an area in Vancouver where many gay men and women live ... you can see many pink flags on the balconies of their apartments which means the residents are gay ... I could not think of this kind of situation in Japan.

Japan is viewed by some gay Japanese men as a constraining environment and Europe or America are seen as more liberated 'others.' Takeshi, a university student studying languages in order to facilitate his escape from Japan, wrote to me that 'Last summer I stayed in Europe for six weeks. I felt that I would be able to live as a gay because Europe is far from Japan ... and one country I stayed in is very large minded in law.' In fact, although Japan has no legislation protecting 'gay rights' neither does it have legislation restricting sexual behaviour between people of the same sex and is therefore more open in a legal sense than most countries in Europe or most states in the US[33].

Japanese gay men who have come out abroad and been socialised into a certain way of being gay find that upon their return to Japan, that side of their personality has to be killed off, or cease to function. This is illustrated in the following messages from Toshi, a Japanese man, posted on the *GayNet Japan* chat line 'The ofuro' (23 June 1996 and 13 July 1996):

> Where do you guys meet young Japanese who are fluent in English and totally out in public? Isn't that impossible or possible? I was away from Japan for four years and have no idea how things work in Japan (e.g. dating and meeting people) ... I don't know if it's possible to be actively gay in Japan ... I am Japanese and don't know if it's possible to be WHO I AM in Japan ... (emphasis in original).

Having come out abroad, Toshi has been socialised into the American gay world and, as he says, has no idea how things work in Japan. Toshi's gay identity ('who I am') is quite literally silenced in Japan, as he explains in a further message:

> All I wanted to say was that people in Japan deny all the way about the normalization of gay cultures. It is always strange and weird in everyone's mind when thinking about gays in general. I am forced not to discuss any matters that relate to gay people at work because talking about it makes people uncomfortable. The culture here is not based on freedom of speech or press ... it is not about the individual issues like the case in the US ... a total individualism is not welcomed in Japan yet.

Had Toshi been socialised into the Japanese gay scene, he would not be so distressed at not being able to discuss his gay life with his colleagues at work. The tension he feels is a tension which comes from the collision of what he sees as the American 'freedom of speech' and 'individual issues' and Japanese society's reluctance to acknowledge difference (especially in a fellow Japanese). His use of the term 'uncomfortable' is significant, for Japanese people are rarely openly hostile to such issues as homosexuality; however by insisting upon introducing heterogeneous, individualistic elements into a work environment where they have no place, Toshi is disrupting the harmony or *wa* of the situation, resulting in an atmosphere of discomfort which anyone who has lived for a time in Japanese society will be able to picture. Toshi has polarised America's 'total individualism' and Japan's groupism. However, his contribution to the Net discussion was challenged in various ways by western gay men such as the American man below who challenged the perception of 'America' as a society which supports a gay individuality:

> Although the US is very aware of the Gay presence it is not an easy thing being Gay. Most larger cities have more tolerance for Gay lifestyle than the smaller cities. It is still very closeted in small rural cities around the US. For one thing the Gays are not very visible in small cities and therefore *most people are not aware that they even exist* (emphasis mine).

This contribution, denying that America was a gay Mecca and asserting that the same kind of invisibility affects gay people in some regions of America as it does throughout Japan was followed by another contribution (this time from a French man) proclaiming Japan as a gay paradise!

Regarding the concerns expressed by Yoshi [sic] I have to say that Japanese culture is much more homosexual than the western one. Not just in the past, as well advertised, but today ... Also, the very fact that talking about gays makes most Japanese uncomfortable is indicative that they are quite homosexual; that's basic psychology. The problem is that, in Japan, the persons do not respect each other the way we do. Much attention is paid to appearance, and whoever does not appear right might be treated like shit ... Anyway if you try to conciliate [sic] the above statements, you will have to conclude that homosexuality in Japan is on the verge of becoming fashionable and respectable. Just because so many people are doing it.

The latter writer seems to be making a distinction between homosexual acts (which, apparently he thinks are common practice in Japan) and homosexual identity (not appearing right) which is not. He seems to think that most Japanese are really homosexual and this is why discussion of the topic causes discomfort. Idiosyncratic though these views might be, this contribution and the preceding comment by the American writer do illustrate the difficulty of setting up binary opposites between a 'permissive' west and a 'repressive' Japan. As argued before, many foreign gay men feel less repressed in Japan than in their country of origin, not because of Japan's tolerance of homosexual behaviour but because all their idiosyncrasies are subsumed under the label of 'foreigner:' they are expected to be different, not to conform. A similar process may be at work in Japanese psychology. When a Japanese gay man leaves Japan and begins to interact as a foreigner in a foreign language, many of the constraints and expectations which are built into Japanese social relations fall away and he or she is enabled to express him- or herself without reference to expected norms and conventions.

Despite the above problems with the discourse of rights, American rights models of sexuality are often stressed in Japanese books which offer apologia for homosexuality: arguing that gays are a persecuted minority. Books such as Kurigi's *Amerika no gei tachi: ai to kaihō no monogatari* (America's gays: a story of love and emancipation) present the level of awareness of sexual rights in America as somehow more advanced than in Japan. Kurigi argues that '[in America] to be gay was to be extremely political' (1997: 1), suggesting that the high public profile of homosexual issues has had an influence upon government, economics, society and culture. Her reading of the situation in Europe is more romantic; she says that of the 'many' European gays she met 'all were freely celebrating their youth in a song of praise' (1997: 1). This may well be true for young, well-educated middle-class gay men living and working in fashionable locations in London, Berlin or Paris but fails to acknowledge the intense homophobia that requires a much larger number of homosexual men either to disguise their same-sex attraction, or leave their friends and family and head for gay-friendly spaces within major metropolises. Texts such as Kurigi's reinforce the image, prevalent in mainstream Japanese media, that western cities such as San Francisco or Sydney are 'gay Meccas' and encourage gay Japanese people to project a fantasy of liberation onto 'America' or 'Europe.' Several of my informants desire to leave Japan and live abroad where they can 'be themselves,' but do not seem to be aware of the very specific and restricted geographical and social locations in which this is possible.

Book stores now carry titles written by Japanese gay men and lesbian women about their real life situations, as opposed to books written about gay men and women as objects of interest. Many of them have adopted the Anglo-American discourse which posits 'homosexuals' as a stigmatised minority within a wider homophobic society and argue for their protection to be legally encoded much as are the rights of ethnic minorities. Itō Satoru (1996) in his *Dōseiai no kiso chishiki* (Basic information about homosexuality) argues such a position and draws parallels between the treatment of homosexuals, and the treatment of women, Japanese-Koreans, and *burakumin* (traditional outcaste class). For Itō, homosexuals are a stigmatised minority (between 3 per cent and 4 per cent of the population) whose civil liberties are ignored by a sexist and heterosexist regime. His book is written for 'parents and teachers' in order to give them a true account of homosexuality and combat the stereotypes found in the media. He refers often to American models of social action, particularly the use of the courts to uphold issues of 'human rights' but unwittingly supports a ghettoising mentality which 'others' same-sex desire onto a minority group. Although he quotes from actual life stories, his informants do not reflect the variety of sexualities which are subsumed under the trope of 'homosexuality' as evidenced in the life stories published by Yajima (1997) and those collected by myself.

The amount of material available in Japanese about homosexuality is now immense. Some of this information can be down loaded from the Internet in the privacy of one's bedroom, mainstream magazines (which can be read without attracting suspicion) still regularly feature discussions of gay-themed issues and book shops and libraries have many books available, both translated from European languages as well as written by Japanese themselves. This information revolution will surely impact upon how the new generation of gay men comes to understand itself. A personal communication from a man in his early twenties illustrates this point:

> Recently there seem to be more gay-related books being published than before but still I think that there are not yet enough. These kinds of books have been very useful in confirming the fact that I'm gay (*jibun ga gei de aru koto*). From now on there are important issues I need to think about in my own gay life (*jibun no gei raifu*). I can say that books which discuss the issue 'Why am I gay?' (*naze jibun ga gei*) are very important to me. Somehow, even with my gay friends I'm not able to discuss questions like 'What do you think about being gay?' or 'How are you going to live as a gay from now on?' I have no idea what other Japanese gays think about these things. Even if the number of other gays thinking [about these things] is small, I still want to know [about them]. So, I'd like you to make the results of your research known soon. I think it would be useful for some people.

I had similar problems as the man quoted above when I came to 'discourse' about sexuality with some of my interviewees. Many told me that this was the first time they had ever had such a conversation with anybody. Many of my informants were unable to vocalise what issues such as 'sexuality' or 'identity' meant for them and, although they had a passive recognition of many of the imported foreign terms for discussing sexuality, seldom used them in reference to themselves. This is largely because, as outlined earlier, sex is considered to be both a very private issue and also a kind of hobby (*shumi*) or play (*asobi/ purei*). Although sex is often joked about on television and is frequently represented in comics and magazines, the treatment is lighthearted and its purpose is entertainment not information. Although there is a large literature in Japanese which utilises academic and sexological concepts for discussing sexuality, it is generally only read by intellectuals or those feminist and gay activist writers who utilise these concepts in their own discussions between themselves and with each other. As this kind of material grows and the number of people coming across it increases, the 'internationalisation' of discourse about homosexuality both through the Internet and print media seems inevitable. However, as with other foreign imports, the American 'rights model' of homosexuality is being variously contested even as it exerts an influence on some homosexual men's self identity.

Another way in which rights-based discourses are beginning to break into mainstream media reporting, is primarily through the efforts of gay-rights pressure groups such as OCCUR (akā)[34] which employ tactics such as litigation, writing letters of complaint and organising parades in order to highlight what they perceive as 'gay issues' and to win increased media visibility. OCCUR is the most vocal organisation which supports a confrontational model of gay rights, and in 1991 became involved in a battle with the Tokyo local authority over its right to use residential youth facilities as a gay organisation (Pinkerton and Abramson 1997: 81–2; Itō Satoru 1996: 91–2; see also my discussion in chapter 2). Their victory in this case was hailed by OCCUR as 'a landmark ruling for homosexual rights in Japan' (OCCUR Internet page) but not all gay men in Japan were impressed by OCCUR's handling of the situation, stressing that it was the unnecessary self-outing of OCCUR's own members which had caused the conflict in the first place. My informant Kazuo, for example, who identifies himself as 'anti-OCCUR' clearly did not feel that OCCUR were fighting for his rights in their court battle and felt that the whole situation could have been avoided by displaying a little discretion.

OCCUR also has the most international profile of Japan's gay rights organisations and frequently sends speakers to overseas lesbian and gay conferences and seminars. Therefore many foreigners' understanding of the situation facing lesbians and gay men in Japan is mediated through OCCUR's own interpretation. Many of OCCUR's writers and speakers argue that in order for lesbians and gay men to achieve increased social visibility, the same strategies that have been used by homosexual communities in Europe and America must be deployed: namely coming out, group mobilisation and the development of a strong 'gay identity.' Yanagihashi Akitoshi put this argument forward at a gay and lesbian rights' conference held in London in 1999. His paper 'Towards legal protection for same-sex partnerships in Japan from the perspective of gay and lesbian identity,' as the title suggests, argued that the development of a gay or lesbian 'identity' was crucial if there were to be any social change. He stressed that 'a strong legal, political, and social movement based on an affirmative gay and lesbian identity' was needed to counter social resistance to change (Yanagihashi 1999).

Hence, some foreign commentators such as Barbara Summerhawk, who cites a number of works by OCCUR authors in her introduction to a collection of interviews with Japanese lesbian, gay, bisexual and transssexual individuals (Summerhawk et al. 1998), tend to give a rather negative evaluation of Japanese society and the social pressures facing lesbians and gay men. For instance, she says 'a majority of Japanese gay men live in contradiction, a constant struggle with their inner self, even to the point of cutting off their emotions and the denial of their own oppression' (1998 10–11). For Summerhawk, Japanese men who are closeted are attempting to hide what she terms their 'true identity' and 'this energy expenditure is often so enormous that it monopolizes their attention and prevents a healthy development' (1998: 11). A number of assumptions underly Summerhawks's negative evaluation of the situation facing Japanese gay men, the most problematic of which is that Japanese men who experience same-sex sexual attraction are somehow hiding their 'true identity' as *gay* men. However, as my own interview data suggests, sexual preference was not understood by my interviewees to be the most meaningful or significant site for personal identity. None of my informants struck me as emotionally repressed or in any way maladjusted. Although they were frank about the limitations that Japanese society placed upon their self-expression, they did not appear to be 'oppressed.' It is not surprising then, that some of my informants who are aware of OCCUR's activities do not see their own experience reflected in this kind of discourse.

Members of OCCUR and those western writers who use OCCUR's texts when reporting the situation facing same-sex desiring individuals in modern Japan do not appear to be aware of the cultural specificity of the terms they deploy. As Knopp points out:

> The gay liberation movement is … a product of ethnically European culture at a specific point in history. It by no means expresses or defines homosexual identities and experience in non-Western or non-contemporary contexts (1990: 21).

Thus, it is not surprising that there are many gay men in Japan who do not see the relevance of this kind of discourse to their own lives. The social realities which contain and condition their expression of same-sex sexuality differ markedly from those in some western countries, hence there can be no universal injustices which all 'gay' men need 'liberating' from. Altman, then, is probably right when he states that in non-western countries 'gay identities may emerge in different ways and without the overtly political rhetoric of the West' (1996: 91).

I found that the number of men in my interview sample who were involved in gay organisations, or expressed an interest in getting involved was extremely small. This is not necessarily to do with passivity or the Japanese tendency to put up with (*gaman suru*) difficult situations, but arises out of a specific understanding of the social significance of same-sex desire. The following personal communication from a man in his early forties is interesting:

> Because I think that being gay is a personal problem (*gei wa pāsonaru na mondai*) I don't think that stressing rights is useful and I cannot agree with gay-lib thinking (*geiribu teki kangae*). It's important to fight against prejudice but it's better to do this quietly. I could live happily if people could just understand that homosexuality (*dōseiai*) isn't especially unusual but is just one kind of love.

This man simply wants his same-sex attraction to be acknowledged by the wider society. He sees his orientation as a personal issue which should not have consequences for how he is treated by others. This man's assertion that 'being gay is a personal problem' is not so different from a point emphasized in Dowsett's study of the Sydney gay community where he notes that many men stressed that 'being gay is simply a personal and emotional state' (1996: 15). Even for many Australian gay men, being gay is about social (who one socialises with) and sexual (who one has sex with) issues and has few implications for a wider 'political' identity.

The issue of 'gay liberation' (*geiribu*) is also frequently debated on the gay activist Itō Satoru's homepage *Sukotan*. One twenty-three-year-old man writes that:

> I know a guy who is involved in 'gay lib' (*geiribu*) and it feels like all he goes on about are 'gay rights' (*gei no jinken*), all he does is argue. If you're gay (*gei datte*) you can do anything you want with regard to love (*ren'ai*) and sex (*sekkusu*), so is it really necessary to go on about gay lib? Why is it necessary to support gay lib?

The man cited above considers 'being gay' to reside in the choice of a same-sex love partner and sex acts and does not seem to feel that there are constraints in Japanese society restricting who you love or have sex with. Itō's lover Yanase Ryūta, who also shares his home page, notices this and comments that the above writer has too narrow a definition of 'being gay.' He suggests that being gay is not limited simply to who you choose to sleep with but has wider social ramifications. He states that 'You say that "you can love and have sex, so what's the problem?" But is it really the case that it's easy to live as a gay man in this world?' Itō himself then adds instances of how gay men are restricted in Japanese society, pointing out that a gay couple cannot walk down the street hand-in-hand, or kiss each other goodbye, or check into a love hotel. Also he says that most gay men must put up a pretence of being straight in front of workmates and neighbours which is an intolerable situation and that 'I want to live as a gay (*gei toshite ikitai*) in a more relaxed manner.' However, as pointed out earlier, Itō and Yanase are very public figures who have become media talents solely on the basis of being an 'out' gay couple[35]. It is not the case that all gay men in Japan necessarily feel the need to be so open about what they consider a private aspect of their lives, for, through coming out, many men feel they are thereby associated with the negative stereotypes about gay men which exist in the wider community. Wim Lunsing also found a similar reluctance among many of his informants to get involved in political activities concerning their sexuality. He comments that 'the reasoning is that homosexuality can be engaged in freely by all those who choose to do so and therefore little need is felt to engage in political activities' (1998: 285). Yet, like Itō and Yanase, Lunsing also points out that this 'freedom' is seriously circumscribed by social conventions regarding time and place and that homosexual behaviour must be engaged in 'wholly privately, beyond the scrutiny of significant others' (1998: 285).

The reluctance to come out and thereby be associated with negative stereotypes is echoed in another personal communication, this time from a man in his late twenties who writes, 'I'm not "a gay" but "a person," (*gei de naku hito deshō*) but the people around me won't think this way.' Just like this man, many other Japanese homosexual men resist the fetishisation of sexual-object choice both by gay organisations as well as society at large, and insist on being viewed simply as people, stressing that their 'same-sex attraction' is not especially unusual or different. These men do not have an agenda on social or family reform. The views of these gay men largely support Jennifer Robertson's contention that 'As long as an individual's sexual practices do not interfere with or challenge the legitimacy of the twinned institutions of marriage and household, Japanese society accommodates – and in the case of males, even indulges – a diversity of sexual behaviors' (1998: 145). What is important is that marriage and the household 'must not be compromised by a politicized sexual identity.' It is for this reason that Lunsing (*in press*) discusses both 'out' gay men and feminist women as facing similar problems in Japan with regard to their freedom of sexual expression, for both groups are stigmatised, not so much because of their chosen sexual acts, but because of their perceived opposition to conventional family role play. One of Yajima's (1997: 121) informants, a left-wing activist, sees just such a political connection between himself as a gay man and feminist women: 'Although I have not had sex with a man at present, if I had to choose between gay (*gei*) and bi (*bai*), politically speaking (*seijiteki ni wa*), I would choose gay,' because, as a label, he says it directly confronts Japan's family system. However, as outlined above, the predominant discourse about sexuality in Japan which constructs sex as a kind of hobby or play, works against the understanding of homosexuality as a political identity.

Young Japanese gay men who might be expected to be more in sympathy with this political discourse are not necessarily more outspoken or radical than older gay men. One personal communication from a man in his late teens states 'In today's Japan (among young Japanese) there's a feeling of anything goes so with regard to homosexuality (*dōseiai*) there's a feeling of tolerance. Sometimes it's made fun of ... but it's not especially rejected.' He looks forward to a time when the changes which are already taking place in Japanese society will mean that 'people won't be disliked simply because they're gay, I think it will become a society in which we can live proudly.' Like many Japanese gay men, he does not think that group action pushing for gay rights will be beneficial. In this respect his opinion is close to that of my twenty-year-old informant Yukio among whose circle of young part-time working friends, his homosexuality was very much a non-issue.

Although there clearly are restrictions in Japan on the extent to which a man can live an openly gay lifestyle, just as there are in Europe or America, it is by no means clear that gay men in Japan necessarily feel repressed or disadvantaged. As argued above, Japan places no legal restrictions on same-sex sexual acts, it does not pass legislation policing what can and can't be said about homosexuality in schools, it does not prohibit gay men from serving in the armed forces and it does not have prominent religious-backed politicians preaching a politics of hate against homosexuals on television and in the newspapers[36]. Incidences of homophobic violence in Japan are also rare. As Lunsing comments, although a man who outs himself to family and colleagues may be regarded as an extra-terrestrial. 'ET is, however, a rather likeable creature, which suggests that even if one is not readily understood, one does not necessarily encounter negative reactions' (*in press*). Thus, the cultural context in which homosexuality exists in Japan is rather different from western countries where homosexual groups must fight against their legally disadvantaged status, where gay men are subject to homophobic attack both in the streets and in the media and where any ground that homosexual organisations are perceived to have won often sets off moral panics.

Conclusion

Some Japanese homosexual men reject the idea that the American 'right's model' is an appropriate strategy for improving the situation for gay men in Japan. For example, Tanaka, interviewed by Yajima (1997: 178) argues that the social situation facing Japanese homosexuals is entirely different from that in Europe and America. Japanese gays do not face the systematic persecution instituted by government, church and legal system which affects many foreign gays. He says that in Japan, men are not punished simply for being gay and so as long as one remains in the closet it is possible to go on living a secret life. This is echoed by an informant of Summerhawk et al.'s who says that 'Japan has a very different history when it comes to discrimination ... I have never had to face termination of employment because I was gay ... I [have] never come across talk of someone being thrown in prison because he was gay ... there is no religious concept of homosexuality as a vice' (1998: 153). Hence, Japanese people find it hard to understand the concept of 'gay rights.' As he says 'For me personally in Tokyo, subscribing to this concept is like carrying someone else's baggage' (1998: 153).

Many of the Japanese gay men I met feel uneasy with the nominalising discourse of 'gay rights' professed by OCCUR and, increasingly, in books written by Japanese gay activists because it associates them with a stigmatised minority surrounded by myths and misrepresentations. Life stories of Japanese homosexual men describe a conflict between the desire for increased social space and visibility and the enforced ghettoisation and stereotyping which often follows upon coming out. Like many stigmatised social groups, individual gay men are often read in terms of the myths and stereotypes which surround the group as a whole. By outing themselves, they do not necessarily create more space and visibility but ally themselves, in the public imagination at least, with a number of negative images and stereotypes which actually hinder their self-expression. No frame exists for the presence of gay men or women in Japan other than the gender-deviant *okama/rezu* of the entertainment world. So far, the 'family' has not been adopted as a possible or even desirable model for gay relationships. This is perhaps why many Japanese gay men and women prefer to keep two faces, a 'straight' face in front of work-mates and family, and a 'gay' face when socialising in the gay community (such as it exists).

Other strategies also exist, such as leaving Japan to live a more open gay lifestyle abroad while maintaining a straight face with family and friends in Japan. It is by no means clear that American-style 'coming out' which accompanies the demand for sexual rights is the most appropriate strategy for creating the space to express same-sex sexuality in Japan. If the diversity which exists among same-sex desiring men in western societies is sufficient to problematise the notion of a coherent gay identity even in the developed gay communities of major cities such as San Francisco and Sydney, positing such an identity in Japan, where no such community exists, is even more difficult.

Afterword

From the preceding discussion of male homosexuality in Japan, it should be clear that I am broadly in agreement with Jennifer Robertson who has analysed the role of lesbianism in popular discourse, particularly that surrounding the all-woman Takarazuka theatre. She argues that:

> Historically in Japan and elsewhere, sexual practices have not presumed a specific sexual orientation or identity, although today, some lesbian and gay activists and homophobic critics alike tend to fuse the two (1998: 174).

Robertson's work on the Takarazuka shows that although many of the women involved in the Revue as either actors or fans will hint at same-sex sexual practices, they will not claim a 'lesbian identity' in their everyday lives (1998: 174). Similarly, I have argued that many 'gay' men deny the fact that their same-sex sexual preference *necessarily* signifies a separate or distinct identity. In so doing, they have much in common with earlier Japanese paradigms of sexuality in which gender performance and not sexual-object choice was considered to be socially significant. What is new in modern Japan is the growing idea that there is a small, discrete number of same-sex desiring men who constitute a social minority. Same-sex desire is considered deviant and it is no longer the case that most Japanese accept same-sex desire in either men or women to be a common occurrence. Indeed, the word 'normal' *(nōmaru* or *futsū)* is commonly used to describe 'heterosexual' people whereas the deviant same-sex desiring 'others' are referred to with a variety of contradictory and confusing terms in which gender-inversion and same-sex desire are often conflated.

However, this 'deviant' model is also contested within popular culture, especially in media directed at women. Here, homosexual men are considered to have an affinity with women, because of some supposed interior androgyny which makes them better dressers, better cooks and even better partners than their straight counterparts. In

Karen Kelsky's (in progress) terms, gay men become 'rhetorical mirrors' reflecting straight men's deficiencies and it is straight men and their desires which are represented as deviant (in the literal sense of deviating from what women actually want). Japanese female consumers in fact provide a large market for a variety of cultural products which dissociate gender from biological sex and disrupt mainstream discourses of normative heterosexuality. In *shōnen'ai* manga, the highly idealised love stories between beautiful young boys live up to the romantic tropes that real heterosexual relationships consistently disappoint. In 'gay boom' movies such as *Okoge* (Murata Takehiro 1992) and *Kira kira hikaru* (Matsuoka George 1992), gay men become women's perfect partners because only a relationship with a gay man can circumvent the sexist scripts which position women as passive objects for male manipulation. The *bishōnen*, cross-dressed boy-band members and Takarazuka *otokoyaku* popular with women, represent idealized, androgynous figures who can embody aspects of both genders while transcending the fixed, normative parameters of mainstream gender roles. Of course, none of these figures really represents actual 'homosexual' men, but then same-sex attraction and gender nonconformism are not the sole possession of such men, and it is only recently in Japanese history that they have become conflated.

The minoritizing discourse of homosexuality professed by some gay rights activists, which posits gay men as a social sub-group identified (and stigmatised) by their same-sex attraction, obscures this widespread interest in and representation of same-sex sexuality and gender nonconformism in Japanese culture. This interest, however, exists only to the extent that these images remain within the frame of the entertainment world. There is much resistance to the politicisation of both sex and gender, whether by gay men, lesbian women or feminists, and it is for this reason that many homosexual men prefer to maintain a conformist outward identity, while enjoying their private gay life.

Among the many social factors identified which condition gay men's self-expression was marriage, a key Japanese institution which many gay men had ambivalent feelings about. However, not all same-sex desiring men necessarily understand their homosexuality as disqualifying them from marriage. Also, some Japanese women clearly do not consider a man's same-sex attraction to render him ineligible as a marriage partner and use the personal ads in gay magazines in an attempt to make contact with gay men. For some women, a man's homosexual inclination renders him more attractive because of his perceived empathy with a woman's subordinate position and supposed willingness to negotiate roles within marriage. However, these women are not supporting homosexuals' right to marry each other but are insisting that such issues as sexual attraction are of minor significance when establishing a marriage relationship with one's life partner. They envisage marriage as transcending not simply gender, but also sex, representing it as a bond between two spirits, not bodies. Such a relationship is very much a fantasy, and is contested by other women who see marriage to a gay man as simply a better deal than marriage to a straight man. Marriage as role play is now being contested by a new model which posits empathy or love as the defining aspect of 'marriage' and 'family.' The gay boom movies represent the relationships between gay men and straight women as authentic because of the empathy which develops between the partners. Women and gay men are seen as natural partners because both are shown to be constrained by the patronising and sometimes violent demands of a sexist and heterosexist society. The conservative nature of this discussion is evident in that mainstream media often discuss the advantages of marriages between gay men and straight women but seldom entertain the idea that gay men might marry each other.

Based on the above, I have argued that the idea that same-sex desire necessarily entails a distinct and separate sexual identity which disqualifies certain individuals from participating in mainstream social institutions such as marriage is expanding, but it is far from universal. Certainly not all the same-sex identified men I spoke to consider this attraction to disqualify them from marriage and living a 'normal' life. There seems to be a split between homosexual men in Japan, some adopting the American-style confrontational model of identity politics and others preferring to negotiate around existing social practices and institutions. Many Japanese men find the idea of two men romantically involved setting up house together and adopting children to be quite strange as the only socially acceptable roles available for cohabiting couples in Japan are those of husband/ father and wife/mother. However, other Japanese men I spoke to would like very much to set up a stable home with a partner but feel unable to do this in Japan where same-sex cohabiting couples are viewed with suspicion and find it hard to rent accommodation. These differences are obviously connected with individual psychology but are also influenced by social discourses. It is not surprising that the 'identity' model discussed above is most prevalent among informants who live or have lived outside Japan, although even these men tend to live in two worlds, an 'out' world incorporating their friends and colleagues abroad and a 'closeted' world including their friends and families in Japan.

In Japanese society the two paradigms of homosexuality as *act* (it is something that you do) and *identity* (it is something that you are) coexist. The traditional nature of personal identity (defined through social role) and the prioritisation of exterior (role) over interior (desire) in Japanese society make it easier for same-sex desiring men to marry women and define themselves through social roles rather than sexual acts. However, a new discourse which prioritises individuality (*jibunrashisa*) has come to challenge this definition, arguing that marriage is not about role but about feeling. This definition actually works to exclude heterosexual men from establishing true relationships with women because, as sexist oppressors, they cannot support a woman's individuality. These two constructions are in conflict. The first suggests that a gay man's sexual preference is irrelevant to the adequate performance of the social roles father/husband because being a father/husband is just that: a role. The latter suggests that a man's same-sex desire somehow regenders him, removing him from the oppressive/patronising role of 'man,' and making him a kind of androgynous intermediary between the sexes and thereby a woman's ideal partner. Homosexual men in Japan are aware of being trapped in someone else's discourse. One man interviewed by Yajima (1997:178) comments that the 'gay boom' is really about Japanese women facing their own sexuality by constructing 'a fantasy which refuses the distortions and bad influences thrust upon them by male society (*dansei shakai*).'

Unlike America or Europe where there are a variety of discourses which seek to define the meaning of same-sex love, some of which are controlled by homosexual people themselves, in Japan these discourses are primarily the product of heterosexual fantasy. Although Japan does have extensive gay media, they reflect the general tendency in Japanese society to treat sexuality as a form of entertainment; this has resulted in homosexual men being largely caught up in other people's projections which either ridicule them or idealize them. Unlike some western countries, Japan has exceedingly few organisations or facilities where gay men can meet for purposes other than sex. If a gay man wants to meet other gay men, he has to go to bars or cruise spots: further emphasising the idea that homosexuality is simply about sex. There is then, little in the way of a gay community, outside of the entertainment industry, where gay men can meet and resist these controlling discourses. To this extent, Japan is not unique but compares with other Asian societies, particularly China (studied by Chou 1997) and Thailand (Miller 1993 and Jackson 1995). Neil Miller comments on his pursuit of gay and lesbian identities throughout Asia and Africa that 'Western dichotomies of "gay" and "straight" just didn't seem to fit in. Attempting to build a Western style gay and lesbian movement in cultures where categories based on sexual identity were traditionally unknown was a dubious venture' (1993: 141). To a certain extent, the same problem with nominalising sexual terminology also applies to Japan where men who experience same-sex attraction do not necessarily prioritise this when developing a self identity or when presenting themselves to the outside world.

Limited though my discussion has been, I hope it is clear that there currently exist a variety of discourses competing to position 'homosexuality' in Japan. There has been a gradual movement away from early-modern understandings of same-sex love as merely one 'way' of loving which could be taken up or cast off much as one might change style in clothes, to a characterisation of homosexuality as a series of deviant and undisciplined acts, and finally to the very recent understanding of the 'gay' man as possessing a specific identity, an identity which he shares with other gay men as a member of a 'minority.' However, cultural representations of same-sex love are extremely varied and receive very different treatment according to the context in which they are portrayed.

Rarely, in any Japanese media outside the gay press and the Internet, are ordinary gay men themselves given a voice. One objective of this book has been to attempt to listen to Japanese homosexual men and let them speak about who they are. Ironically, this attempt has been flawed from the outset because there is no genuine, univocal 'homosexual' standpoint from which such subjectivity can be elucidated. I do not mean to suggest that we are totally free agents like the heroes of the morph cartoons who can change identities at will; identities *are* negotiated, but not from an infinite range of choices. Rather, choice must be made from the very limited number of blueprints available in specific cultures and time periods. I hope I have been able to go some way in describing the resources currently available in Japanese culture which homosexual men variously appropriate and resist in constructing and negotiating who they are.

Notes

1 At this time France was one of the few European nations which did not legislate against sex between men. Laws relating to consenting sexual acts between men had been dropped after the Revolution and the Code Napoleon of 1810 did not reinstate them, instead it became 'the model for the repeal of the medieval [sex] laws throughout the civilised world' (Johansson and Percy 1990: 424).

2 For example, Murray (1994: 420) describes him as 'a gay man with a taste for rough trade despite the fact that he was married with two children.' He describes Mishima's novel *Kinjiki* (Forbidden colours) as 'a gay love story,' a bizarre reading given that the only characters who can be described as 'in love' are the two women whom the gay 'hero' leads on only to betray.

3 However, my informant D.J. told me of a school-boy experience exactly paralleled by an incident described by Mishima in *Kamen no kokuhaku* (Confessions of a mask) where the hero is electrified by the sight of an older boy's under-arm hair as he worked out on the cross bar. When D.J. read this book he was struck by the many similarities between the homoerotic environment of the hero's school and his own.

4 A collection of photos of Mishima, either naked or clad only in a traditional *fundoshi* (loin-cloth) in a variety of painfully self-conscious 'erotic' poses was published by the photographer Hosoe Eikō under the title *Barakei* (Ordeal by roses) in 1963. Long (1996: 221) suggests that the argot term for homosexuals, *barazoku* or 'rose clan' (now the title of Japan's oldest gay magazine) derives from this collection.

5 *Seken* is an important term which constantly recurs in the biographies of my interviewees as well as in published literature about the difficulties of living a gay, or indeed any nonconformist lifestyle in Japan. It suggests the prying eyes of the neighbourhood or the community who use peer pressure to enforce social conformity by stigmatising not just the nonconformist individual but also his or her family. One of Ōhama's (1994) non-gay informants gives a graphic definition of how concern about *seken* interfered with his life:

> I just hate this word (*sekentei* [social respectability]). You can't do anything when you are stuck with social respectability ... I made a mistake in my entrance exams for university: you know I spent two years trying to pass entrance exams. I was so concerned about my parents' reputation and I thought it would be a shame for my parents if I didn't go to university. I wanted to tell them that I didn't

want to go ... but I didn't have the guts to say it ... Finally I had to betray them ... I knew I liked cooking and wanted to become a cook ... however my parents expected me to go to a respectable university ... I tried to fit in but everything they thought good for me was what the society (*seken*) would think good ... I don't buy the idea of social respectability as the only way to make my life meaningful.

6 Lunsing (1997: 275–6, note 51), however, states that the age of consent for boys is 'implicitly' thirteen and mentions the local rules in different municipalities termed *jōrei* prohibiting such things as prostitution or the seduction of people under the age of eighteen.

7 I am not suggesting a politically correct world in which humour at the expense of any group should be rejected. There are also plenty of examples in Japanese media where mainstream understandings of 'masculinity' and 'femininity' are parodied. Nor do I mean to suggest that representing 'gay' men as feminine is necessarily a bad thing. 'Masculinity' is not reducible to male genitalia just as 'femininity' cannot be reduced to the possession of a female body. The problem with these representations is their ubiquity, and the lack of a public forum where other 'homosexualities' are acknowledged.

8 The other context in which I have come across the term *rezupurei* is on gay Internet sites where participants describe their first sexual experiences. I have read several accounts where young school boys dressed up as girls in order to perform 'lesbian sex.' As 'lesbian sex' is a common fantasy trope in male pornography, it is possible that the boys picked up the idea from looking at these media.

9 Osugi and Piiko are brothers and media *tarento* who both write in magazines and appear on panel shows commenting on things such as films and fashion. They do not wear flamboyant clothing but their speech is 'feminine' as are their mannerisms. I once watched a panel show on which Piiko was a guest and was able to identify him immediately from the way in which he spoke. Hiratsuka (1994: 130) describes their speech and movements as having a 'different feeling from usual people.' He sees the fact that they appear as gay (*nanshoku*) alongside heterosexual (*ishoku*) talents as a sign of liberalisation in the mass media. He thinks that the 'dark shadow' of homosexuality is being dispelled and that the gay world (*nanshoku kai*) is becoming brighter. However, Osugi and Piiko are very much 'token gays;' they are still to a certain extent transgendered (in speech and mannerisms) and their inclusion on the occasional panel discussion hardly represents a challenge to the dominant image of homosexual men as *okama*. Piiko himself would probably not agree with Hiratsuka's analysis either. In an *ASIAWEEK* article on homosexuality in Japan (3 August 1998) he mentions how, when he came out as 'a very ordinary looking man telling the Japanese people that he ... loves other men,' he was no longer asked to be a television host or do commercials because 'sponsoring companies didn't want a gay person associated with their products as the image of homosexuals is ugly.' He adds that

'mainstream newspapers also shunned me.' Thus the only role left to him was that of minor *tarento* on panel discussions and the occasional column in magazines.

10 This point was reinforced for me when I visited an *okama* bar in Roppongi called Laki Laki. The clientele seemed to be made up of salarymen and a few female office workers who were out for the night. The 'hostesses' at the club were divided into two clear groups: *okama* who made no attempt to pass as women and 'new-half' who passed very convincingly. The show which was part of the night's entertainment reflected this division. The *okama* were the comedians who engaged with the audience in a witty repartee of jokes mainly connected with sex and going to the toilet (regular staples of Japanese humour). The new-half hostesses, however, took part in separate dance numbers which were highly erotic. Several of the performers had breasts and may even have had sex-change operations; however, even those without breasts seemed not androgynous, but definitely female. On several occasions I winced at the intrusive and brutal questioning which was aimed at the hostesses by drunken (male) guests. However, this kind of harsh and patronising treatment is also aimed at female hostesses in regular clubs (*see* Allison 1994) who are likewise treated as a marginal group in Japanese society (Mock 1996). Although the entertainment business *(mizu shōbai)* may act as a refuge for certain disenfranchised groups, it comes at a price to their self-esteem.

11 Nomura and I obviously move in radically different social circles for I have never seen any of the things which she thinks indicate homosexuality in any gay man's apartment. Perhaps these things can be found in the apartments of rich and famous gay *tarento* with whom Nomura can be expected to socialise. However, regular gay men, having been socialised as *men*, are not much better than their straight counterparts at taking care of themselves. Hence, many of the gay men's apartments I visited were not particularly clean or well kept, and like the apartments of single Japanese people generally, were highly functional, with little money or effort being put into decoration. Most of the homosexual men I know in Japan are attempting to pass as straight with colleagues and parents and therefore avoid the display of anything that might suggest a homosexual inclination. Also, having regular jobs, they tended to wear the same kind of conservative suits and white shirts which *all* salarymen wear. It is true that in Shinjuku Ni-chome there are many neatly-turned out young men in fashionable clothes smelling of expensive deodorant; however, they are hardly typical of homosexual men in general.

12 McGregor (1996: 243) argues that 'promiscuous' Japanese women are penalized by the media in a way that Japanese men never are. He points to a television documentary which used staged footage to prove the supposed loose morals of groups of OLs (office ladies) travelling to Hawaii. Karen Ma (1996) also points out how, in the late-1980s, the Japanese media carried sensationalised stories about OLs travelling abroad for sex with foreign men (and thereby introducing AIDS to Japan) whereas the widespread sex tourism of Japanese men to South-East Asia 'went unmentioned' (1996: 64). Lunsing (personal communication) mentions an AIDS-awareness poster put up in Japanese airports in the late-1980s

which showed a Japanese man inside a condom hiding his face behind a passport. This poster would seem to condone male sex tourism; i.e. if you are going abroad for sex, at least use a condom.

13 This perplexes many foreign gay men in Japan such as this man who posted the following message on GayNet Japan (11 September 1997): 'Could anyone tell me why Japanese fanzines about homosexuality ... are always made and read by GIRLS?'

14 For example, see *YAOI webring for girls* which contains 'pictures and stories about beautiful youths (*bishōnen*) and homosexual love (*dōseiai*)' at http://www.home4.highway.ne.jp/t-mei/yaoi/. For a discussion of Japanese women's boy-love sites on the internet see my paper 'No climax, no point, no meaning? Japanese women's boy-love sites on the Internet,' in *The Journal of Communication Inquiry*, 24:3 (July 2000).

15 'Fantasy' seems an integral element of most women's popular culture in Japan, and is underlined by Jennifer Robertson when she states that with regard to the Takarazuka 'Generally speaking, with the exception of wartime reviews, contemporary Japan and Japanese were not and are not now represented on the Takarazuka stage, which instead offers audiences a chance to dream of other lives in other worlds' (1998: 7). The crossover from manga to stage fantasy is thus easily achieved. Kelsky (1999) also points out that the 'discourse of internationalism' in many Japanese women's media posits a largely illusory 'West' which is held up as a 'rhetorical mirror' to reflect the 'backward' attitudes supposed character-istic of Japan's patriarchal society.

16 I must thank Megumi Maderdonner for pointing this out to me.

17 The difficulties Japanese women face in gaining access to effective contraception are outlined in Hardacre (1997). McGregor (1996: 230) also states that 'Japanese women cannot buy the Pill.' The medical establishment argues that it is not available because it is unsafe, whereas feminist organisations argue it is because the medical establishment runs a booming abortion business. Hatano and Shimazaki (1997: 830) state that as of January 1997 'only a medium-strength form of the pill was available in Japan for medical (non-contraceptive) purposes.' McLauchlan (1998) also cites the government's fear of an increase in AIDS if oral contraceptives were to be made available. However, at the time of writing legislation legalising the pill has just been passed.

18 There is also a crossover readership for *shōnen'ai* manga of young men who (in print at least) do not identify as 'gay.' The December 1994 special issue of *B-boy*, entitled 'Students who Changed Schools' (*Tenkōsei*), has a selection of letters from young men under the heading 'Strive on, male readers!' (*Gambare dansei shokun*) where male fans of the comic write about the embarrassment they feel when buying it because of the strange looks they get from the cashier. Several mention that they are not gay (*homo*). One high-school boy says that 'It's not that I'm gay' which in the text of his letter is followed by the picture of a tear (was this added by the editor, does it signify the writer's or the editor's or the reader's regret?). He goes on to say that he and a group of two or three girls buy these magazines and share them. The girls ask him 'Mā-kun [his name], how about turning gay (*homo ni nachaeba?*)', to which he replies 'they say such

irresponsible things but, basically, if it's beautiful then either is OK,' a statement which is followed by the character *warai*, signifying laughter (presumably the speaker is suggesting an ironic stance to his last statement). Such letters, if they are genuine, signify a certain playfulness on the part of the readers. Just as a consumer of fantasy fiction is willing to suspend disbelief about the parameters of the possible, the reader of *shōnen'ai* fiction is also willing to suspend the normally constraining parameters of gender, at least within the world or community produced by reading the magazine. Some men who read *shōnen'ai* fiction do so in a context which brings them into proximity with women (as in the reading circle described above). These men are exposed to very different constructions of masculinity than those they would find in a reading circle comprised of other men. Moreover, the images of masculinity present in *shōnen'ai* fiction are obviously attractive to many women, so a man who is sexually attracted to women may, either consciously or unconsciously, seek to cultivate them.

19 As the Asahi poll cited earlier in the chapter shows, young women are the group most likely to accept the idea that homosexuality is just one way of loving. Studies have also shown this to be true of western nations. *See* Kite and Whitley (1998).

20 The number of men who are 'really' homosexual in any community is obviously impossible to calculate as it is unclear exactly what the boundaries of 'homosexual' are and how they might be empirically validated. The only statistics I have found relating to the prevalence of homosexuality in Japan are cited by Hatano and Shimazaki (1997: 821) who refer to a 1987 survey which found that 4.5 per cent of male college students were 'active homosexuals.' However, as my interview data suggests, many gay men in Japan start with a heterosexual phase before moving into same-sex relationships later in life which would suggest that a survey based only on college students underestimates the prevalence of homosexual behaviour in Japan.

21 Jennifer Robertson's (1998) work on sexual politics within the Takarazuka also points to the widespread use of vertical kinship terms within that homosocial subculture: 'When kinship terminology is used to denote relationships between individual Takarasiennes, it is based both on age or seniority, as 'elder sister' (*onēsan* or *ane*) and 'younger sister' (*imōto*), and on gender, as 'older brother' (*aniki*) and 'younger sister', without regard, necessarily to literal age or seniority. Both sets of kinship terms are applied by Takarasiennes and their fans to identify both homosocial and homosexual relations between females' (1998: 16).

22 Clammer (1995: 200) comments that 'A characteristic of much of the Japanese periodical press is its mixing of genres, with text, advertisements, visuals and comics all in the same publication.' It is clear that this also holds true for Japanese gay publications which not only mix genres but levels, including film and book reviews, interviews and news items sandwiched between pornographic stories and comics.

23 Of course these are also important functions of gay magazines in other societies. Take, for example, this excerpt from a letter to the American gay porn magazine *Torso* (1995, vol. 12, no. 12, p. 4): 'I was browsing in the

bookstore when I saw copies of *Torso*, *Mandate*, *Honcho*, etc., and it surprised me when I saw the pages . . . I learned a lot from these magazines and it helped make it easier to accept myself, and I discovered I am not alone anymore.'

24 Many Japanese men confided to me that they were self-conscious about both the size and appearance of their penises. To have the foreskin completely cover the glans is considered to be a sign of sexual immaturity (because this is how most boys' penises appear) whereas to have the glans stand out clearly above the foreskin is a sign of adult, masculine sexuality. For this reason, various men's clinics offer circumcision services. Also men who have at one time or other contracted a sexual disease can attend these men's clinics which specialise in treating such problems in a discrete manner. Recently, techniques for lengthening penises have been developed and such services are also offered by these clinics. The clinics advertise extensively in the gay press and also in magazines and comics directed at straight male readers as well as on the Internet. Their flexible opening hours, central locations and exclusively male staff make them attractive to busy salarymen.

25 It was also pointed out to me that *Gaten* is the title of a recruitment magazine specialising in blue-collar occupations but my informants were unsure whether the nuance attached to the term predated its publication or was, instead, attributable to the magazine's influence.

26 As the video copies I received were already copies of copies, the credits were either absent entirely or so blurred as to be impossible to read. Thus I am unable to provide such information as year of production, name of production company etc. Also, Lunsing (personal communication) suggests that I have been overly-influenced by the *shumi* or tastes of the gay man who provided me with the videos and that my account of Japanese video pornography should not be taken as representative.

27 The issue of Thai homosexuality/bisexuality further complicates the hetero/homo binary mode of classifying human sexuality. Jackson (1995) argues that Thai culture has traditionally had three genders: man, woman and man-woman (*kathoey*). The *kathoey* is a biological man who dresses as and acts like a woman and has an exclusive sexual interest in men. The status of the *kathoey* is somewhat ambivalent but men, generally, do not lose status by engaging in 'active' sex with them. Jackson suggests that the very public and obvious existence of this 'third gender' allows gender normative men to engage in sex with both women and other men without raising suspicion about their 'sexual identities.' However, he also outlines how exposure to western models of gay identity is opening space for a new kind of sexual actor: the gender normative man who is also exclusively interested in other men. Traditionally, exclusive interest in other men has meant adopting the transgender attributes of the *kathoey*.

28 *Shunga* (erotic prints) from the Tokugawa period often feature a third-party who is peeping in at the action. There are also *nozoki* or 'peeping' image clubs (*imekura*) where men can pay to peep at either the staged action being performed by club employees, or the action of other clients (*see* Altbooks 1998).

29 Doi has been roundly criticised by, among others, Peter Dale (1986) as being a typical *nihonjinron* (Japanese uniqueness) theorist. However, I

have found the connection he makes between *amae* and homosexual feelings (*dōseiai kanjō*) to be useful.

30 However, other reasons why foreign gay men find Japan so easy to live in are that in Japan, being a foreigner (*gaijin*) is such an all-embracing signifier of the 'other' that personal idiosyncrasies are rendered invisible. Thus, any personal characteristics which contradict expected patterns of behaviour are likely to be explained in terms of a person's foreignness rather than in terms of his or her sexuality. Also, as outlined earlier, Japan's vertical society places great emphasis on senior/junior relationships and older men often find themselves targeted by men much younger. This seems very different from the gay scene in Anglo-America which is much more youth oriented and many older foreign gay men feel more appreciated on Japan's gay scene. It is ironic, then, that many western-oriented Japanese gay men perceive such cities as San Fransisco or Sydney as gay Meccas whereas, for some, especially older western gay men, Tokyo is a preferable gay destination.

31 Of course this kind of website where men seek intergenerational contacts is not specific to Japan but can be found in the west also. For example, the American site *Gay Boys Like Men* is a website for young men to write in about their fantasies and experiences with older men. On this site too, sex is not foregrounded but other more emotional aspects of the relationships are stressed. One twenty-six-year-old man writes that he appreciates 'the charm, the security, the confidence, the manliness' of older men. An older man (age unspecified) writes in to say that 'It is my view that the majority of [older] men here are here to help and encourage these young men and give them the very best of our years of experience.' What is different in the case of Japan is the very common use of kinship terminology to define these relationships and their ubiquity (they appear on a wide variety of different websites).

32 Largely absent from the above discussion is a consideration of the published views of gay activists and organisations in Japan which can also be understood as representing part of Japan's 'gay media.' I do not consider the influence of the discourse of gay rights in this chapter because of its extreme marginality. Although Japan has numerous gay organisations, membership is small (Lunsing [1999b: 306] cites membership figures for several organisations, the largest number being only 550), and their views are not generally represented in the more popular gay media which, as I have argued, are primarily entertainment oriented. I do, however, discuss some of these individuals and organisations and their published works in chapters 8 and 9.

33 For example, Britain prosecuted 213 youths for underage sex with men in 1993 (*World Press Review*, September 1993, vol. 40, Issue 9, p. 24). Had Takeshi been brought up in England, he would have been breaking the law (by committing an act of 'gross indecency') when, at age sixteen, he allowed himself to be masturbated by a school friend.

34 While in Japan in July/August 1998, I attempted to arrange an interview with some members of OCCUR, hoping to hear from them more about their activities. However, after repeated telephone calls, I was told that everyone was too busy to meet me but that any questions I had would be

answered by fax. Unfortunately, I never received a response to my list of questions (inquiring about things such as membership numbers) and, after my phone messages remained unanswered, I finally gave up. Lunsing (personal communication) reports a similarly cool response from members of the organisation to his requests for information. This may be because OCCUR's membership number cited in an *ASIAWEEK* article (3 August 1998) as 35,000 is a complete fabrication. Lunsing (personal communication) estimates that the number is less than 300 based on information he has received from ex-OCCUR members.

35 After the success of Itō and Yanase's 1994 book *Otoko to otoko no ren'ai nōto* (Love notes of men who love men) where they discuss the problems they have living together as a family with Itō's invalided mother, the production team for the television comedy show *Denpa shōnen* (Young airwaves) turned up at their home and asked that the well-known television personality Matsumura Kunihiro, who was dressed as a kindergarten student, be allowed to stay the night 'as a child of the family;' the implication being that Itō and Yanase might like to play the role of parents, because, of course, 'real' families have children (*see* the account given in Itō and Ochiai 1998: 12; and also Summerhawk et al. 1998: 91).

36 An impressive catalogue of legal and institutional oppression of gay men and lesbians in the United States is given in Signorili's (1994) *Queer in America*; Goode (1997) gives a catalogue of recent hate crimes committed against men suspected of being gay in America. Legal discrimination against gay men (but not lesbians) continues in Britain where in 1998, the House of Lords rejected a Common's Bill recommending that the age of consent for homosexual acts between men, currently eighteen, be brought into line with the age for heterosexual acts, which is sixteen. Furthermore, in 1988 in Britain, Clause 28 of the Local Government Act was passed which states that a local authority should not: '(a) intentionally promote homosexuality or publish material with the intention of promoting homosexuality; (b) promote the teaching in any maintained school of the acceptability of homosexuality as a pretended family relationship' (cited in Spencer 1995: 383).

References

Abelove, Henry, et al. (eds) (1993) *The Lesbian and Gay Studies Reader*, New York: Routledge.

Abramson, Paul and Hayashi, Haruo. (1984) 'Pornography in Japan: Cross-Cultural and Theoretical Considerations,' in: N. Malamuth (1984).

Adam, Barry. (1987) *The Rise of a Gay and Lesbian Movement*, Boston: Twayne Publishers.

Adam, Barry, et al. (eds) (1999) *The Global Emergence of Gay and Lesbian Politics: Nationwide Imprints of a Worldwide Movement*, Philadelphia: Temple University Press.

AERA. (1999, March 1) '*Mēru de bakeru "otoko ga onna" "onna ga otoko"*' (Men who appear as women and women who appear as men on e-mail), pp. 28–30.

Akā (OCCUR). (ed.) (1992) *Gei repōto: dōseiaisha wa kōgen suru* (Gay report: homosexuals speak out), Tokyo: Tottōri shinsha.

Akizuki, Koh, and Nakata, Aki. (1997) *Rasuto zōn* (Last zone), Tokyo: June Comics.

Allison, Anne. (1994) *Nightwork: Sexuality, Pleasure, and Corporate Masculinity in a Tokyo Hostess Club*, Chicago: Chicago University Press.

Allison, Anne. (1996) *Permitted and Prohibited Desires: Mothers, Comics, and Censorship in Japan*, Boulder, Colorado: Westview Press.

Altbooks. (1998), v. 14, *SEX no arukikata: Tōkyō fūzoku kanzen gaido* (How to find your way around sex: the complete guide to Tokyo's sex scene), Tokyo: Mediawākusu.

Altman, Dennis, et al. (1988) *Homosexuality, Which Homosexuality?: International Conference on Gay and Lesbian Studies*, London: GMP Publishers.

Altman, Dennis. (1996) 'Rupture or Continuity? The Internationalization of Gay Identities,' *Social Text* 48, vol. 14, no. 3, Fall 1996, pp. 77–94.

AMPO. (ed) (1996) *Voices from the Japanese Women's Movement*, New York & London: M.E. Sharpe.

Aogi, Yūji. (1992) *Naniwa kin'yūdō* (Osaka's money trade), Tokyo: Kōdansha.

Aoyama, Tomoko. (1988) 'Male Homosexuality as Treated by Japanese Women Writers,' in: G. McCormack and Y. Sugimoto (eds) (1988).

Asahi Shimbun. (1998, January 1) *Otoko to onna kawaru ai no katachi* (The changing shape of love between men and women), pp. 24–25.

Asai, Haruo. (1997) '*Dansei to sekushuaru raitsu*' (Men and sexual rights), in: N. Yamamoto (ed.) (1997).

Ashby, Janet. (1994) *Read Real Japanese*, Tokyo: Kodansha International.
ASIAWEEK. (1998, August 3) special report: 'Gays in Asia.'
ASIAWEEK. (1998, May 22) 'Isolated in their Grief,' pp. 40–41.
Asupecto. (1998), v. 41, *Kono shōjo manga ga kiku* (These girls comics are influential), Tokyo: Asupecto.
Ayres, Tony. (1999) 'China Doll–The Experience of Being a Gay Chinese Australian,' *The Journal of Homosexuality*, vol. 36, nos 3/4, pp. 87–97.
B-boy, various writers. (1994) v. 18, *Tenkōsei tokushū* (Students who changed schools, special edition), Tokyo: Biburosu.
Bessatsu Takarajima. (1992, August) *Gei no okurimono* (A gay present), Tokyo: Takarajimasha.
Bessatsu Takarajima. (1994, February) *Gei no rakuen tengoku* (Gay playland paradise), Tokyo: Takarajimasha.
Bessatsu Takarajima. (1998) v. 382, *Ura Tōkyō kankō* (Backstreet Tokyo sightseeing), Tokyo: Takarajimasha.
Blakemore, Thomas. (transl.) (1954) *The Criminal Code of Japan as Amended in 1954*, Tokyo: Charles Tuttle.
Bornoff, Nicholas. (1991) *Pink Samurai: The Pursuit of Politics and Sex in Japan*, London: Grafton Books.
Brinton, Mary. (1992) 'Christmas Cakes and Wedding Cakes: the Social Organization of Japanese Women's Life Course' in: T.S. Lebra (ed.) (1992).
BRUTUS. (1998, August 1) *'Boku tachi wa mesuka shiterun desuka?'* (Are we men becoming feminized?).
Buckley, Sandra. (1991) 'Penguin in Bondage: a Tale of Japanese Comic Books' in: C. Penley and A. Ross (eds) (1991).
Buckley, Sandra. (1994) 'A Short History of the Feminist Movement in Japan,' in: J. Gelb (1994).
Buckley, Sandra. (1997) *Broken Silence: Voices of Japanese Feminism*, Berkeley, Los Angeles, London: University of California Press.
Buruma, Ian. (1984) *Behind the Mask: On Sexual Demons, Sacred Mothers, Transvestites, Gangsters and other Japanese Cultural Heroes*, New York: Meridian.
Butler, Judith. (1990) *Gender Trouble: Feminism and the Subversion of Identity*, New York: Routledge.
Cabezon, José. (ed.) (1992) *Buddhism, Sexuality and Gender*, New York: State University of New York Press.
Chamberlain, Basil. (1905) *Things Japanese*, London: Kelley and Walshe.
Childs, Margaret. (1980) 'Chigo Monogatari: Love Stories or Buddhist Sermons?' *Monumenta Nipponica* 35:2, pp. 127–151.
Chou, Wah-Shan. (1997) *Tongzhi Come Home: Politics of Same-Sex Eroticism in Chinese Societies*, unpublished book manuscript.
Clammer, John. (1995) 'Consuming Bodies: Constructing and Representing the Female Body in Contemporary Japanese Print Media,' in: L. Skov and B. Moeran (eds) (1995).
Constantine, Peter. (1993) *Japan's Sex Trade: A Journey Through Japan's Erotic Subcultures*, Tokyo: Charles Tuttle.
Cooper, Michael. (ed.) (1965) *They Came to Japan: An Anthology of European Reports on Japan, 1543–1640*, Berkeley: University of California Press.

Coxon, Anthony. (1996) *Between the Sheets: Sexual Diaries and Gay Men's Sex in the Era of AIDS*, London: Cassell.

CREA. (1991, February) *'Gei runessansu 91'* (Gay renaissance '91).

Da Vinchi. (1999, March) *'Utsukushi sugiru otoko wa suki desu ka?'* (Do you like men who are too beautiful?), pp. 14–27.

Dalby, Liza. (1985) *Geisha*, New York: Vintage.

Dalby, Liza. (1993) *Kimono: Fashioning Culture*, New Haven: Yale University Press.

Dale, Peter. (1986) *The Myth of Japanese Uniqueness*, London and New York: Routledge.

Derichs, Claudia, and Oziander, Anja. (eds) (1998) *Soziale Bewegungen in Japan*, Hamburg: Mitteilungen der Vereinigung fur Natur und Volkenkunde.

De Vos, George, et al. (1973) *Socialization for Achievement: Essays on the Cultural Psychology of the Japanese*, Berkeley: University of California Press.

Doi, Takeo. (1985) *Amae no kōzō* (Anatomy of dependence) (2nd. ed.), Tokyo: Kōbunsha.

Dollimore, Jonathan. (1991) *Sexual Dissidence and Cultural Change: Augustine to Wilde, Freud to Foucault*, New York: Oxford University Press.

Dorenkamp, Monica, and Henke, Richard. (eds) (1995) *Negotiating Lesbian and Gay Subjects*, New York: Routledge.

Douglas, Nick, and Slinger, Penny. (1981) *The Pillow Book: The Erotic Sentiment and the Paintings of India, Nepal, China and Japan*, New York: Deshny Books.

Dowsett, Gary, W. (1996) *Practicing Desire: Homosexual Sex in the Era of AIDS*, Stanford: Stanford University Press.

Duberman, Martin, et al. (eds) (1989) *Hidden From History: Reclaiming the Gay and Lesbian Past*, New York: Meridian.

Dunn, Charles, and Torigoe, Bunzo. (transl.) (1969) *The Actors' Analects (Yakusha rongo)*, Tokyo: University of Tokyo Press.

Dynes, Wayne. (ed.) (1990) *Encyclopedia of Homosexuality*, New York: Garland Publishing.

Edwards, Walter. (1989) *Modern Japan Through Its Weddings: Gender, Person and Society in Ritual Portrayal*, Stanford: Stanford University Press.

EG. (1994) *Onna no ko no himitsu monogatari* (Girls' secret love stories), Tokyo: Easy Books.

Epstein, Steven. (1998) 'Gay Politics, Ethnic Identity: the Limits of Social Constructionism,' in: P. Nardi and B. Schneider (eds) (1998).

Eureka. (1993, May) *Gei karuchā* (Gay culture).

Fiske, John. (1989a). *Reading the Popular*, London: Routledge.

Fiske, John. (1989b). *Understanding Popular Culture*, London: Routledge.

Flowers, Paul et al. (2000) 'The Bars, the Bogs, and the Bushes: The Impact of Locale on Sexual Cultures,' *Culture, Health and Sexuality*, vol. 2, n. 1, pp. 69–86.

FOCUS. (1998, April 1) *'Mata ōkurashō! Kakuseizai taiho shokuin no homo konekushon: afutā 5 no hisokana "shumi"'*(The Finance Ministry again! An employee arrested for stimulants' homo connection: his secret after five 'hobby'), pp. 6–7.

Foucault, Michel. (1990) *History of Sexuality Volume 1: An Introduction*, London: Penguin.

Francoeur, Robert. (ed.) (1995) *The International Encyclopedia of Sexuality*, New York: Continuum Publishing Company.

Fujimura-Fanselow, Kumiko, and Kameda, Atsuko. (eds) (1995) *Japanese Women: New Feminist Perspectives on the Past, Present, and Future*, New York: The Feminist Press.

Fukasaku, Kinji. (1968) *Kuro tokage* (Black lizard), motion picture.

Fukushima, Jirō. (1998) *Mishima Yukio: tsurugi to kankō* (Mishima Yukio: sword and winter-blossom), Tokyo: Bungei shunjū.

Furukawa, Makoto. (1994) 'The Changing Nature of Sexuality: The Three Codes Framing Homosexuality in Modern Japan,' *U.S.-Japan Women's Journal English Supplement*, no. 7, pp. 98–126.

Fushimi, Noriaki. (1991) *Puraibēto gei raifu* (Private gay life), Tokyo: Gakuyō shobō.

Fushimi, Noriaki, and Saito, Ayako. (1997) *Kairaku no gijutsu* (The art of pleasure), Tokyo: Kawade bunko.

Fushimi, Noriaki. (1998a) *Gei sutairu* (Gay style), Tokyo: Kawade bunko.

Fushimi, Noriaki. (1998b) *Sūpārabu* (Super love), Tokyo: Shodensha.

Gelb, Joyce, and Lief Palley, Marian. (1994) *Women of Japan and Korea: Continuity and Change*, Philadelphia: Temple University Press.

Gendai no esupuri. (1990, August), *Toransujendā genshō* (Transgender images), Tokyo: Shibundō.

Gendai shisō. (1997, November) *Rezubian/gei sutadiizu* (Lesbian/gay studies), Tokyo: Seidosha.

Goode, Erich. (1997) *Deviant Behavior*, 5th Edition, New York: Prentice Hall.

Greenberg, David, F. (1988) *The Construction of Homosexuality*, Chicago: University of Chicago Press.

Gunew, Sneja, and Yeatman, Anna. (1993) *Feminism and the Politics of Difference*, Boulder: Westview Press.

Guth, Christine. (1987) 'The Divine Boy in Japanese Art,' *Monumenta Nipponica*, 42:1, pp. 1–23.

Hagio, Moto. (1997) *Zankokuna kami ga shihai suru* (A cruel god reigns), 9 vols., Tokyo: Shōgakkan.

Hall, John. (1968) *Studies in the Institutional History of Early Modern Japan*, Princeton: Princeton University Press.

Halperin, David. (1995) *Saint Foucault: Towards a Gay Hagiography*, New York: Oxford University Press.

Hanasaki, Kazuo. (1980) *Edo no kagema chaya* (Edo's *kagema* teashops), Tokyo: Gannando Inc.

Hanawa, Yukiko. (1996) 'Inciting Sites of Political Interventions: Queer 'n' Asian,' *Positions*, 4:3, pp. 459–489.

Hara, Minako. (1996) 'Lesbians and Sexual Self-Determination,' in: AMPO (ed.) (1996).

Hardacre, Helen. (1997) *Marketing the Menacing Fetus in Japan*, Berkeley: University of California Press.

Hatanaka, Jun. (1997)*Ryōta*, v. 1, Tokyo: Bungei Shunjū.

Hatano, Yoshiro, and Shimazaki, T. (1997) 'Japan' in R. Francoeur (ed.) (1997).

Hatfield, Elaine, and Rapson, Richard. (1996) *Love and Sex: Cross-Cultural Perspectives*, Boston: Allyn and Bacon.

Heaphy, Brian, et al. (1998) '"That's Like my Life": Researching Stories of Non-heterosexual Relationships', *Sexualities*, vol. 1, n. 4., pp. 453–470.

Hendry, Joy. (1981) *Marriage in Changing Japan*, London: Croom Helm.

Herek, Gregory. (ed.) (1998) *Stigma and Sexual Orientation: Understanding Prejudice against Lesbians, Gay Men and Bisexuals*, Thousand Oaks: Sage.

Hidaka, Noboru. (1982) *Sex in Japan*, New York: Vantage Press.

Hiratsuka, Yoshinori. (1994) *Nihon ni okeru danshoku no kenkyū* (Research on male homosexuality in Japan), Tokyo: Ningen no kagakusha.

Hot Dog. (1994, October 1) '*Dōseiai saishin jōhō*' (Homosexuality: the latest news).

Ihara, Saikaku. (1956) *Five Women Who Loved Love*, transl. W.M. Theodore de Bary, Tokyo: Charles Tuttle.

Ihara, Saikaku. (1964) *Life of an Amorous Man*, transl. Masakazu Kuwata, Tokyo: Charles Tuttle.

Ihara, Saikaku. (1983) *Tales of Samurai Honor*, transl. Caryl Ann Callahan, Tokyo: Monumenta Nipponica, Sophia University.

Ihara, Saikaku. (1990) *The Great Mirror of Male Love*, transl. Paul Gordon Schalow, Stanford: Stanford University Press.

Ikegami, Chizuko. (1995) *Adamu to ibu wa naze kaikan wo shinka saseta no ka* (Why did Adam and Eve evolve pleasure?), Tokyo: Daiwa shobō.

Ikegami, Eiko. (1995) *The Taming of the Samurai: Honorific Individualism and the Making of Modern Japan*, Cambridge MA: Harvard University Press.

imago. (1995, November) *Gei riberēshon* (Gay liberation), Tokyo: Seidosha.

imago. (1996, May) *Sekushuariti* (Sexuality), Tokyo: Seidosha.

Imamura, Anne. (ed.) (1996) *Re-imagining Japanese Women*, Berkeley: University of California Press.

Inagaki, Taruho. (1993) *Shōnen no bigaku* (The aesthetics of boy love), Tokyo: Kawade bunko.

Ishino, Sachiko, and Wakabayashi, Naeko. (1996) 'Japan' in: R. Rosenbloom (ed.) (1996).

Itō, Kimio. (1996) *Otokorashisa no yukue* (The whereabouts of masculinity), Tokyo: Shin'yōsha.

Itō, Satoru, and Yanase, Ryūta. (1994) *Otoko to otoko no ren'ai nōto: ai to kurashi to shigoto no pātonāshippu* (Notes on love between men: a partnership of love, living together and work), Tokyo: Tarōjirōsha.

Itō, Satoru. (1996) *Dōseiai no kiso chishiki* (Basic information about homosexuality), Tokyo: Ayumi shuppan.

Itō, Satoru, and Ochiai, Keiko. (1998) *Jibunrashiku ikiru: dōseiai to feminizumu* (Live more like oneself: homosexuality and feminism), Kyoto: Kamogawa booklet.

Iwao, Sumiko. (1993) *The Japanese Woman: Traditional Image and Changing Reality*, New York: The Free Press.

Jackson, Peter. (1995) *Dear Uncle Go: Male Homosexuality in Thailand*, Bangkok: Bua Lung Books.

Johansson, Warren, and Percy, William. (1990) 'France' in W. Dynes (ed.) (1990).

Jolivet, Muriel. (1997) *Japan: The Childless Society? The Crisis of Motherhood*, London: Routledge.

Jones, Sumie. (ed.) (1996) *Imaging/Reading Eros: Proceedings from the Conference, Sexuality and Edo Culture, 1750-1850*, Bloomington: Indiana University Press.

Kawai, Hayao. (1997) 'The Message from Japan's Schoolgirl Prostitutes,' *Japan Echo*, June 1997, pp. 47–50.

'Kazuya.' (1998) *Gei seikatsu manyuaru* (Gay lifestyle manual), Tokyo: Data House.

Kelsky, Karen. (1999) 'Gender, Modernity, and Eroticized Internationalism in Japan,' *Cultural Anthropology*, 14(2), pp. 229–255.

Kelsky, Karen (in progress) *Women on the Edge: Gender, Race and the Erotics of the International in Japan*, Durham, NC: Duke.

Kinmouth, Earl. (1981) *The Self-Made Man in Meiji Japanese Thought*, London: University of California Press.

Kinsella, Sharon. (1995) 'Cuties in Japan' in: L. Skov and B. Moeran (eds) (1995).

Kinsella, Sharon. (1998) 'Japanese Subculture in the 1990s: Otaku and the Amateur Manga Movement,' *Journal of Japanese Studies*, 24:2, Summer, 1998, pp. 289–316.

Kinsey, A.C. et al. (1948) *Sexual Behavior in the Human Male*, Philadelphia: W.B. Saunders.

Kirby, Stewart, and Hay, Iain. (1997) '(Hetero)sexing Space: Gay Men and "Straight" Space in Adelaide, South Australia,' *The Professional Geographer*, August 1997, vol. 49 no. 3, p.295–.

Kite, Mary, and Whitely, Bernard, Jr. (1998) 'Do Heterosexual Women and Men Differ in Their Attitudes Towards Homosexuality? A Conceptual and Methodological Analysis,' in G. Herek (ed.) (1998).

Kiyohara, Muneaki. (1994) *Homotaimu* (Homo time), Tokyo: Ōta Shuppan.

Knopp, Lawrence, M., Jr. (1990) 'Social Consequences of Homosexuality,' *Geographical Magazine*, May 1990, pp. 20–25.

Kuia sutadiizu '97. (1997) (Queer Studies '97), Tokyo: Nanatsumorishokan.

Kurigi, Chieko. (1996) *Amerika no gei tachi: ai to kaihō no monogatari* (America's gays: a story of love and liberation), Tokyo: Chūōkōronsha.

Lebra, Takie Sugiyama. (1984) *Japanese Women: Constraint and Fulfillment*, Honolulu: University of Hawaii Press.

Lebra, Takie Sugiyama. (ed.) (1994) *Japanese Social Organization*, Honolulu: University of Hawaii Press.

Lent, John. (1989) 'Japanese Comics' in: R. Powers (ed.) (1989)

Leupp, Gary. (1992) *Servants Shophands and Laborers in the Cities of Tokugawa Japan*, Princeton: Princeton University Press.

Leupp, Gary. (1995) *Male Colors: The Construction of Homosexuality in Tokugawa Japan*, Berkeley: University of California Press.

Leupp, Gary. (1996) 'Male Homosexuality in Edo during the Late Tokugawa Period 1750–1850: Decline of a Tradition,' in: S. Jones (ed.) (1996).

Levy, Howard. (1973) *Japanese Sex Jokes in Traditional Times*, Washington DC: Warm-Soft Village Press.

Lewin, Ellen, and Leap, William. (eds) (1996) *Out in the Field*, University of Illinois Press.

Livia, Anna, and Hall, Kira. (eds) (1997) *Queerly Phrased: Language, Gender and Sexuality*, New York and Oxford: Oxford University Press.

Long, Daniel. (1996) 'Formation Processes of Some Japanese Gay Argot Terms,' *American Speech*, 71.2, pp. 215–224.

Lunsing, Wim. (1995) 'Japanese Gay Magazines and Marriage Advertisements,' in: Gerald Sullivan (ed.) (1995).

Lunsing, Wim. (1997) '"Gay Boom" in Japan: Changing Views of Homosexuality?' *Thamyris*, vol. 4, n. 2, Autumn 1997, pp. 267–293.

Lunsing, Wim. (1998) 'Lesbian and Gay Movements–Between Hard and Soft,' in: C. Derichs and A. Oziander (eds) (1998).

Lunsing, Wim. (1999a) 'Life on Mars: Love and Sex in Fieldwork on Sexuality and Gender in Urban Japan,' in: F. Markowitz and M. Ashkenazi (eds) (1999).

Lunsing, Wim. (1999b) 'Japan: Finding its Way?' in: Adam et al. (1999).

Lunsing, Wim. (in press) *Beyond Common Sense: Negotiating Constructions of Sexuality and Gender in Contemporary Japan*, London: Kegan Paul International.

Ma, Karen. (1996) *The Modern Madame Butterfly: Fantasy and Reality in Japanese Cross-Cultural Relationships*, Tokyo: Charles Tuttle.

Malamuth, N. (ed.) (1984) *Pornography and Aggression*, Orlando: Academic Press.

Manderson, Lenore, and Jolly, Margaret. (1997) *Sites of Desire, Economies of Pleasure: Sexualities in Asia and the Pacific*, Chicago: Chicago University Press.

Marco Polo. (1994, February) '*Fudangi no gei*' (Gays in normal clothes).

Markowitz, Fran, and Ashkenazi, Michael. (eds) (1999) *Sex, Sexuality and the Anthropologist*, Chicago: University of Illinois Press.

Matsumoto, Toshio. (1968) *Bara no sōretsu* (Funeral procession of roses), motion picture.

Matsuoka, Hiroshi. (1981) *Kore kara no seikyōiku: shō chū kōkōsei no nayami ni kotaeru* (Sex education from now on: [you] can reply to junior-, middle- and high-school students' troubles), Tokyo: Yūhikaku shinsho.

Mc Cormac, Gavan, and Sugimoto, Yoshio. (1988) *The Japanese Trajectory: Modernization and Beyond*, Cambridge: Cambridge University Press.

McGregor, Richard. (1996) *Japan Swings: Politics, Culture and Sex in the New Japan*, St Leonards: Allen and Unwin.

McLauchlan, Alastair. (1998) 'One More Bitter Pill for Japanese Women to Swallow,' *New Zealand Journal of East Asian Studies*, vol. 6, no. 1, pp. 97–104.

Miller, Neil. (1993) *Out in the World: Gay and Lesbian Life from Buenos Aires to Bangkok*, New York: Vintage Books.

Miller, Stephen. (ed.) (1996) *Partings at Dawn: An Anthology of Japanese Gay Literature*, San Fransisco: Gay Sunshine Press.

Minakata, Kumagusu. (1991) *Jō no sekusorojii* (Sexology of purification), Tokyo: Kawade bunkō.

Mishima, Yukio. (1973) *Zenshū* (complete works), vol. 3: *Kamen no kokuhaku* (Confessions of a mask); vol. 5: *Kinjiki* (Forbidden colours), Tokyo: Shinchōsha.

Mishima, Yukio. (1977) *Yukio Mishima on Hagakure: the Samurai Ethic and Modern Japan*, transl. Kathryn Sparling, London: Souvenir Press.

Mishima, Yukio. (1996) 'Onnagata,' transl. Donald Keene, in: S. Miller (ed.) (1996).

Mizushima, Keiichi. (1973) 'Criminality and Deviancy in Premodern Japan,' in: G. DeVos (1973).

Mock, John. (1996) 'Mother or Mama: The Political Economy of Bar Hostesses in Sapporo' in: A. Imamura (ed.) (1996).

Mori, Ōgai. (1971) *Zenshū* (complete works), vol. 1: *Wita sekusuarisu* (Vita sexualis), Yoshida Seiichi (ed.).

Mori, Yōko. (1994) *'Nigashita sakana wa ōkikatta'* (The fish she let get away was big), in: J. Ashby (1994).

Munro, Donald, et al. (eds) (1997) *Motivation and Culture*, New York and London: Routledge.

Murano, Inuhiko. (1996) *Gakuran tengoku* (Tumultous heaven), vols. 1 and 2, Tokyo: Takeshobō.

Murakami, Ryū. (1977) *Almost Transparent Blue*, transl. Nancy Andrew, Tokyo: Kodansha International.

Murakami, Ryū. (1998) *Coin Locker Babies,* transl. Stephen Snyder, Tokyo: Kodansha International.

Murray, Raymond. (1994) *Images in the Dark: An Encyclopedia of Gay and Lesbian Film and Video*, Philadelphia: TLA Publications.

Namihira, Emiko. (1987) 'Pollution in the Folk Belief System,' *Current Anthropology Supplement*, vol. 28, no. 4, August-October, 1987, pp. S65–S73.

Napier, Susan. (1990) *The Fantastic in Modern Japanese Literature: the Subversion of Modernity*, London and New York: Routledge.

Nardi, Peter, and Schneider, Beth. (eds) (1998) *Social Perspectives in Lesbian and Gay Studies: A Reader*, London: Routledge.

Newsweek. (1996, December 23) 'Innocence for Sale,' pp. 15–18.

Newsweek. (1996, December 23) 'The Joy of Abstinence,' p. 18.

Nishino, Kōji. (1993) *Shinjuku Ni-chome de kimi ni attara* (When I meet you in Shinjuku Ni-chome), Tokyo: Takarajimasha.

Nitta, Tomoko. (1997) *Okama in the office: Umi-chan, his life as a woman*, Tokyo: Bara iro kampanii.

Nomura, Sachiyo. (1995) *Anata otoko no kantei dekimasuka? chekkupointo wa kono 17 ka sho* (Can you judge men? 17 check points), Tokyo: Kuresutosha.

Ochiai, Emiko. (1996) *The Japanese Family System in Transition: a Sociological Analysis of Family Change in Post-war Japan*, Tokyo: International Library Foundation.

Offord, Baden, and Cantrell, Leon. (1999) 'Unfixed in a Fixated World: Identity, Sexuality, Race and Culture,' *Journal of Homosexuality*, vol.36, nos. 3/4, pp. 207–220.

Ōhama, George. (1994) *Male Homosexuality and its Social Acceptance in Modern Japanese Society*, unpublished B.A. thesis submitted to International Christian University, Tokyo.

Oki, Hiroyuki. (1989) *Yūei kinshi* (Swimming prohibited), motion picture.

Oki, Hiroyuki. (1990) *Kankei* (Infection), motion picture.

Oki, Hiroyuki. (1992) *Matsumae-kun no senritsu* (Melody for Buddy Matsumae), motion picture.

Oki, Hiroyuki. (1994) *Hachigatsu no kuchibiru* (Lips of August), motion picture.
Oki, Hiroyuki. (1994) *Anata ga suki desu dai suki desu* (I love you I love you very much), motion picture.
Penley, C, and Ross, A. (eds) (1991) *Technoculture*, Minneapolis: University of Minnesota Press.
Pinkerton, Steven, and Abramson, Paul. (1997) 'Japan,' in D. West and R. Green (eds) (1997).
Powers, R. and Kato, H. (eds) (1989) *Handbook of Japanese Popular Culture*, Westport, Conn: Greenwood Press.
Purojekuto G. (1992) *Otoko no ko no tame no bōifurendo gei handobukku* (A gay boyfriend handbook for boys), Tokyo: Shōnensha.
Ragawa, Marimo. (1998) *New York New York*, 4 vols., Tokyo: Hakusensha.
Rayns, Tony. (1995) 'Japan: Sex and Beyond,' *Sight and Sound*, June 1995 vol. 5, no. 6, pp. 26–30.
Richie, Donald. (1991) *A Lateral View: Essays on Contemporary Japan*, Tokyo: The Japan Times Ltd.
Robertson, Jennifer. (1998) *Takarazuka: Sexual Politics and Popular Culture in Modern Japan*, Berkeley: University of California Press.
Rosenbloom, Rachel. (ed.) (1996) *Unspoken Rules: Sexual Orientation and Women's Human Rights*, London and New York: Cassell.
Rubin, Gayle. (1998) 'Thinking Sex: Notes for a Radical Theory of the Politics of Sexuality,' in: P. Nardi and B. Schneider (eds) (1998).
Schalow, Paul. (1992) 'Kukai and the Tradition of Male Love in Japanese Buddhism,' in: J. Cabezon (ed.).
Schalow, Paul. (1996) 'Wild Azaleas,' in: S. Miller (ed.) (1996).
Schulman, Sarah. (1994) *My American History: Lesbian and Gay Life During the Reagan and Bush Years*, London: Cassell.
Screech, Timon. (1998) *Shunga* (transl. Takayama Hiroshi), Tokyo: Kōdansha.
Sedgwick, Eve. (1990) *The Epistemology of the Closet*, London: Penguin.
Seigle, Cecilia Segawa. (1993) *Yoshiwara: The Glittering World of the Japanese Courtesan*, Honolulu: University of Hawaii Press.
Shibayama, Hajime. (1993) *Edo danshoku kō* (History of Edo homosexuality), 3 vols. Tokyo: Hihyōsha.
Shiveley, Donald. (1968) 'Bakufu versus Kabuki' in: J. Hall (ed.) (1968).
Shiveley, Donald. (1970) 'Tokugawa Tsunayoshi: the Genroku Shogun,' in: D. Shiveley and A. Craig (eds).
Shiveley, Donald, and Craig, Albert. (eds) (1970) *Personality in Japanese History*, Berkeley: University of California Press.
Signorili, Michelangelo. (1994) *Queer in America: Sex, the Media, and the Closets of Power*, New York: Anchor Books.
Skov, Lise, and Moeran, Brian. (eds) (1995) *Women, Media and Consumption in Japan*, Richmond: Curzon Press.
SPA! (1998, March 18) '*Onna wo sentaku suru gei to gei wo sentaku suru onna*' (Gays who choose women and women who choose gays), pp. 20–21.
Spence, Jonathan. (1985) *The Memory Palace of Matteo Ricci*, London: Faber and Faber.
Spencer, Colin. (1995) *Homosexuality: A History*, London: Fourth Estate.
Starrs, Roy. (1994) *Deadly Dialectics: Sex, Violence and Nihilism in the Works of Yukio Mishima*, Folkestone: Japan Library.

Statler, Oliver. (1961) *Japanese Inn*, Honolulu: University of Hawaii Press.

Stone, Lawrence. (1977) *The Family, Sex and Mariage in England 1500 – 1800*, London: Wiedenfeld and Nicolson.

Sullivan, Gerald. (1995) *Gays and Lesbians in Asia and the Pacific: Social and Human Services*, Binghampton NY: Haworth Press.

Summerhawk, Barbara, et al. (eds) (1998) *Queer Japan: Personal Stories of Japanese Lesbians, Gays, Transsexuals and Bisexuals*, Norwich: New Victoria Publishers.

Tagami, Gengoroh. (1994) *Naburimono* (Laughingstock), Tokyo: B purojekuto.

Takada, Masatoshi. (1994) 'Changing Patterns in Sexuality and Sex-based Roles,' in: A. Ueda (ed.) (1994).

Takarajima. (1993, December 9) '*Gei jishin ga katari tsukushita otoko to otoko ga aishi au imi*' (Gays themselves tell all about the real meaning of male/male love).

Tamaki, Yuri. (1993) *Partners*, Tokyo: Takeshobō.

Tokyo Shimbun. (1997, December 10,11,12) '*Onna no kokoro wo motsu seitō kaichō*' (The student chairperson with a woman's heart) (3–part series).

Totman, Conrad. (ed.) (1990) *Tokugawa Japan: the Social and Economic Antecedents of Modern Japan*, Tokyo: University of Tokyo Press.

Treat, John. (1994) 'Aids Panic in Japan: or How to Have a Sabbatical in an Epidemic,' *Positions* 2:3, Winter, 1994, pp. 629–679.

Treat, John. (1995) 'Yoshimoto Banana's *Kitchen*, or the Cultural Logic of Japanese Consumerism,' in L. Skov and B. Moeran (eds) (1995).

Tsunoda, Ryusaku, et al. (eds) (1965) *Sources of the Japanese Tradition*, New York and London: Columbia University Press.

Ueda, Atsushi (ed). (1994) *The Electric Geisha: Exploring Japan's Popular Culture*, Tokyo: Kodansha International.

Ueno, Chizuko. (1987) 'The Position of Japanese Women Reconsidered,' *Current Anthropology* (Supplement), v. 28, n. 4, August-October, 1987, pp. S75–S82.

Ueno, Chizuko. (1992) *Sukāto no shita no gekijō* (Theatre under the skirt) Tokyo: Kawade bunko.

Ueno, Chizuko. (1994a) 'Women and the Family in Transition in Post-industrial Japan,' in: J. Gelb (ed.) (1994).

Ueno, Chizuko. (1994b) *Seiairon* (Discussions on sex and love), Tokyo: Kawade bunko.

Ueno, Chizuko. (ed.) (1995) *Nihon no feminizumu*, vol. 6, *Sekushuariti* (Japanese feminism vol. 6, Sexuality), Tokyo: Iwanami shoten.

Ueno, Chizuko. (1997) 'Interview' in: S. Buckley (1997).

Ujiie, Mikito. (1996) 'From Young Lions to Rats in a Ditch: the Decline of *Shudō* in the Edo Period,' in: S. Jones (1996).

Valentine, James. (1997a) 'Pots and Pans: Identification of Queer Japanese in Terms of Discrimination,' in: A. Livia and K. Hall (eds) (1997).

Valentine, James. (1997b) 'Skirting and Suiting Stereotypes: Representations of Marginalized Sexualities in Japan,' in *Theory, Culture and Society*, 14:3, pp. 57–85.

Valentine, James. (1997c) 'Conformity, Calculation and Culture,' in: D. Munro et al. (eds) (1997).

264   REFERENCES

Voller, Peter. (1986) 'Gaisen–Naisen: Gay Male Attitudes in Japan,' unpublished M.A. paper, Temple University Japan.

Watanabe, Tsuneo, and Iwata, Jun'ichi. (1989) *The Love of the Samurai: A Thousand Years of Japanese Homosexuality*, London: GMP Publishers Ltd.

Watanabe, Tsuneo. (1995) *Datsudansei no jidai* (The age of missing men), Tokyo: Keisōshobō.

West, Donald, and Green, Richard. (eds) (1997) *Sociolegal Control of Homosexuality: a Multi-Nation Comparison*, New York and London: Plenium Press.

Wittig, Monique. (1992) *The Straight Mind and Other Essays*, Brighton: Harvester Wheatsheaf.

Yajima, Masami. (1997) *Dansei dōseiaisha no raifuhisutorii* (Homosexual men's life histories) Tokyo: Gakubunsha.

Yamamoto, Hideo. (1996) *Okama repōto (Okama* report*)*, Tokyo: Shōgakkan.

Yamamoto, Jōchō. (1979) *Hagakure*, transl. William Scott Wilson, Tokyo: Kodansha International.

Yamamoto, Naohide. (1997) *Sekushuaru raitsu* (Sexual rights), Tokyo: Akashi shoten.

Yamamoto, Yasuhito. (1995) *Tetsujin ganma* (The ironman) vol. 9, Tokyo: Kōdansha.

Yanagihashi, Akitoshi. (1999) 'Towards Legal Protection for Same-Sex Partnerships in Japan from the Perspective of Gay and Lesbian Identity,' paper presented at the conference *Legal Protection for Same-Sex Partnerships*, King's College, London 1–3 July, 1999.

Yanagisawa, Kimio. *Iro otoko iro onna* (Randy man, randy woman), vol. 1, Tokyo: Bungei Shunjū.

Yoshimoto, Banana. (1993) *Kitchen*, transl. Megan Backus, London: Grove Press.

Index